THE COMPOSITION OF LUKE'S GOSPEL

BRILL'S READERS
IN BIBLICAL STUDIES

VOLUME 1

THE COMPOSITION OF LUKE'S GOSPEL

Selected Studies from Novum Testamentum

COMPILED BY

DAVID E. ORTON

BRILL
LEIDEN · BOSTON · KÖLN
1999

This book is printed on acid-free paper.

Cover design: BEELDVORM, Leidschendam

On the cover: the evangelist Luke. Manuscript Patmos 80,
13th century, evangeliarion, fol. 131 vo.

ISSN   1389-1170
ISBN   90 04 11157 3

PRINTED IN THE NETHERLANDS

CONTENTS

Preface vii

Places of Original Publication ix

B.M.F. van Iersel, The finding of Jesus in the temple 1

C.T. Ruddick, Jr, Birth narratives in Genesis and Luke 14

D. Hill, The Rejection of Jesus at Nazareth (Luke IV 16-30) 20

P.S. Minear, Jesus' Audiences, According to Luke 40

L.T. Johnson, The Lukan Kingship Parable (Lk. 19:11-27) 69

L. Alexander, Luke's Preface in the Context of Greek Preface-
Writing 90

D.P. Moessner, "The Christ must suffer": New Light on the
Jesus-Peter, Stephen, Paul Parallels in Luke-Acts 117

J.B. Green, Preparation for Passover (Luke 22:7-13):
a Question of Redactional Technique 154

R.J. Shirock, The Growth of the Kingdom in Light of
Israel's Rejection of Jesus: Structure and Theology in
Luke 13:1-35 169

W.C. van Unnik, The "Book of Acts"—the Confirmation of
the Gospel 184

Index of Authors 219

Index of Biblical References 223

PREFACE

This is the first in a series of publications designed—in something of a departure from the traditional policy of Brill Academic Publishers— to make previously published journal material available in a more convenient and accessible form. The material presented in this series, then, though it certainly contains some previously neglected but valuable studies, does not claim to be more than a convenient selection. However, convenience can easily translate into usefulness and indeed use, and many university and seminary teachers will find the selections suitable not only for their personal use, but also for their classes.

The present selection has been made from the best articles on Luke's literary work to have appeared to date in the journal, *Novum Testamentum*. An attempt has been made to offer a balanced representation of the discussion over a period of four decades. Since opinions on the value of particular pieces of scholarship always vary, and inevitably some studies become dated more quickly than others, doubtless some teachers would have preferred a different selection. The constraint of maximum international usefulness has meant that only English-language articles could be included. Had this not been the case the present volume would also have included the following articles: G. Braumann, "Die lukanische Interpretation der Zerstörung Jerusalems" (*NT* 6, 1953, 12-127); W. Wilkens, "Zur Frage der literarischen Beziehung zwischen Matthäus und Lukas" (*NT* 8, 1956, 48-57); G. Sellin, "Quellen und Funktion des Lukanischen Reiseberichtes (Lk. ix 51-xix 28)" (*NT* 20, 1978, 100-135); R. Kany, "Der Lukanische Bericht von Tod und Auferstehung Jesu aus der Sicht eines hellenischtischen Romanlesers" (*NT* 28, 1986, 75-90). Those interested in a complete listing of articles published in this field in *Novum Testamentum* may be referred to the relevant entries in *An Index to Novum Testamentum Volumes 1-35* (ed. W.E. Mills & J.H. Mills; Brill, 1994).

As the compiler of this collection, I must bear responsibility for the choice. I am not, of course, responsible for the original publication of the articles, which resulted from the due process of peer review and editorship by the incumbent editorial boards of *Novum Testamentum*. The present selection is not the responsibility of the editorial board. I would like, however, to acknowledge with gratitude the kind and encouraging advice of Professor David Moessner, a member of the current editorial board of the journal, and a leading international scholar on the subject of this collection, in response to my draft table of contents. It was his suggestion that the article by W.C. van Unnik, "The 'Book of Acts' the Confirmation of the Gospel" might be usefully included in this collection, since it is relevant to Luke's work as a literary composer.

The articles in this selection speak for themselves, and are offered without editorial comment, in conformity with the ethos of the journal. I shall merely note that individually and together, the articles clearly demonstrate that interest in Luke's literary artistry is not merely a feature of the most recent biblical study. Readers will find here many insights from decades past which are entirely relevant to current modes of biblical appreciation.

DEO
Leiden, 1998

PLACES OF ORIGINAL PUBLICATION

The articles of this book first appeared in *Novum Testamentum*.

B.M.F. van Iersel, 'The Finding of Jesus in the Temple,' *NT* vol. IV (1960), pp. 161-173.

C.T. Ruddick, Jr, 'Birth Narratives in Genesis and Luke,' *NT* vol. XII (1970), pp. 343-348.

D. Hill, 'The Rejection of Jesus at Nazareth (Luke IV 16-30),' *NT* vol. XIII (1971), pp. 161-180.

P.S. Minear, 'Jesus' Audiences, According to Luke,' *NT* vol. XVI (1974), pp. 81-109.

L.T. Johnson, 'The Lukan Kingship Parable (Lk. 19:11-27),' *NT* vol. XXIV (1982), pp. 139-159.

L. Alexander, 'Luke's Preface in the Context of Greek Preface-Writing,' *NT* vol. XXVIII (1986), pp. 48-74.

D.P. Moessner, '"The Christ must suffer": New Light on the Jesus-Peter, Stephen, Paul Parallels in Luke-Acts,' *NT* vol. XXVIII (1986), pp. 220-256.

J.B. Green, 'Preparation for Passover (Luke 22:7-13): a Question of Redactional Technique,' *NT* vol. XXIX (1987), pp. 305-319.

R.J. Shirock, 'The Growth of the Kingdom in Light of Israel's Rejection of Jesus: Structure and Theology in Luke 13:1-35,' *NT* vol. XXXV (1993), pp. 15-29.

W.C. van Unnik, 'The "Book of Acts"—the Confirmation of the Gospel,' *NT* vol. IV (1960), pp. 26-59.

THE FINDING OF JESUS IN THE TEMPLE

SOME OBSERVATIONS ON THE ORIGINAL FORM OF LUKE ii 41-51a

BY

B. VAN IERSEL

H. Landstichting 14, Nijmegen

I.

The story of the finding of Jesus in the temple, Luke ii 41-51a [1]), is according to R. BULTMANN "eine ursprüngliche Einzelgeschichte, die die vorangegangenen nicht voraussetzt". The story has two points, viz. "1. die überraschende Weisheit des jugendlichen Jesus (V. 47); 2. sein Weilen im Tempel, das seine religiöse Bestimmung kundtut" [2]). The story may have originated in Christian-Hellenistic circles of Jewish origin [3]), whereas its central theme [4]) has possibly been taken from pagan Hellenism and applied to Jesus [5]). About the nature of the story he writes elsewhere: "Dass die Gestalt Jesu unter dem Gesichtspunkt des Glaubens, des Kultus und des Mythos gesehen wird, das ist auch der Grund dafür, dass diese Gestalt nicht zum Gegenstand der eigentlichen Heiligenlegenden geworden ist. Es fehlen Geschichten, die ihn als Muster frommer Lebensführung darstellen . . ., das Interesse an seinem βίος fehlt nicht nur im Sinne der Historie, sondern auch im Sinne der Heiligenverehrung. Eine Ausnahme ist nur die Geschichte vom zwölfjährigen Jesus Lk 2, 41-52 . . ." [6]). Accordingly this story would be the only specimen of a legend.

M. DIBELIUS holds a similar view. To his opinion the narrative is a typical case of a "Personallegende", i.e. a story about a person who, on account of his exceptional virtue or holiness, is particularly

---

[1]) Cf. the bibliography in R. LAURENTIN, *Structure et théologie de Luc I-II*, Paris 1957, 189-226. To my knowledge there are no other important works that should be added to this list, exc. A. S. GEYSER, *The Youth of John the Baptist*, NT I (1956) 70-75.

[2]) *Die Geschichte der synoptischen Tradition*, Göttingen 1958⁴, 327.

[3]) *Op. cit.*, 330.

[4]) B. does not specify which of the two themes is the main motive of the *pericopa*.

[5]) *Op. cit.*, 331.

[6]) *Op. cit.*, 334.

privileged by God [1]). Jesus is represented here as the acme of piety, because He surpasses his parents' piety in staying longer in the temple than they did [2]). The legendary structure shows at the same time that the origin of the story does not lie in the milieu of preaching but in the milieu of story-telling. Since the story represents Jesus as an example to be imitated [3]), its religious value is in its edifying character.

In the following a critical analysis of the text will put these statements to the test, and at the same time serve as a starting-point for some observations pointing to another direction.

2.

Is it probable that originally the story existed in the tradition as an "Einzelgeschichte"?

From the purely formal point of view the passage stands out from its context, and is separated from it by a framework that makes it fit into the whole of Luke i-iii. The editorial seams are easily visible. On one side it is v. 40, and on the other v. 51c-52. Both verses are akin to i 80, and form a kind of inclusion, a frame in its literal sense. They do not only correspond with each other, but are also in keeping with the narrative in between them, because one of its two themes, the σύνεσις of young Jesus, re-echoes in both the frame-verses, in either of which his σοφία is emphasized [4]).

Within this editorial framework [5]) (to which v. 51c belongs too) [6]),

---

[1]) *Die Formgeschichte des Evangeliums*, Tübingen 1933², 101-102.

[2]) *Op. cit.*, 103-106.

[3]) *Op. cit.*, 128-129.

[4]) This naturally raises the question why σοφία is used in the framework, and σύνεσις in v. 47. Σοφία is doubtless a loftier word than σύνεσις and is also used in relation to God, whereas the latter in the New Testament means a specifically human knowledge. For the rest both words are not unfrequently synonymous: Mt. xi 25 par; 1 Cor. i 19; Col. i 19; ii 2-3. Why v. 47 has σύνεσις could be explained by οὐ συνῆκαν in v. 50. So the σύνεσις of young Jesus is contrasted with the lack of σύνεσις of his parents. As a result of the use of σοφία in the framework instead of σύνεσις, the ordinary 'intelligence' is put on a level more in keeping with the other things that are said of Jesus in these frame-verses.

[5]) It is still open to question what does and what does not belong to the editorial frame. DIBELIUS e.g. *op. cit.*, 103ff., thinks that v. 50 belongs to the editorial framework, since it does not fit in with a legend "die auf einem beglückenden Schluss hinausläuft".

[6]) The information about Jesus' mother certainly belongs to it. As to how far v. 51b, καὶ ἦν ὑποτασσόμενος αὐτοῖς, belongs to the editorial framework or the original story, is doubtful. The word ὑποτάσσειν does not

the story itself begins and ends with verses that are related to one another: a) v. 41 καὶ ἐπορεύοντο . . . εἰς Ἰερουσαλήμ contrasts with v. 51 καὶ ἦλθεν εἰς Ναζαρέθ; b) v. 42 ἀναβαινόντων αὐτῶν with v. 51 καὶ κατέβη μετ' αὐτῶν [1]). Thus the story itself, being circumscribed by two corresponding verses, is made into a formal unit.

These points are undoubtedly positive indications to justify the hypothesis that Luke ii 41-51a is "eine ursprüngliche Einzelgeschichte".

The same holds true, if we examine the relation of Luke ii 41-51a to Luke i 5-ii 39. For the latter forms a well-defined structure [2]), in which there is no place for the end of the second chapter, that, therefore, is generally held to be an epilogue [3]). Considering the difference of style and the lack of traces of a Hebrew original [4]), R. LAURENTIN thinks it quite probable that the *pericopa* in question is "une pièce plus tardive [5]), ajoutée après coup" [6]).

─────────

occur in the gospels but in Lk., and is much used by Paul. Since the original story itself was rewritten by Luke (cf. pp. 166-167), it is, however, impossible to derive anything definite from this.

[1]) Probably the change of subject is not due to mere coincidence. In the first part (vv. 41-45) Jesus' parents are the principal characters, whereas from v. 47 onwards Jesus himself is the centre of the story. V. 46 forms the transition.

[2]) Cf. for the structure R. LAURENTIN, *op. cit.*, 23-42, where also the views of E. BURROWS, P. GÄCHTER and S. LYONNET are summarized.

[3]) Cf. e.g. R. LAURENTIN, *op. cit.*, 33 and 141. A. GEYSER, *op. cit.*, holds, however, that the story of the finding in the temple formed part of a written source containing the parallel narratives of Jesus and the Baptist. The lack of a parallel of Lk ii 41-51a in the story of the Baptist would be a "break in the parallel account of the Lucan infancy story". Accordingly G. tries to reconstruct the subject-matter of this missing part. To my opinion the parallelism is broken not because a section was left out, but because ii 41-51a was added.

[4]) This is disputable. There are first the two hebraisms καὶ ἐγένετο and ἐν τῷ with the infin., which are frequent with Lk., and occur here likewise. But one could also point out the fact that the story in spite of a number of participles, v. 44, 45 (bis), 46 (terties), 47, 48 (bis), and a gen. absol., 42-43, continues to show a very paratactic structure. Nearly all the sentences start with καὶ, followed immediately, or almost immediately, by the verb; only twice another conjunction is used, viz. in v. 44 and v. 47. For this reason I would not be too positive about the non-Hebrew origin of the story.

[5]) I would not be so certain about this. If our hypothesis is correct, the *pericopa* though added later, is older than the component parts of the rest of Lk. i-ii. This might be corroborated by the fact that Jesus' virgin-birth is in no way supposed here.

[6]) *Op. cit.*, 141-142.

There is indeed an important difference of style and inspiration,
first because the midrash-character of Luke i 5-ii 39 [1]) is wanting
here [2]), and secondly because this is the only story in these chapters
that does not owe its impulse and spiritual impact to the words
of heavenly messengers [3]) or prophets [4]), but to a word of Jesus
himself.

Finally, it is of great importance that this story, as R. BULTMANN
has rightly pointed out, "die vorangegangenen nicht voraussetzt,
wie besonders V. 48 und 50 zeigen, wo die Eltern noch keine Ahnung
von der Bedeutung des Kindes verraten" [5]). In order to understand it the reader need not be acquainted with the preceding
parts of the Birth-Stories. Moreover, it is very well possible that
the isolated story was part of the tradition before the primitive
church had become conscious of Jesus' virgin-birth and its implications, to which Matthew i and Luke i—doubtless more recent
compositions—bear witness so evidently [6]).

BULTMANN's opinion as to the isolated pre-existence of Luke ii
41-51a in the tradition before it was incorporated into Luke i-ii is,
consequently, borne out by an analysis of the text.

3.

Is this also the case with his opinion that Luke ii 41-51a is a
typical specimen of a legend? We cannot but admit that the story
shows some characteristics of a novel or legend, and that it belongs
to the genre of story-telling rather than catechetical instruction.
In this connexion two things need mentioning.

The first is the great interest taken in the human side of the
events. The description of the search of Jesus is packed with details,
and especially v. 44 presents us with a number of particulars that
are irrelevant to the preacher or catechist, but are of paramount

---

[1]) Cf. for this R. LAURENTIN, *op. cit.*, 43-119.

[2]) LAURENTIN's reference, *op. cit.*, 142, to Mal. iii 1, seems to be far-
fetched. It is a matter rather of *staying* in the temple than of *coming* into the
temple, and it would, therefore, be more obvious to think of young Samuel
(1 Sam. ii), to which the framework clearly refers, although there are no
references or allusions in the story itself and both the situations differ
completely.

[3]) i 11-20, 26-38, ii 9-12, 13-14.

[4]) Elisabeth i 41, Zachary i 67, Simeon ii 25, 26, 27, Anna ii 36.

[5]) *Op. cit.*, 327. Up to now it has never been proved convincingly that this
episode excludes Jesus' virgin-birth.

[6]) Cf. p. 163 n. 5.

importance to the narrator, who wants to enliven his story and to represent the scene in clear and vivid terms. It is also notable that so much attention is being paid to the feelings of the persons concerned (v. 47, 48a and 48b), and that the text shows a great interest in the minor actors, Jesus' parents (v. 41-45).

The other remarkable fact is the profane character of v. 47, which would be appropriate to a narrative but not to a piece of ecclesiastical catechesis. The audience is amazed at Jesus' σύνεσις and his answers. The best translation for this Greek word is 'in-telligence' [1]), for there is nothing in the context to suggest that Jesus' σύνεσις is of a religious nature [2]). The whole sentence should, therefore, be translated: 'all those who heard him were amazed at his intelligent answers'. The profane character of v. 47 is also manifest in the reactions of the listeners, and can only be realized to the full if one compares the verse with similar synoptic passages in which the reactions to a pronouncement or miracle of Jesus are recorded [3]). Far more often than not these reactions are of a religious character, e.g.: people praise God [4]) or fall down at Jesus' feet [5]), and in one case a man who has been cured sets out to proclaim the Lord [6]). In most cases people are said to be

---

[1]) How neutral the meaning of σύνεσις really is appears from Mk. xii 33 (a quotation from Dt. vi 5, where σύνεσις is the translation of שׂכל; in the LXX שׂכל is never rendered in this way) and from 1 Cor. i 19, where it is used in a derogatory sense (cf. also Mt. xi 25 par., where the adj. συνετός has the same meaning). The meaning 'intelligence' is similar to the use of συνετός in Acts xiii 7, where Luke calls Sergius Paulus 'an intelligent man'. The noun σύνεσις is everywhere else specified (Eph. iii 4, Col. i 9, ii 2, 2 Tim. ii 7). The verb συνιέναι is frequently used in the synoptic tradition to signify that one does *not* understand the Lord: Mt. xiii 13 parr., the quotation in Mt. xiii 14-15 (cf. also Acts xxviii 26), Mt. xiii 19. It is also used to denote the fact that one *does* understand: Mt. xiii 23 par., xv 10 par., xvi 12, Mk. viii 17, 21. Besides in viii 10 and xxiv 25, Luke also uses it in xviii 34, after the third prediction of Jesus' passion. After the second prediction he uses ἀγνοεῖν (ix 45), in correspondence with Mk. ix 32.

[2]) The διδάσκαλοι speak of course about religious subjects in the temple, particularly about the Torah. But this is the very σύνεσις τῶν συνετῶν which is rejected.

[3]) Mk. i 22 parr., 1 27 par., ii 12 parr., iv 41 parr., v 20, v 42 parr., vi 51 par., vii 37 par., x 24-32, xi 18, xii 17 parr., xv 5 par., Mt. ix 33 par., xii 23, xxii 33, Lk. ii 18, iv 22, ix 43. Sometimes they also occur in the middle of a *pericopa*: Mk. v 15, vi 2 par., Mt. xxi 20, Lk. i 21, 63, ii 33, xxiv 37, 41.

[4]) Mk. ii 12 parr., Mt. xv 31.

[5]) Lk. v 8, Mt. xiv 33.

[6]) Mk. v 20.

overcome with awe and fear in the presence of the superhuman [1]). The *pericopae* that compare best with the description given in Luke ii 47 are those which inform us of people's amazement at Jesus' teaching [2]). But even then there are a few striking differences. In Luke ii 47 Jesus does not act as a διδάσκαλος, but on the contrary as a disciple, who 'sits, listens and asks questions' [3]). Moreover, there is no other text in which people are said to be amazed at his 'intelligence'. One gets the impression that young Jesus is depicted here as a sort of child prodigy, who strikes his listeners by his unusual intelligence. This motive is nowhere to be found in the catechetical tradition; it is legendary rather than anything else, and occurs quite frequently in the apocrypha [4]).

Accordingly, one cannot easily deny the legendary, or at least novellistic, character of the story. It is worth noticing that the novellistic characteristics, though not altogether absent from the rest of the text, are concentrated in v. 44 and 47.

4.

There is, however, a serious objection against the view that Luke inserted this novellistic or legendary story between the Birth-Stories and the body of his gospel, in such a form as he had found it in the tradition. Luke's text bears unmistakable evidence of his authorship. Of the 67 words which R. MORGENTHALER mentions in his list of Lukan words [5]), no less then 13 occur in Luke ii 41-51a, viz.: πορεύεσθαι, ἔτος, Ἰερουσαλήμ, γίνεσθαι,

---

[1]) Mk. iv 41 parr., v 15, vi 51 par., vii 37, x 24-32, Mt. ix 33 par., xii 23, xxi 20, Lk. iv 22, ix 43, xxiv 37, 41.

[2]) Mk. i 22 parr., i 27 par., vi 2, Mt. xxii 33.

[3]) K. BORNHÄUSER, *Die Geburts- und Kindheitsgeschichte Jesu, Beiträge zur Förderung christlicher Theologie* II/23, 140, holds that the fundamental differences between Jesus and the scribes already emerged at this first meeting. That would be the explanation of their astonishment at Jesus' answers. In this hostile atmosphere he would have been found by his parents, and that would have been the reason why they were frightened. However interesting this opinion may be, there is nothing in the text to support it. The attitude towards Jesus described by ἐξίσταντο ... ἐπὶ τῇ συνέσει ... αὐτοῦ, seems to have been more favourable than BORNHÄUSER supposes.

[4]) Cf. esp. the apocryphon about the Childhood of Jesus, attributed to Thomas, ed. E. HENNECKE-W. SCHNEEMELCHER, *Neutestamentliche Apokryphen in deutscher Übersetzung*, I, Tübingen 1959, 293-298. Cf. for an English edition W. HAYES, *The gospel according to Thomas*, 1921.

[5]) *Statistik des neutestamentlichen Wortschatzes*, Zürich-Frankfurt am Main 1958, 181.

ἡμέρα, ὑποστρέφειν, ζητεῖν, εὑρίσκειν, μέσος, ἐρωτᾶν, πρός, δεῖ, ῥῆμα. Out of a total of 170 words in the passage, 22 belong to this list, which means a proportion of 22:170, or more than 1:8. Besides, a number of other words are more or less characteristic of Luke [1]:

	Mt.	Mk.	Lk.	John	Acts	Paul	Hebr.	else-where
γονεῖς	1	1	6	6	—	6	—	—
κατά	37	23	43	8	90	194	41	35
ἔθος	—	—	3	1	7	—	1	—
ὑπομένειν (stay on) [2])	—	—	1	—	1	—	—	—
νομίζειν	3	—	2	—	7	3	—	—
ἀναζητεῖν	—	—	2	—	1	—	—	—
γνωστός [3])	—	—	2	2	10	1	—	—
infin. εἶναι	6	8	23	3	20	54	3	8
ἱερόν	11	9	14	10	25	1	—	—
ἐξιστάναι	1	4	3	—	8	1	—	—
ἐπί	120	73	160	33	165	131	30	166
ὀδυνᾶσθαι	—	—	3	—	1	—	—	—

Including these the total number of typically Lukan words amounts to 43:170, which is a little more than 1:4.

Finally one could point out the expressions κατὰ τὸ ἔθος [4]) and τί ὅτι [5]), which are exclusively Lukan, and ἐν τῷ with the infinitive [6]), καὶ ἐγένετο [7]) and ἐν μέσῳ [8]), which are more frequent with Luke than with Mark and Matthew.

In the light of these data we have to accept the fact that Luke either composed the whole story himself or at least rewrote an account he had found in the tradition.

[1]) The statistical data are from R. MORGENTHALER, op. cit.
[2]) So A. PLUMMER, A critical and exegetical commentary on the gospel according to S. Luke, Edinburgh 1956⁵, 75.
[3]) Usually the neuter γνωστόν; for persons only in Lk. ii 44, xxiii 49, John xviii 15, 16.
[4]) Viz. i 9, ii 42, xxii 39. Cf. A. PLUMMER, op. cit., 10.
[5]) M. J. LAGRANGE, Évangile selon Saint Luc, Paris 1948⁷, 96, refers also to Lk. iv 36; F. BLASS-A. DEBRUNNER, Grammatik des neutestamentlichen Griechisch, Göttingen 1954⁹, Nr. 298, thinks that it is an abbrev. of τί γέγονεν ὅτι (John xiv 22), and F. M. ABEL, Grammaire du Grec biblique, Paris 1927, § 35 l, of τί ποτέ ἐστιν ὅτι.
[6]) Cf. F. M. ABEL, op. cit., § 70 g; F. BLASS-A. DEBRUNNER, op. cit., Nr. 404.
[7]) Cf. A. PLUMMER, op. cit., 75; M. J. LAGRANGE, op. cit., XLVII-XLIX.
[8]) Cf. A. PLUMMER, op. cit., 218-219.

5.

The choice between a story written by Luke himself on the one hand, and a story adapted by him from a written source or an oral tradition on the other, cannot be decided in favour of the latter unless we are able to prove convincingly that Luke ii 41-51a, as it stands now, is uneven with regard to subject-matter or form. And indeed, the actual version of the story is unsatisfactory in both respects.

As for the contents there is a certain lack of balance in the account, which is due to the fact that the story has two points. These are, according to BULTMANN: "1. die überraschende Weisheit des jugendlichen Jesus (V. 47); 2. sein Weilen im Tempel, das seine religiöse Bestimmung kundtut" [1]. And he adds: "Beide Motive sind immerhin so verwandt, dass die Annahme, sie hätten einmal isoliert in literarischer Fassung existiert, nicht notwendig ist" [2]. But is this definition of the two motives correct? The second and main motive is obviously concerned with Jesus' stay in the temple, but its real point is the opposition between the one Jesus' mother calls ὁ πατήρ σου (v. 48), and the one Jesus himself calls, without transition, ὁ πατήρ μου (v. 49). The dialogue between Jesus and his mother (v. 48-49) stresses this opposition as strongly as possible, and states firmly that Jesus' belonging to God, his Father, is his only rule of conduct. In this saying of Jesus (v. 49) centres the main interest of the second motive. The first (v. 47) is only of secondary importance. And if Jesus dissociates himself from his father in order to make clear that God is his Father, is it then still correct to say that both the motives of the story are in a direct line with each other? Are the boy's σύνεσις and his sonship of the divine Father related to one another? Apparently, Jesus' parents do not understand anything of his exclusive relationship with God, which is expressed by the words οὐ συνῆκαν (v. 50). Thus Jesus' σύνεσις and his parents' lack of σύνεσις are somehow opposed to each other. But this does not necessarily mean that both have the same object, viz. Jesus' relationship with his heavenly Father. For in case the boy would have spoken about that in the temple, the διδάσκαλοι would certainly have been horrified at his pretensions instead of being astonished at his intelligence [3].

---

[1] *Op. cit.*, 327.
[2] *Ad loc.*
[3] In that case it would be right to describe the situation in the sense of K. BORNHÄUSER. Cf. p. 166 n. 3.

Actually, in the story Jesus' σύνεσις is not connected with his particular relation to God, but with something else. There is, consequently, no connection between the two motives of the story [1]).

The opposite is more likely. The theme of v. 47 is totally absent from the catechesis of the primitive church, whereas that of v. 49 is there of considerable importance [2]). Moreover, the first motive diverts the reader's attention from the logion, and so weakens the total effect of the story. This warrants the supposition that the theme of v. 47 was interpolated during a later stage of the tradition. In any case, on account of its double motive the structure of the story is neither well-balanced nor altogether clear, and this fact needs explaining.

There is, indeed, a flaw in the narrative showing that the present version of the story is an adaptation. The subject of v. 47 is πάντες οἱ ἀκούοντες αὐτοῦ. The sentence runs on in v. 48, so that, at least from the point of view of syntax, we are supposed to read both sentences as having the same subject: 'all those hearing him were amazed at his intelligence and answers, and seeing him were astonished'. One gets the impression that at first they only heard him, without yet seeing him. Quite rightly this verse is generally held to refer to his parents [3]). But one does not seem to be sufficiently aware of the fact that the syntax does not allow of this interpretation. The only way out of the difficulty is to drop v. 47. In that case the subject of v. 43 and of all the following sentences, οἱ γονεῖς αὐτοῦ, would also be the subject of v. 48. With this corresponds a flaw in the subject-matter. In v. 47 Jesus is said to be listening and asking questions. In v. 48, however, one is amazed, not at his questions, but at his answers, which have not been mentioned.

The very fact that both the flaw in the subject-matter and the one in the syntax have reference to the same verse, and so confirm

---

[1]) This does not, of course, simply imply that the two motives have existed in the tradition in a form which R. BULTMANN calls "literarischer Fassung".

[2]) The really ultimate point of the motive seems to be that Jesus cannot be understood and comprehended as long as one judges him by his antecedents and milieu. This idea recurs in the catechetical tradition in several forms, particularly in the logia in which Jesus dissociates himself from his relatives, and declares explicitly that consanguinity does not matter, because those who believe in him are his relatives: Mk. iii 20-21, 31-35 parr., Mk. vi 2-4 parr., Lk. xi 27-28, John ii 4, vii 3-10.

[3]) PLUMMER, op. cit. 77; LAGRANGE seems to take it so much for granted that he does not mention it.

one another, should not be underestimated. It follows as a matter of course that v. 47 is to be regarded as a secondary addition to the story, which implies that the story originally had one point only, viz. the logion of v. 49.

6.

It has gradually become clear that Luke ii 41-51a is indeed an adapted version of an original "Einzelgeschichte", which presumably originated from the catechetical tradition [1]). What then was the original form of the story, and what was being added in the process of its adaptation? We have come to the conclusion that Luke must have rewritten the story completely [2]), but it is of course not possible for us to restore the original. The matter is too complicated for that. Nevertheless, there are a few verses of which the secondary character can be easily demonstrated, and which therefore may be left out.

Starting with v. 47, of which the secondary character has already become clear, we may suppose that it was added by Luke himself on the analogy of similar editorial verses which are firmly rooted in synoptic passages containing a logion or miracle of Jesus [3]). This presumption can be corroborated by Luke xx 26, the only text of the synoptic tradition which states explicitly and in terms remindful of Luke ii 47 that people were amazed at an answer of Jesus: καὶ θαυμάσαντες ἐπὶ τῇ ἀποκρίσει αὐτοῦ ἐσίγησαν. The word ἀπόκρισις does not occur anywhere else in the synoptic tradition, and only twice in the rest of the New Testament, viz. in John i 22, xix 9. On the other hand, supposing Luke himself has added the verse, we are left with the problem why he did not

---

[1]) Unlike the kerygmatic phase of the tradition which concentrates on Jesus' death and resurrection, the catechetical phase is much more interested in his life, i.e. his words and miracles, by which one can enter into the meaning of Jesus and his mission.

[2]) Even the logion may have been tampered with, as might appear from the presence of δεῖ, for which Lk is known to have a predilection. Cf. H. CONZELMANN, *Die Mitte der Zeit*, Tübingen 1960³, 141-144. The word also occurs in the other parts of the synoptic tradition. The divine 'must' which is expressed by the impersonal form of this verb, is in this tradition connected either with Jesus' passion and death (Mk viii 31 parr.) or with the eschatological events (Mk ix 11 parr., xiii 7 parr., xiii 10). There does not seem to be here a direct connexion with either of them.

[3]) Cf. p. 165 n. 3.

smooth away the resulting syntactic irregularity between v. 47 and v. 48 [1]).

The presence of v. 44 may also be due to Luke's interference. The Lukan words are particularly numerous in this verse [2]). Moreover, the details show a novellistic tendency, and the account of the search is rather circumstantial, while the repetition of the verb ἀναζητεῖν in v. 44 and v. 45 deepens the impression that the verse is a detailed and novellistic elaboration of what in v. 48 is said about the anxious search of Jesus' parents. Such novellistic elaborations are not uncommon with Luke [3]).

A curious detail seems to verify this hypothesis. Luke has evidently tried to change the original paratactic structure of the narrative into a more syntactic one [4]). His attempt, however, has not been quite successful. For all the sentences start with καὶ, followed immediately or almost immediately by the verb [5]). The only two exceptions are the verses 44 and 47, which are linked with the preceding verses by the particle δέ. As above it is a formal criterion

---

[1]) There are three possibilities: 1. This addition is not by Lk, but by somebody before him, in which case the irregularity resulting from the process of adaptation would have been overlooked by Luke. 2. The addition is by Luke; but having been interpolated rather clumsily it is still easily recognizable as such. 3. The addition is by Luke or somebody else, but after the adaptation had been made.

The curious thing, however, is that there are strong objections against each of the three possibilities, and it is therefore still very much an open question as to what exactly happened. This uncertainty, however, does not justify the conclusion that v. 47 has always formed part of the story.

[2]) Νομίζειν; εἶναι; συνοδία is a *hapaxlegomenon*, but the verb συνοδεύειν occurs only once, viz. Acts ix 7; if we take into account Luke's preference for the prep. σύν and for the verbs with the prefix συν, we may consider this noun as a Lukanism too. Cf. the tables in R. MORGENTHALER, *op. cit.*, 160; ἡμέρα; ἀναζητεῖν; συγγενεύς (this word recurs only twice, viz. here and in Mk vi 4, but συγγενής occurs in Lk i 58, xiv 12, xxi 16, Acts x 24; once in John and four times in Paul; and συγγένεια only in Lk i 61 and Acts vii 3, 14); γνωστός. These are all the verbs but one (ἦλθον) and all the nouns but one (ὁδός).

[3]) Cf. the following specimens, which belong to the Lukan *Sondergut*,: vii 11-17, vii 36-viii 3, xix 1-10, xxiii 6-12, xxiv 13-35, and from texts Lk has in common with the others, esp. Lk iv 16-30 (esp. v. 17, 20, 29), v. 18-19, vii 1-10. It is hardly a coincidence that BULTMANN in the chapter on the technique of the story, takes most of his examples from Lk, *op. cit.* 335-346.

[4]) As appears from the many participles and the two genitivi absoluti (cf. p. 163 n. 4).

[5]) This points to a Hebrew original (see p. 163 n. 4).

again which confirms what has been put forward as a hypothesis on account of the subject-matter [1]).

7.

Although it is not possible for us to restore the exact wording of the original story, we might venture to say a few things about its original shape. If we take the story out of its framework (v. 40, 51b-52) and drop the verses 44 and 47, we are left with a unit that has all the structural qualities of the synoptic *pericopa* which DIBELIUS has called a *Paradigma*, BULTMANN an *Apophthegma*, and English scholars a pronouncement-story. The formal features of this kind of pattern may be summarized as follows [2]):

a. The text is concise and sober.
b. At the beginning and at the end it is rounded off with literary devices (v. 41-42 καὶ ἐπορεύοντο . . . εἰς Ἰερουσαλὴμ . . . καὶ . . . ἀναβαινόντων αὐτῶν v. 51 καὶ κατέβη μετ' αὐτῶν καὶ ἦλθεν εἰς Ναζαρέθ).
c. The narrative supplies a brief sketch of the situation, which generally has an introductory function (v. 41-43, 45-46).
d. At the end usually stands the logion or the dialogue which transcending the particular situation, is the real point of the story (v. 49).
e. The logion is often followed up by a summary account of the reactions either of the listeners or of the participants of the dialogue (v. 50).

The paradigmatic form of the original narrative is not without importance. It shows that the primitive story was neither legendary nor novellistic. At the same time it makes clear that the story has its *Sitz im Leben* in the catechetical instruction, and it makes it probable that Luke ii 41-51a, in its paradigmatic form, belongs to a primitive stage of the tradition, which, also according to BULTMANN and DIBELIUS, provides us with the most reliable

---

[1]) It is notable, however, that v. 51c begins also with καί, whereas in v. 19 the same information is connected with the foregoing by δέ. V. 52 starts with καί too, whereas the related texts i 80 and ii 40 make the connexion with δέ. It is possible that Lk, being under the influence of his source, unconsciously continued to use καί.

[2]) Cf. M. DIBELIUS, *op. cit.*, 34-66; R. BULTMANN, *op. cit.*, 66-72.

information about Jesus that can be derived from the synoptic gospels.

The purport of the original *paradigma* coincides with that of the present version of the story, but with all attention being focussed on the short dialogue of vv. 48-49 it probably came there more to the fore. The fact that the logion is not quite clear in its details is due to the problematic ἐν τοῖς [1]). Of one thing, however, we may be sure, viz. that the real issue of the story is the opposition between Jesus' putative father (Luke iii 23) and his real Father, as is clear from the formal opposition in vv. 48-49, where the boy Jesus dissociates himself clearly from Joseph and declares that he must be in 'the affairs' or 'the house' of his real Father [2]).

The *paradigma* and the logion are related with other fragments of the catechetical tradition, particularly with those in which Jesus is said to dissociate himself from his family [3]). The problem of Joseph's fatherhood is sensed in texts such as Matthew xiii 55 par. and John vi 42. But there is not one logion in the gospels that deals with it explicitly, unless we are to take the saying of Matthew xi 27 as to have originally been the answer to the question of Matthew xiii 54-56, as we have proposed elsewhere [4]).

---

[1]) Cf. P. TEMPLE, *What is to be understood by* ἐν τοῖς (Lk. 2,49)?, The Irish Theological Quarterly 17 (1922) 248-263, who examines especially the old translations and the interpretations of the Fathers, without reaching, however, any definite conclusion.

[2]) The christological import of ii 49 is denied by P. WINTER, *Lc.* 2,49 *and Targum Yerushalmi*, ZNW 45 (1954) 145-179; cf. also ZNW 46 (1955) 140. His argumentation does not seem to be convincing. Cf. the criticism of R. LAURENTIN, *op. cit.*, 143-146.

[3]) Cf. p. 169 n. 2.

[4]) '*Der Sohn*' *in den synoptischen Jesusworten, Christusbezeichnung der Gemeinde oder Selbstbezeichnung Jesu?*, Part III Chapter 4 (to appear shortly).

BIRTH NARRATIVES IN GENESIS AND LUKE

BY

C. T. RUDDICK, Jr.
Providence

Lucan scholarship has become increasingly conscious of the influence of the Old Testament scriptures on the composition of the gospel, especially in the nativity stories [1]. It is now clear that such influence extends far beyond direct quotations and obvious parallels to rather subtle verbal reminiscences and allusions. Most attention has hitherto been directed to parallels from the prophetic books, but it would seem reasonable to expect the birth narratives of Genesis to provide an obvious model for the evangelist. In fact, the language and events of some fifteen chapters of Genesis, from the birth of Jacob's children through their migration to Egypt (xxvii-xliii) are remarkably paralleled by Luke i-ii.

The three canticles (i 46-55; i 68-79; and ii 29-32) already point us back to the patriarchs, for each one speaks of Jacob:

> 'He has helped his servant Israel' (i 54)
> 'Blessed be the Lord God of Israel' (i 67)
> '. . . and the glory of his people Israel' (ii 32)

Whether these were pre-Christian psalms taken over by Luke or original compositions, they seem only slightly adapted to their ostensible settings. Mary's hymn is a jubilant thanksgiving for a reversal of fortunes—more appropriate, in fact, to Elizabeth (to whom a few MSS attribute it) or equally to Rachel, who was barren (Gen. xxix 31) but conceived when God 'remembered' her (xxx 22; cf. Luke i 54). The hymn of Zechariah similarly dwells on deliverance 'from those who hate us' and the sending of one ahead to prepare the way: 'to guide our feet into the way of peace'. In terms of Genesis, one is reminded of Jacob's escape from Laban (xxxi 17ff.) and his preparations, including sending ahead messengers, for his potentially hostile encounter with his brother Esau (xxxii 3 ff.).

---

[1] Cf. e.g. R. LAURENTIN, *Structure et Théologie de Luc I-II*, Paris, 1957, pp. 64 ff.

With these hints to go on, a number of verbal and thematic parallels can be discovered:

Luke i-ii	Genesis xxvii-xliii
An angel appears to Zechariah in the temple and promises that his wife will bear a son.	Isaac blesses Jacob and sends him to Laban to find a wife.
Mary is visited by the angel Gabriel, who is sent 'from God':	Jacob in a dream sees a ladder with the angels of God:
ὁ ἄγγελος Γ. ἀπὸ τοῦ θεοῦ (26)	οἱ ἄγγελοι τοῦ θεοῦ (xxviii 12)
The angel says, 'Hail, O favoured one, the Lord is with you':	The angel says, 'I am the Lord . . . I am with you':
ὁ κύριος μετὰ σοῦ (28)	ἐγὼ κύριος (13) . . . ἐγὼ μετὰ σοῦ (15)
(at 48b Mary says, 'all generations shall call me blessed')	He says 'by you all the families of the earth shall bless themselves' (14)
Mary is afraid, but the angel reassures her, 'Be not afraid':	Jacob is afraid (vv. 16-17), but the angel reassures him, 'Be not afraid':
μὴ φοβοῦ (30)	μὴ φοβοῦ (13)
Mary is to bear a son and call his name Jesus:	Jacob sets up a pillar and calls the name of the place Bethel:
καὶ καλέσεις τὸ ὄνομα αὐτοῦ Ἰησοῦν (31)	καὶ ἐκάλεσεν Ἰακωβ τὸ ὄνομα τοῦ τόπου ἐκείνου Οἶκος θεοῦ (19)
He will reign over the house of Jacob for ever:	Jacob prays to return to his father's house in peace:
ἐπὶ τὸν οἶκον Ἰακωβ (33)	εἰς τὸν οἶκον τοῦ πατρός μου (21)
Moreover, her kinswoman Elizabeth 'has conceived':	(at xxix 25 Jacob mistakes Leah for Rachel, and she conceives:
ἰδοὺ Ἐλισάβετ . . . αὐτὴ συνείληφεν,	ἰδοὺ ἦν Λεια . . . συνέλαβεν Λεια (32)
although she 'was called barren':	although Rachel 'was barren':
τῇ καλουμένῃ στείρᾳ (36)	Ραχηλ δὲ ἦν στείρα (31)
Mary says, 'Behold the handmaid of the Lord':	(Cf. xxx 3, 'Behold my handmaid':
ἰδοὺ ἡ δούλη κυρίου,	ἰδοὺ ἡ παιδίσκη μου,
and 'let it be to me according to your word':	and xxx 35, 'let it be according to your word':
γένοιτό μοι κατὰ τὸ ῥῆμά σου (38)	ἔστω κατὰ τὸ ῥῆμά σου.)
Mary arises and goes into the hill country:	Jacob journeys to the land of the east:
ἐπορεύθη εἰς τὴν ὀρεινήν (39),	ἐπορεύθη εἰς γῆν ἀνατολῶν (xxix 1)
where her kinswoman Elizabeth greets her warmly (vv. 40 ff.) and says, 'Blessed is the fruit of your womb':	where his kinsmen greet him warmly (vv. 4 ff.). Rachel has been deprived of 'the fruit of the womb':
ὁ καρπὸς τῆς κοιλίας (42),	καρπὸν κοιλίας (xxx 2)

and 'blessed is she who believed':

μακαρία ἡ πιστεύσασα (45)

Mary sings a song of exultation:
καὶ εἶπεν Μαριάμ . . . (46),

and says, 'all generations shall call me blessed.:

μακαριοῦσίν με (48),

'for (the Lord) has looked upon the lowliness of his handmaiden':

ὅτι ἐπέβλεψεν ἐπὶ τὴν ταπείνωσιν,

and 'now all generations shall call me blessed':

ἀπὸ τοῦ νῦν μακαριοῦσιν . . .

God is praised for 'remembering' his mercy:

μνησθῆναι (54).

He has reversed the fortunes of the meek and has helped his servant Israel (Jacob).

Mary remains with Elizabeth three months and returns to her home (56).

Elizabeth's son is born and named not Zechariah but John:

οὐχί, ἀλλὰ κληθήσεται Ἰωάννης (61) . .
Ἰωάννης ἐστὶν ὄνομά σου (63)

His father speaks, blessing God:

εὐλογῶν τὸν θεόν (64).

The 'dwellers-around' are afraid:

ἐγένετο ἐπὶ πάντας φόβος (65),

for 'the hand' of the Lord was with him:

χείρ κυρίου ἦν μετ'αὐτοῦ (66).

Zechariah praises the God of Israel (Jacob) for delivering his people 'from the hand' of all their enemies:
ἐκ χειρὸς πάντων . . . (71).

God is praised for 'showing mercy' on our fathers:

ποιῆσαι ἔλεος μετὰ τῶν πατέρων,

and for 'remembering' his covenant:

μνησθῆναι διαθήκης (72).

God has 'sworn to deliver us without fear':

ὤμοσεν . . . ἀφόβως (73).

---

but Leah says, 'Blessed am I':

μακαρία ἐγώ (xxx 13)

Leah exults after the birth'of each son:
καὶ εἶπεν Λεια . . . (xxx 13),

and says, 'women shall call me blessed':

μακαρίζουσίν με (xxx 13)

(at xxix 32, Leah says, 'for the Lord has seen my lowliness':

διότι εἶδέν μου κύριος τὴν ταπείνωσιν,

and 'now my husband will love me':

νῦν με ἀγαπήσει . . .)

God 'remembers' Rachel and she also conceives:

ἐμνήσθη . . . τῆς Ραχηλ (xxx 22).

She says, 'God has taken away my reproach' (23) With God's help Jacob outwits Laban (vv. 25 ff.).

Jacob escapes from Laban and returns to his home (xxxi 17ff).

Jacob wrestles with an angel, and his name is changed to Israel:

οὐ κληθήσεται . . . Ἰακωβ, ἀλλὰ Ἰσραηλ ἔσται τὸ ὄνομά σου (xxxii 29)

Jacob compels the angel to bless him:

ηὐλόγησεν αὐτὸν (xxxii 30).

Jacob praises 'the fear of Isaac':

ὁ φόβος Ἰσαακ ἦν μοι (xxxi 42),

who delivered him from 'the hand' of his brother:

ἐκ χειρὸς τοῦ ἀδελφοῦ μου (xxxii 11).

(Cf. above)

(at xxxiii 11 Jacob says, 'God has had mercy upon me':

ἠλέησέν με ὁ θεός.)

(Cf. xxx 22, where 'God remembered Rachel')

(Jacob has 'sworn by the fear of Isaac':

ὤμοσεν Ἰακωβ κατὰ τοῦ φόβου . . .)

They are to worship God with 'righteousness before his face':

ἐν δικαιοσύνῃ ἐνώπιον αὐτοῦ (75).

The boy is to 'go before the face of the Lord to prepare his way':

προπορεύσῃ ἐνώπιον κυρίου (76).

God gives light to 'those who sit in the shadow of death' and guides their feet 'into the way of peace' (79).

Mary and Joseph journey to the city of David (where Mary is to bear her son), 'which is called Bethlehem':

ἥτις καλεῖται Βηθλέεμ (ii 4).

Shepherds, having seen a heavenly vision of angels, come to worship Jesus:

οἱ ποιμένες (15).

All who hear are surprised, but Mary 'kept all these words in her heart':

ἡ δὲ Μαρία πάντα συνετήρει τὰ ῥήματα ταῦτα (19).

The child is called Jesus, as he was named before he was conceived:

ἐκλήθη τὸ ὄνομα αὐτοῦ Ἰησοῦς . . . πρὸ τοῦ συλλημφθῆναι αὐτὸν (21).

When the days of Mary's purification were fulfilled, they take Jesus to Jerusalem:

ἀνήγαγον αὐτὸν εἰς Ἱεροσόλυμα (22).

There Jesus is recognized as 'having the grace of God in him':

χάρις θεοῦ ἦν ἐν αὐτῷ (40).

Jesus' parents go up to Jerusalem to the feast and return leaving Jesus there.

At the end of a day's journey they find he is missing.

Jesus is 'listening' to the rabbis:

ἀκούοντα αὐτῶν,

and 'questioning' them:

ἐπερωτῶντα αὐτούς (46).

All are amazed:

ἐξίσταντο δὲ πάντες (47).

(at xxx 33 Jacob boasts of his 'righteousness before your face':

ἡ δικαιοσύνη μου . . . ἐνώπιόν σου).

Jacob, on his way to meet Esau, sends some of his flocks ahead as a present:

προπορεύεσθε ἔμπροσθέν μου (xxxii 17).

Jacob, who fears death from his brother, is allowed to go his way in peace (xxxiii 1 ff.).

Jacob journeys to the city of Shechem; Rachel dies giving birth to Benjamin and is buried at Bethlehem:

αὕτη ἐστὶν Βηθλεεμ (xxxv 19).

Joseph dreams that the heavenly bodies worship him while he is shepherding the flock with his brothers:

Ἰωσηφ . . . ἦν ποιμαίνων (xxxvii 2).

His brothers are jealous, but his father 'kept this word in mind':

ὁ δὲ πατὴρ αὐτοῦ διετήρησεν τὸ ῥῆμα (xxxvii 11).

Judah's wife conceives, bears a son, and calls his name Er:

συλλαβοῦσα ἔτεκεν υἱὸν καὶ ἐκάλεσεν τὸ ὄνομα αὐτοῦ Ηρ (xxxviii 3).

Joseph, having been sold into slavery, is taken to Egypt:

Ἰωσηφ δὲ κατήχθη εἰς Αἴγυπτον (xxxix 1).

There Pharaoh recognizes Joseph as 'having the spirit of God in him':

ἔχει πνεῦμα θεοῦ ἐν αὐτῷ (xli 28).

Joseph's brothers go down to Egypt to buy grain (xlii 1 ff.) and return leaving Simeon there.

At the end of a day's journey they discover the money in their sacks.

Joseph 'listens' to his brothers:

ἀκουει Ἰωσηφ (xlii 23).

and questions them:

ἐπηρώτησεν ἡμᾶς (xliii 7).

Joseph's brothers are amazed:

ἐξέστη ἡ καρδία αὐτῶν (xlii 28).

Jesus' parents, when they find him, ask, 'Why have you done this to us?':	Joseph's brothers, when they find the money, ask, 'Why has God done this to us?':
τί ἐποίησας ἡμῖν οὕτως; (48).	τί τοῦτο ἐποίησεν ὁ θεὸς ἡμῖν; (xlii 28)
Jesus goes down with his parents and is subject to them:	Benjamin goes down with his brothers, though Jacob at first objects:
κατέβη μετ' αὐτῶν (51).	οὐ καταβήσεται . . . μεθ' ὑμῶν (xlii 38).

Not only does this cursory survey reveal some 30 direct verbal parallels between Luke and the Greek of the Septuagint, but most of these also occur in the same order in both documents. The framework, as well as many details, of the Lucan nativity narrative would appear to have been determined by the sequence of events narrated in Genesis xxvii-xliii. One cannot help speculating how this came about.

We know that the reading of the Gospel in the Christian assembly took over the place of honour held by the *Torah* in the synagogue and was surrounded by similar ceremonies. Is it not possible that Luke was consciously writing a Christian *Torah* to replace or supplement the Pentateuch? Or did the gospel originate in a series of homilies preached in the primitive Christian assemblies and influenced by the lessons read from the Pentateuch? [1]) Ancient Jewish homilies were related to the lessons of the synagogue by just the sort of verbal connections we have detected above in Luke [2]). The Palestinian triennial lectionary spread the story of Jacob from which our parallels have been drawn over some fifteen Sabbaths [3]). When the text of Luke 1-2 is divided into matching sections, these appear to correspond almost perfectly with the natural divisions of the narrative. The numbered chapter-divisions of Codex B, in fact, will serve very well for this purpose.

Codex B: Masoretic Text:

Luke				Seder Gen		
1	i 1-4	Introduction		25	xxvii 1	Story of Jacob
2	5-25	Zechariah's vision		26	xxvii 28	Jacob's blessing
3	26-38	Annunciation		27	xxviii 10	Vision of angels
		(i 26 = xxviii 12; i 28				
		= xxviii 13-15; i 30 =				
		xxviii 30; i 31 = xxviii				
		19; i 33 = xxviii 21)				

---

[1]) I have made a similar suggestion with regard to the Fourth Gospel in 'Feeding and Sacrifice', *Expository Times* LXXIX (1968), pp. 340 f.

[2]) Cf. J. MANN, *The Bible as Read and Preached in the Old Synagogue*, Cincinnati, 1940, pp. 11 ff.

[3]) MANN, *op. cit.*, pp. 208 ff.

4	39-45	Visitation (i 42=xxx 2; i 45= xxx 13)	28	xxix 31	Leah gives birth
5	45-46	Mary's song	29	xxx 22	God remembers Rachel
6	57-66	Naming of John Baptist (i 65=xxxi 42)	30	xxxi 3	God names Jacob
7	67-end	Zechariah's song (i 71=xxxii 12; i 76= xxxii 17)	31	xxxii 4	Messengers sent
8 ii	1-5	Journey to Bethlehem	32	xxxiii 18	Journey to Shechem
9	6-14	Birth of Jesus	33	xxxv 9	Death of Rachel
10	15-20	Shepherds (ii 15=xxxvii 2; ii 19 =xxxvii 11)	34	xxxvii 1	Shepherds
11	21	Naming of Jesus (ii 21=xxxviii 3)	35	xxxviii 1	Judah's incest
12	22-24	J. taken to Jerusalem (ii 22=xxxix 1)	36	xxxix 1	J. taken to Egypt
13	25-35	Simeon's prophecy	36b	xl 1	J. interprets dreams
14	36-38	Anna's prophecy	37	xli 1	J. interprets dreams
15	39-41	Jesus has grace of God (ii 40=xli 38)	38	xli 38	J. has spirit of God
16	42-end	J's. parents come to him (ii 46=xlii 23 & xliii 7; ii 47-8=xlii 28; ii 51=xlii 38)	39	xlii 18	J's. brothers come to him

It would appear to be more than accident that 20 verbal parallels fall within the sections thus arranged. It is possible that Codex B (the earliest complete MS of the gospels we have) preserves the original units of composition, by which the evangelist has consciously matched the lessons of the triennial cycle?

THE REJECTION OF JESUS AT NAZARETH
(Luke iv 16-30)

Sheffield

If we suspend judgment temporarily on the historicity of the Rejection of Jesus at Nazareth as recorded by Luke, the main problems raised by the narrative may be listed as:

I. The relation of the pericope to Mark vi 1-6.
II. The apparent incongruity between the initial friendly response to Jesus on the part of the synagogue audience and its subsequent hostility and rejection.
III. The meaning of the pericope as a whole for Luke and its significance in his theology.
IV. The relation between the Scripture from Isaiah and the teaching or 'sermon' which follows.

After investigating these problems we may be able to offer some tentative suggestions on the historicity of the narrative. It should be said that these problems, together with opinions on and possible answers to them, cannot easily be treated serially because they are interrelated from the beginning: nevertheless, in the interests of clarity we shall attempt to discuss each in turn.

I

The position of the Rejection narrative in Luke is very different from that in which it appears in Mark (and Matthew). In Mark, the episode is placed just before the Galilean ministry draws to its close (Mark vi 1-6), and in Matthew it has a similar location (Matt. xiii 53-58): but in Luke, the Rejection pericope appears to stand as a programmatic preface to the public ministry. Moreover, there is little verbal similarity between Luke iv 16-30 and Mark vi 1-6: most of the Lukan passage is in fact peculiar to the third evangelist. In spite of these significant differences the over-all structure of the

Markan and Lukan episodes is the same: Jesus comes to his own country (or town); he visits the synagogue on the sabbath and teaches; there is an astonished reaction from the people, followed by comments on his origin; Jesus utters the logion about 'the prophet in his own country'; he is rejected by his own people; the refusal to work miracles (Mark vi 5) is possibly presupposed, though rather awkwardly, in the complaint which Jesus attributes to his hearers (Luke iv 23) [1]. In view of the general similarity DIBELIUS and BULTMANN correctly suppose that in his account of the Rejection Luke has given us a scene patterned after Mark vi 1-6 [2]. That he supplemented the Markan record of the 'scene' with traditional material drawn from other sources is possible [3]; but more probable is the view that Luke regarded his own version of the Rejection as a substitute—a rearranged and largely rewritten substitute—for the Markan narrative [4].

II

Luke's rewriting of the Markan episode raises problems of its own. The most striking of these is that, by his omission from verses 22-24 of the Markan words ,,and they were offended at him'', he appears to leave unbridged the gap between the initial friendly response of the people and their subsequent violent hostility. Jesus is presented

[1] Luke's independence of Mark at this point may be questioned on the grounds that Luke iv 23 seems to imply earlier healing works of Jesus in Capernaum, and that city has not been mentioned by Luke up to this point, but had been alluded to by Mark as early as i 21. This is not conclusive evidence: activity in Capernaum could be included, by implication, in Luke iv 14-15. In support of Luke's dependence on Mark it should be noted that in the passage linking the Temptation story and the Rejection (Luke iv 13-15) verse 14 seems to take its geographical (but not its temporal) details from Mark: cf. A. R. C. LEANEY, *Commentary on the Gospel according to St Luke*, p. 51.
[2] M. DIBELIUS, *From Tradition to Gospel*, p. 110, and R. BULTMANN, *The History of the Synoptic Tradition*, pp. 31-32, 386-87. We need not concern ourselves here with BULTMANN's claim (shared by DIBELIUS in the first edition of his book, but not in its second and revised edition) that the Markan narrative represents an ideal scene constructed out of the Oxyrhynchus saying: "A prophet is not accepted in his own country and a physician works no cures on those who know him" (Pap. Oxy. 1 lines 21-26): suffice it to say that it seems more probable that the Oxyrhynchus logion actually depends on Luke's narrative: the words "Physician, heal thyself" (Luke iv 23) certainly seem like the original underlying the second half of the developed Oxyrhynchus saying.
[3] This is the view taken by R. H. LIGHTFOOT, *History and Interpretation in the Gospels*, pp. 204, 208.
[4] LEANEY, *op. cit.*, p. 51.

as himself taking the initiative against the people and (in the
Elijah and Elisha analogies of verses 25-27) as criticizing their
inability or refusal to acknowledge him. LEANEY remarks that Luke
has left us "an impossible story" [1]). The difficulty cannot be
resolved by arguing that Mark's statement about the people being
offended at Jesus is included or implied in the Lukan words, "Is not
this Joseph's son?" (v 22). These words are probably intended to
express sheer surprise: they need not imply malice or contempt [2]).
Nor is it satisfying to resolve the paradox in the narrative by recourse
to LAGRANGE's view that Luke conflated records of two visits by
Jesus to his own town and that this is the reason for the obscurity
in the sequence of the narrative [3]).

The most interesting attempt to resolve the apparent inconsistency
in the Lukan scene is made by JEREMIAS in his monograph *Jesus'
Promise to the Nations* [4]): his suggestion forms part of his argument
that Jesus removed from Jewish eschatological expectation the
idea of vengeance on the Gentiles. JEREMIAS regards verse 22 as
the key to the solution of the paradoxical nature of the whole
pericope. As they stand, the first two clauses of this verse appear
to express entranced wonder, while the third implies disbelief and
criticism. In order to restore unity of thought to the verse JEREMIAS
builds upon the suggestion of B. VIOLET that the verse has an
Aramaic origin and could be translated as "And they all testified
against him and were aghast at the words of grace which proceeded
from his mouth". According to JEREMIAS the verb μαρτυρεῖν (like
the Hebrew הֵעִיד and the Aramaic אַסְהֵד עַל) may be followed by
either a dative of advantage (to bear witness *on behalf of* a person)
or a dative of disadvantage (to bear witness *against* a person). The
correct meaning in verse 22 can only be decided by the interpretation
given to the second clause. In this connection, JEREMIAS points out
(i) that θαυμάζειν can express both admiring astonishment and
bewildered opposition to what is strange, and (ii) that οἱ λόγοι τῆς
χάριτος in this Semitic Greek will not mean "words full of charm"
or "gracious words", but "words of (God's) mercy". The people

---

[1]) LEANEY, *op. cit.*, p. 52.
[2]) It is likely that Mark's words "Is not this the carpenter, the son of Mary"
are contemptuous, for it is contrary to Jewish custom to name a man after
his mother, even when the father was dead, except in insulting terms (cf.
Jud. xi 1 f.): cf. LIGHTFOOT, *op. cit.*, pp. 187 f.
[3]) M.-J. LAGRANGE, *Évangile selon Saint Luc*, (8me ed. 1948) pp. 146 ff.
[4]) J. JEREMIAS, *Jesus' promise to the Nations*, pp. 44 f.

(he argues) were amazed and annoyed that Jesus spoke only of the grace of God by omitting from the scripture reading the words "and a day of vengeance of our God" which in Isaiah follow "to proclaim the acceptable year of the Lord". Jesus left out the day of vengeance and the people were aghast. "They protested with one voice (πάντες ἐμαρτύρουν αὐτῷ) and were furious (καὶ ἐθαύμαζον) because he (only) spoke about (God's year of) mercy (and omitted the words about the Messianic vengeance)". The scornful third clause would then follow aptly. There is therefore no break in the attitude of Jesus' audience in verse 22: from the outset unanimous rage was their response.

Attractive though this reconstruction is, there are strong arguments against it [1]).

(a) The Semitic character of Luke's language is still very much an open question. The view that most of his 'Semitisms' are really 'Septuagintalisms' is cogently argued by H. F. D. SPARKS [2]), and the Rejection pericope itself contains evidence of Luke's attention to the words and phrases of the LXX [3]). In this narrative Sparks can find only one obvious Aramaism, the periphrastic ἦν ἀνατεθραμμένος in verse 16 which looks like a Semitic pluperfect; but even this is not certain evidence of an Aramaic source [4]). The idea of an Aramaic original behind Luke iv 22 remains merely a conjecture.

(b) If it had been Luke's intention to describe unmixed feelings of rage on the part of Jesus' audience would he have given us two phrases (or three, if we include ἐπὶ τοῖς λόγοις τῆς χάριτος) so ambiguous as JEREMIAS claims they are?

(c) Luke does not seem to use μαρτυρεῖν in the negative sence, i.e. to witness or protest *against* [5]).

---

[1]) Most of the points are listed by H. ANDERSON, "Broadening Horizons: The Rejection at Nazareth Pericope of Luke iv 16-30 in Light of Recent Critical Trends", *Interpretation*, XVIII (1964), 259-75, especially pp. 267-69.

[2]) H. F. D. SPARKS, "The Semitisms of St Luke's Gospel", *JTS* XLIV (1943), 129 ff.

[3]) The phrase in verse 26 εἰς Σάρεπτα τῆς Σιδωνίας πρὸς γυναῖκα χήραν corresponds closely to the LXX of 1 Kg. xvii 9; and twenty-four of the twenty-six words of the Isaiah quotation are exactly identical with the LXX.

[4]) E. HAENCHEN, *Die Apostelgeschichte* (10. Aufl. 1956) p. 119 note 7 thinks that Luke's predilection for the use of periphrasis does not betray the reproduction of Semitic sources, but may correspond to the outlook and art of the author who took equal pleasure in portraying the concrete background situation and in coining picturesquely individual expressions.

[5]) Cf. the review of New Testament usage by H. STRATHMANN, *T.W.N.T.* (Eng. version) vol. IV, pp. 496 f.

(d) As we pointed out earlier, it is not at all certain that the third clause of verse 22, "Is not this Joseph's son?" denotes disbelief and criticism. JEREMIAS' attempt to unify the attitudes described in the verse requires that the comment be derogatory.

(e) Even if verse 22 as a whole were to be construed as denoting hostility, we would still have to face the problem posed by the last clause of verse 20, which describes the first reaction of the people to Jesus' words: "the eyes of all in the synagogue were fixed on him". The verb ἀτενίζω—a favourite of Luke's—appears always to mean for him the gaze of expectant faith or trust [1]). Instead of the attitude of the people being one of hostility from the outset, may it not have been one of warm responsiveness to the end of verse 22?

(f) JEREMIAS attributes the hostility of the synagogue audience to the fact that Jesus had removed from the Isaiah passage read the reference to vengeance on the Gentiles. But did Jesus speak or read on this occasion precisely and only the words of Isaiah recorded in Luke iv 18-19 [2])? It is not inconceivable that Luke had an oral tradition to that express effect, but we must not overlook the fact that it would have been an odd *reading*: the quotation is in fact composite, made up of Isaiah lxi 1 (with the omission of "to heal the broken in heart"), lviii 6 and the first four words of lxi 2. Perhaps Luke had a document in which these passages had already been brought together: perhaps, as ANDERSON suggests [3]), he was citing freely from memory the LXX text of Isaiah lxi 1-2 into which he inserted the words ἀποστεῖλαι τεθραυσμένους ἐν ἀφέσει (from lviii 6) as a substitute for "and a day of vengeance of our God", which would neither have suited the situation not have harmonised with his own general theological conception, *viz.* that on its rejection by the Jews the gospel was sent to the Gentiles. JEREMIAS' rationale for the people's antagonism (itself questionable) depends on the presumption of the precise historical accuracy of Luke's narrative.

For these reasons the attempt by Jeremias to rid the Lukan rejection narrative of its apparent inconsistency by means of linguistic reconstruction can scarcely be judged persuasive.

Is the 'inconsistency' resolved by discovery of the evangelist's own

---

[1]) Cf. Acts i 10, vi 15: also iii 4, vii 55, xi 6, xiii 9, xiv 9 and Luke xxii 56.

[2]) In any case, is it certain that the omitted words denote God's vengeance on the Gentiles? The Isaiah passage may describe favour *and* judgment for Israel.

[3]) ANDERSON, *op. cit.*, 269.

purpose and theology? Later in this essay we shall consider the *redaktionsgeschichtliche* approach to this narrative, but at this point a few remarks may be made on what this method of Gospel criticism has to say on the particular problem of the seemingly inexplicable *volte-face* of the Nazareth audience. CONZELMANN, who is more interested in the geographical details contained in the story and their theological significance, does not raise the problem [1]: to do so would probably be regarded by him as an unwarranted attempt to probe to historical facts [2]. In his discussion of the pericope HELMUT FLENDER also resists the attempt to discover the historical facts [3], but he does try to explain how Luke himself understood the reaction of the people of Nazareth. In Luke's intention the narrative has a twofold purpose. It reveals, first of all, the people's concentration on what is superficial: their astonishment is for the externals, the 'winsome words' of the infant prodigy from their own town, the local carpenter's son. This astonishment should have turned from a hankering after sensation into an adoration of God for his miracles, but in fact it did not so develop: the audience could not make up their minds (which is implied in the use of θαυμάζειν): all they saw in Jesus was Joseph's son. So in verse 23 Jesus actually provokes the rejection (by refusing to oblige them as they wish) and exposes their unbelief, or their inability to decide to believe. But in Luke's writing straightforward narrative and the kerygmatic appeal to faith form a dialectical unity. Therefore the second aspect of Luke's intention in this pericope is to reveal its contemporary relevance for himself and his readers. "The first reaction evoked by the preaching of the gospel is that ordinary human curiosity is aroused. Then the extraordinary quality in Jesus' words and deeds"

---

[1] On verse 23 (which for him is the crucial verse) CONZELMANN says: "The general opinion, that the verse represents a reminiscence of previous events, rests on an inadmissible interpretation of history. It is a view which is not suggested by the text, is scarcely conceivable from the point of view of literary criticism and is disproved by Luke's structure." *The Theology of St Luke*, p. 34.

[2] "We have to leave aside the question as to what the historical facts were if we are to understand Luke's account", says CONZELMANN (*op. cit.*, p. 31): when he goes on to say that "we are concerned with its inner consistency and meaning", but does not look at the apparent inconsistency in the audience's reaction to Jesus, one wonders how he understands ,,consistency".

[3] "To reconstruct the scene historically bars the way to a true understanding of the pericope", H. FLENDER, *St Luke: Theologian of Redemptive History*, p. 153.

—for λόγοι τῆς χάριτος is deliberately ambiguous: 'winsome words' is the superficial assessment, but 'message of grace' is the deeper and demanding significance—"challenges his audience to a decision of faith. Either they accept in faith the heavenly power of Jesus as the disciples accept it, or they remain open-minded..... or they reject Jesus' claim like... the people of Nazareth" [1]). With FLENDER's suggestion about the two layers of meaning in the story we are not now concerned: we wish only to draw attention to the way in which he irons out the problem of the sudden change in the people's attitude as it is presented in the narrative. The audience is so preoccupied with the human aspect of his person that Jesus himself provokes their hostility by anticipating their demand for miracles and refusing to accede to it. Whereas JEREMIAS claimed that Jesus provoked the audience's hostility from the beginning by omitting mention of God's vengeance on the Gentiles, FLENDER argues that he deliberately turned their acceptance of him into rejection by refusing to work the miracles they wanted. The narrative, as it stands, lends support to this commonly-held view, but is it a sufficiently precise and penetrating explanation of the dramatic change in attitude?

In his review of recent treatments of the Rejection story ANDERSON suggests that the explanation of the apparently inconsistent narrative lies in its paradoxical character for Luke himself. The evangelist is following an account of rejection and failure, akin to or the same as Mark's [2]), and on this he is superimposing a "success" theme suitable for the opening of a description of Jesus' public ministry, and this "success" theme, in Luke's total theological conception, is the direction of the gospel beyond the bounds of the Jewish nation towards the Gentiles [3]). This theme is signified or symbolized in advance by the lack of success at

---

[1]) FLENDER, op. cit., pp. 156-57.

[2]) Whereas BULTMANN claims that Mark's story (vi 1-6) was originally, in the main, a record of a successful appearance of Jesus, altered later by the addition of the logion about the prophet (verse 4), ANDERSON suggests — following F. W. BEARE, *The Earliest Records of Jesus*, p. 124 and W. L. KNOX, *The Sources of the Synoptic Gospels*, I, pp. 47 ff. — that the earliest form of the story in Mark was one of complete failure and hostility, later toned down (by the evangelist) by adding in verse 2 the conventional note of astonishment and by the inconsistent insertion of verse 5b (*op. cit.*, 265)

[3]) Cf. ANDERSON, op. cit., pp. 266, 272: also LEANEY, op. cit., pp. 51, 52 who regards the story as one about a triumphant visit combined with a tradition concerning rejection.

Nazareth. But if Luke's purpose in presenting the story demands Jesus' rejection (as part of a "success" theme), why does he begin the account with the mention of his warm reception, especially if he is in touch with Mark's story which is one of virtually outright hostility? Is the favourable response recorded simply in order that the provocative words of Jesus (in verse 23) can be included? The difficulty inherent in the narrative is not really taken away by ANDERSON's suggestion.

Must we then remain content to say that Luke has in fact left us with an "impossible" story? Let us look again at the narrative, as given by the evangelist, to see if we can find a logical sequence in its development. Jesus reads or quotes in the synagogue at Nazareth verses drawn from Isaiah which announce relief and release for the captives and poor: it is like a year of Jubilee (cf. Lev. 25 and particularly verse 10): it is the "year of the Lord's favour", שְׁנַת־רָצוֹן לַיהֹוָה, ἐνιαυτὸς κυρίου δεκτός, and the use of δεκτός in the LXX requires that this be rendered as "a year well-pleasing or acceptable *to God*" because chosen by him (cf. LXX Isa. xlix 8, lviii 6) [1]. The year that is acceptable to God is the year of favour and active blessing for men. The synagogue audience expectantly awaits what the 'preacher' will say. His message to them is, "Today this scripture is fulfilled in your ears". The time of divine election, acceptance and presence is realised in the prophetic affirmation they have heard. And the people respond to the declaration with enthusiasm and surprise: they are spellbound by "the words of grace", and οἱ λόγοι τῆς χάριτος can hardly be construed in any other way. "As Luke shows by the way he uses the term elsewhere (Acts xiv 3; xx 24, 32), we have here a technical term with the unequivocal meaning of 'message of grace'" [2]. The message that release and redemption had come to them, in Nazareth, was indeed sufficient to make the people both enthusiastically excited and expectant: their blind, poor and captives will now win relief. The audiende's reaction—and a very understandable one it is—is actually voiced by Jesus himself: since the year of release has come to us, let us see it in action, here and now. "Assuredly, you will say to me this proverb, 'Physician, heal thyself': what we

---

[1] "In the LXX δεκτός . . . means 'acceptable' or 'pleasing' on the basis of a divine act of will", W. GRUNDMANN, *T.W.N.T.* (Eng. version), vol. II, p. 58.
[2] FLENDER, *op. cit.*, p. 153.

have heard you did at Capernaum, do here also in your own country",
that is, in this place and among us to whom you have just announced
the arrival of the era of fulfilment. There does not seem to be any
serious impediment to understanding the proverb as "Heal the ills
of your own town", with much the same meaning as "Charity
begins at home", i.e. "let us now see relief and release and redemption *here*". At this point Luke introduces the Markan logion, "A
prophet is not without honour except in his own country", but
with a difference which is surely significant: he does not use the
adjective ἄτιμος, but says "A prophet is not δεκτός in his own
country": now δεκτός is the word used earlier to describe the year
of the Lord and may be open to (if it does not actually require) the
interpretation "acceptable *to God*" [1]). Is it possible that Luke is
declaring that for a prophet to be acceptable to God he must go
outside his own country? This is suggested by the evangelist's two
illustrations from the Old Testament. There were many needy
widows in Israel in Elijah's time, and many lepers in Israel in
Elisha's time, and it was not necessarily their hostility to or lack
of acceptance of the prophets which failed to gain relief for them:
the purpose of God was that the activities of his servants should
transcend the limits of their own land and people. To no one of
the widows of Israel was Elijah sent (on the divine initiative [2]) but
to a non-Israelite, a poor woman to whom God's blessing and
provision were communicated by the prophet: the lepers of Israel
did not receive cleansing, but a Syrian—an enemy of Israel—was
cleansed and restored. Is Luke implying that Jesus will be carrying
out a ministry acceptable to God only if he does not confine his
work and words to his own people—contrary to their expectations:
he must be among and available to those not of his own people.
If this idea is present, even as an overtone of meaning in the
narrative, it is no surprise that the parochially-minded Jews of
Nazareth were filled with anger and murderous intent and attacked
Jesus in a manner which (in Luke's description) recalls in advance
the final rejection of Jesus and also the death of Stephen, the martyr
who challenged the parochialism and exlusiveness of Jewish religion.

---

[1]) The ARNDT-GINGRICH *Greek-English Lexicon of the New Testament*
notes that only here does δεκτός (an almost exclusively Biblical-Greek word)
seem to be used to mean "acceptable to men": elsewhere it is always used of
acceptability to God — a fact which should give us pause in interpreting
the adjective here.

[2]) The passive voice may well imply the divine action.

On this reading, Luke's narrative is consistent and fairly logical. There is no need to seek consistency by means of JEREMIAS' linguistic reconstruction. To FLENDER's view that Jesus provoked hostility by by refusing to work miracles we would add the suggestion that, according to Luke, Jesus, by refusing to do miracles for his own people and by his words, is affirming that his acceptability to God, his place in God's purpose, requires him to bring relief and release to these outside Israel, and it was this that really created the resentment and antagonism.

III

In presenting the case for the coherence of Luke's story we have implied a certain amount about the significance of the narrative for the evangelist's theology. The programmatic prologue to the ministry of Jesus would suggest (i) that the gospel of redemption and release will achieve "success" outside the confines of Judaism [1]), and (ii) that its rejection by Jews and acceptance by Gentiles do not depend solely on their choice; they belong to the purpose of God (even so far as its proclaimer is concerned); they are in fact part of a Lukan *Heilsgeschichte*.

To understand the meaning of the narrative for Luke in this way is to admit that for the evangelist the story had a symbolic significance. In this connection, however, we do well to remember CONZELMANN's claim that "there is no unrestrained symbolism in Luke; only what is in his opinion a historical event can possess genuine typological meaning" [2]). Despite his many valuable insights on this particular narrative, CONZELMANN's insistence on Luke's symbolical use of geographical details to present his theological attitudes to Jesus and the church fails to convince simply because he does not follow the implications of the words just quoted. For CONZELMANN the sequence Nazareth-Capernaum-Call of the disciples is of great theological importance [3]), but for it to have this

---

[1]) It is significant that in Luke's gospel Jesus himself does not go to the Gentiles. The Rejection narrative proclaims *in advance* his lack of success among his own people: the rest of the gospel bears this out. The move towards the Gentiles and the success of the gospel belong to the mission and ministry of the Church.

[2]) CONZELMANN, *op. cit.*, p. 34.

[3]) In CONZELMANN's view, the sequence conveys important insights on the priority of miracle to preaching, on election ("one can only be a relative of Jesus *sola gratia*") and on the Lukan conception of the witness (*op. cit.*, pp. 34-38).

significance the verb ἐρεῖτε (in iv 23) must refer to the *future* in Capernaum. There can be no question of any reference in the verse to past events in that city. The future tense therefore becomes a literary artifice, pointing the reader of the story forward to what *will be done and said* in Capernaum, i.e. to iv 31 ff. If this is the case, can Luke have regarded the Nazareth pericope as a record of a genuine historical event? If Luke thought of Jesus as speaking with real people in a real situation (as CONZELMANN's words would allow us to assume), the verb ἐρεῖτε and the content of verse 23 cannot refer only to future events in Capernaum: they must apply to the audience's *present* situation ("you will now say") and the reference to activity in Capernaum can of course be considered to be covered in verses 14-15. CONZELMANN's contribution at this point is vitiated by an over-subtle dependence on geographical details and their theological importance.

FLENDER deduces from the Rejection narrative support for his theory that Luke's theology is structured around a dialectical pattern of concepts through which reality may be seen under different aspects or on different levels. The account of the earthly life of Jesus is combined with testimony to the eschatological salvation in Christ, the mystery of which is disclosed only to faith. Accordingly, the appearance of Jesus at Nazareth illustrates the vulnerable character of Jesus' claim: he evokes curiosity and presents a challenge to decision, and he may be rejected or accepted. The "today" of Jesus' affirmation is confirmed in the "today" of the preaching to which hearers may give the same responses. To argue in this way presupposes that Luke is consciously writing on these two levels (the past and the contemporary) and necessitates the attribution to him of a cunning ambiguity in the use of words and phrases: in this case οἱ λόγοι τῆς χάριτος means "winsome words" on one level and "message of grace" on the other, and θαυμάζειν suggests a suspension of judgment, bringing out the either/or nature of the challenge [1]. Again the *redaktionsgeschichtlich* method seems to be deducing from details a theological motif and a spiritual message (with existential overtones) which are not subject to adequate controls by the text as a whole. It is the position of the Rejection narrative in Luke's gospel and its over-all content (which is not necessarily marred by inconsistency or incongruity) that reveal and confirm the evangelist's theological purpose.

[1] Cf. FLENDER, *op. cit.*, pp. 153, 155-56.

IV

Thus far we have been concerned to examine the Rejection pericope for its consistency as a narrative and to see its significance, as a structured unit, in Luke's theological scheme. But is the story wholly a Lukan creation? The question of historicity requires investigation. Broadly speaking, this issue may be considered in two steps: (i) the chronology of the event narrated, and (ii) the traditional content of the passage.

(i) It seems highly improbable that a visit to the Nazareth synagogue which resulted in rejection was in fact the first act in Jesus' public ministry, which is what the Lukan story asserts. Preference for Luke's chronology at this point over against his fellow evangelists could be justified only on the basis of assumptions about the absolute reliability of Luke as a historian and about his access to sources of more antiquity and originality than Mark's.

(ii) The possibility that *on some occasion* during his ministry Jesus visited Nazareth and read and spoke in the synagogue, as Luke records, cannot be dismissed so peremptorily. That Jesus visited and taught in the synagogues of his people is widely affirmed in the tradition; that he did so at Nazareth, after he had gained a considerable following elsewhere, is attested by Mark vi 1-6 (cf. Matt. xiii 54 ff.) and is inherently likely; but only Luke gives details of what took place in the synagogue. Are these details conceivably accurate as a report of *a* synagogue visit? One approach to affirming the historicity of what is recorded by Luke is made through the appeal to synagogue lectionaries. It is not our purpose to enter into discussion of the evidence on which the existence of an annual or triennial lectionary system is postulated: [1]) we wish to consider how the lections are used to illumine the sequence and unity of Luke iv 16-30 [2]). It is suggested (a) that Jesus preached a sermon at Nazareth at the end of the month Tishri or the beginning of Cheshvan and that the sermon reflects in its contents the Old Testament passages which were read at that time of the year in

---

[1]) The outstanding recent work in this field is A. GUILDING, *The Fourth Gospel and Jewish Worship* (1960). Far-reaching criticisms of the work are made by L. MORRIS, *The New Testament and the Jewish Lectionaries* (1964).

[2]) For this section of this essay I am indebted to L. C. CROCKETT, "Luke iv 16-30 and the Jewish Lectionary Cycle: A Word of Caution", *Journal of Jewish Studies* XVII (1966), 13-46. The first part of this study presents a careful review of the evidence for and against the existence and use of a lectionary cycle in the first century A.D.

the Palestinian triennial cycle; and (b) that Luke was acquainted with this lectionary and was influenced by its language in his description of the sermon and the reaction it provoked. The part of the reconstructed triennial cycle which is relevant to the argument is set out below, with the readings used as a background for Luke iv 16-30 in italics.

	Year 1	Year 2	Year 3
Tishri Week 3	Gen. xxxv 9	Lev. ix 1	Deut. vii 12
	Isa. xliii 1-21	1 Kg. viii 56-8	Isa. iv 6
	Isa. lxi 1 (?)		
Tishri Week 4	Gen. xxxvii 1	Lev. xii 1	Deut. ix 1
	Isa. xxxii 18-	Isa. lxvi	Jer. ii
	xxxiii 15		
Cheshvan Week 1	Gen. xxxviii 1	Lev. xiii 29	Deut. x 1
	2 Sam. xi 2	2 Kg. v	*2 Kg. xiii 23*
Cheshvan Week 2		*Lev. xiv 1*	*Deut. xi 10*
		2 Kg. vii	Isa. liv 11-lv 6

On what basis are these lections so designated? The readings from the Pentateuch (*sedarim*) are arranged according to a three-year cycle beginning in Nisan, and that still remains a problematical scheme. The most important passages are the prophetic readings (*haftaroth*). How do we know that these particular *haftaroth* were linked with their respective *sedarim*? Dr GUILDING tells us that they are so designated "according to BÜCHLER" [1]: but on investigation of BÜCHLER's claims CROCKETT finds that his sources for designating these particular *haftaroth* are widely separated in time and place: his deductions are in fact indefinite and not always convincing [2]. For example, the inclusion of Isa. lxi 1-2 as a *haftarah* is not supported by any lectionary list but depends on an inference by JACOB MANN from the homily to Gen. xxxv 9 [3]. It should be noted that the passages used to illumine the Lukan pericope are selected from a large number of possible passages with considerable longitude as well as latitude allowed: this increases the uncertainty of the use of the reconstructed cycle as a background for the passage. Furthermore, CROCKETT demonstrates that the connections

---

[1] That is, according to A. BÜCHLER, "The Reading of the Law and Prophets in a Triennial Cycle", *Jewish Quarterly Review* V (1893), 420-68; VI (1894), 1-73.

[2] CROCKETT, *op. cit.*, 41-42.

[3] J. MANN, *The Bible as read and preached in the Old Synagogue*, vol. I (1940), pp. 283-85; MANN in fact concluded that the *haftarah* commenced, not with verse 1, but with verse 2.

drawn between the Old Testament passages and the text of Luke iv 16-30 are frequently artificial. The suggested links are as follows.

(i) Isa. lxi 1-2 is quoted in Luke iv 18-19. But was Isa. lxi 1 f. ever a *haftarah*? Even if it was, the lectionary background offers no explanation of the peculiar form of the quotation, *viz.* the omission of a line from verse 1, the interpolation of a line from Isa. lviii 6—and since the Rabbis did not allow skipping *backwards* in the reading of the minor prophets, B. Meg. 24a, they probably did not permit it in the other prophets—together with the omission of the final phrase in Isa. lxi 2. It is in fact doubtful if we are dealing with a *haftarah* at all [1]).

(ii) Luke iv 27 contains an allusion to 2 Kg v, and the phrase πολλοὶ λεπροί in verse 27 is an allusion to 2 Kg. vii 3 ("the four lepers sitting by the gate"). But does one have to have in mind a specific Old Testament reference when saying simply that there were many lepers in Israel? And if verse 27 recalls 2 Kg. v, then verse 25 must recall 1 Kg. xvii—and for that 'allusion' the lectionary system offers no assistance. The linking of the references must depend on something other than the fixed lectionary suggested.

(iii) The phrase "the heavens were shut up" (Luke iv 25) is found as a metaphor for drought in Deut. xi 17, in the proposed *seder* for the second week of Cheshvan. But the expression "shutting up the heavens", as a periphrasis for "drought" is fairly common in the Bible: in addition to Deut. xi 17, it appears at 1 Kg. viii 35, 2 Chron. v 26; vii 13 and Rev. xi 6, and it is probably implied by the context in 2 Kg. v. The assumption of an explicit reference to Deut. xi is unnecessary.

(iv) The words κατακρημνίζω and ὀφρῦς ("brow" of a hill) in Luke iv 29 are both *hapaxlegomena* in the New Testament: the former appears only once in the LXX, at 2 Chron. xxv 12 which is a parallel account of material in 2 Kg. xiii 23, the proposed third year *haftarah* for the first week of Cheshvan; and ὀφρῦς appears in the LXX only at Lev. xiv 9 (meaning "eye-brow"!) which belongs

---

[1]) In his contribution to the volume *Historicity and Chronology in the New Testament*, entitled "The Gospels as evidence for First-Century Judaism" (pp. 28-45) A. R. C. LEANEY takes up Dr GUILDING's suggestion about the background to Luke iv 16-30, but thinks that the Isaiah passage represents the "text" (*petiḥta*) to which Jesus related the lessons from Deut. xi (*seder* for first week of Cheshvan) and either 2 Kg. v or 2 Kg. vii. The required linguistic link between "text" and *haftarah* could be forged by לְבַשֵּׂר in Isa. lxi 1 and יוֹם־בְּשׂרָה in 2 Kg. vii 9.

to a *seder* for the second week in Cheshvan in the second year of the cycle. But both these words are fairly common in Hellenistic Greek (with their Lukan meanings), and, as CROCKETT remarks, "since not many people are thrown off cliffs in the New Testament, or in the Old for that matter, it is not surprising that this term occurs only once in each" [1]. Has not the search for, and discovery of allusions become both artificial and uncritical?

But even if the suggested connections with the proposed triennial lectionary system were more convincing than they are, we would still have to face a problem of great importance in using them to explain Luke iv 16-30. Presumably Jesus' sermon at Nazareth (at whatever time or season it was uttered)was given in Aramaic, or possibly Hebrew, and was later translated, probably in a condensed form, into the Greek version in which we have it. Yet it is to the *Septuagintal* renderings of lections for the end of Tishri - beginning of Cheshvan that recourse is had in the lectionary hypothesis. In addition to the initial assumption that Jesus read the lections for the day and preached on them, this appeal to the LXX makes sense only if we assume also that Luke (in writing of the attempt on Jesus' life) and those for whom he wrote were familiar with the lectionary system and using a Greek translation of the cycle which was textually identical with our LXX. Neither of these assumptions has any other support than the hypothesis of the reconstructed triennial cycle itself [2]. The assumption or, in the case of LEANEY, the affirmation of the unity and historicity of the reading and sermon at Nazareth by means of an appeal to a reconstructed lectionary system is made on the basis of "a strained and tenuous reasoning which has piled one hypothesis on another" [3])—the hypothesis of fixed *haftaroth*, of the reconstructed cycle of readings, known and used by Jesus, and familiar (in Greek translation) to Luke and his readers. In addition the lectionary background offers no word of assistance in the solution of the important literary

---

[1]) CROCKETT, *op. cit.*, 43.

[2]) Cf. CROCKETT, *op. cit.*, 39-40. In the course of his discussion of the possibility — or likelihood — that a lectionary cycle of Law and Prophets (when established) did not *create* connections between passages but made use of such connections already uncovered by midrashic exegesis, CROCKETT suggests that many New Testament passages which Dr GUILDING has interpreted by reference to a reconstructed lectionary cycle may be equally and more simply explicable in terms of acquaintance on the part of Jesus or the authors of the Gospels with Jewish exegetical traditions (p. 35).

[3]) CROCKETT, *op. cit.*, p. 45.

problem in the Rejection pericope which engaged our attention earlier in this essay, *viz.* the change in the audience's attitude. The embarassment caused by this to the proponents of a lectionary explanation is very clear in the case of LEANEY. After arguing that the passage from Isaiah is the "text" rather than a reading, he says:

> Nevertheless verse 16 states clearly that Jesus stood up "to read" and the "sermon" does not appear to begin until verse 21. In fact we do not at first hear the sermon, for which is substituted, by a device like that of the modern cinematograph film, its effect on the congregation (verse 22). ... After Jesus has, rather curiously, anticipated opposition which the people have so far been far from showing... he continues the sermon which occupies verses 24-8 [1]).

Confronted by an "explanation" like this, one begins to wonder whether the writer is on the right track at all in thinking that verses 24-28 constitute a "sermon" or condensed sermon on lections for a particular sabbath in Cheshvan.

A different approach to the Lukan passage is made by ASHER FINKEL [2]). He claims that while Isa. lxi 1 ff. represents a prophetic lection (a possible *haftarah* to Gen. xxxv 9) which would be followed by a proem-homily, the actual content of Jesus' sermon is not recorded in Luke at this point, but can be reconstructed from other sources in the Synoptics. The homily—a kind of *pesher* interpretation of Isa. lxi 1 ff.—is in fact the Beatitudes (Matt. v 3-12, Luke vi 20 23).

> Apparently both Matthew and Luke drew from a common source where the statements of blessings followed the proem text of Jesus' homily at Nazareth on the Sabbath day as recorded in Luk. iv 16-20. In presenting the blessings, Luke records the materialistic interpretation of the text and Matthew the abstract and spiritual [3]).

The linguistic parallels between the Beatitudes and the Isaiah passage listed by FINKEL are well-known and striking [4]): they may

---

[1]) LEANEY, *History and Chronology in the New Testament*, p. 38.

[2]) A. FINKEL, *The Pharisees and the Teacher of Nazareth* (Leiden, 1964), pp. 155 ff. and in his contribution to the Michel *Festschrift*, *Abraham unser Vater* (Leiden, 1965) pp. 106-115, entitled, "Jesus' Sermon at Nazareth (Luke iv 16-30)".

[3]) FINKEL, *The Pharisees and the Teacher of Nazareth*, p. 158.

[4]) The "poor" (or "poor in spirit") and the "meek" are indeed the עֲנָוִים of Isa. lxi 1: the "mourners" are referred to in Isa. lxi 3: the desire for "righteousness" could also be an allusion to Isa. lxi 3 and to the character of the year of God's favour. FINKEL links "hunger and thirsting" with Isa. lxi 5-6 and other Beatitudes with verses from the Psalms (*Abraham unser Vater*, p. 113).

even be added to if M. BLACK's observation that "the pure in heart" (Matt. v 8) when rendered into Aramaic gives דכי לב which (consonantly) comes very near to an Aramaic equivalent of Isaiah's נִשְׁבְּרֵי לֵב (Aram. דכיכי לב), the "broken hearted" (Isa. lxi 1) is allowed to influence our judgment[1]). It is undoubtedly an attractive hypothesis that the Beatitudes represent a *pesher* on Isa. lxi 1-7 (or part of it) in which the prophetic words are projected into the the life of Jesus' hearers and disciples: it cannot of course be proved that it was, nor that it was the "sermon" following the reading in the Nazareth synagogue. Moreover, it does not explain the form of Luke's narrative as it stands. FINKEL says very little on verses 25-28. They cannot be part of the "sermon": they must belong to the *Auseinandersetzung* with the synagogue audience *after* the sermon, when Jesus, on proclaiming himself an anointed prophet, is rejected: "therefore", says FINKEL, "he will continue his ministry in other villages, as told of the two great prophets Elijah and Elisha"[2]). But is it only to justify going to "other villages" that we have the introduction of references to Old Testament prophetic ministries to non-Israelites? The illustrations surely mean more than that. And if they do, and if we were to try to maintain the historicity of the whole section, we would have to ask, "Did Jesus, at an early stage or at any stage in his teaching, so directly imply the necessity of his mission to the Gentiles?" This is a problem which would have to be faced and answered by those who attempt to argue for the historicity of verses 24-28 either by having recourse to the lectionary hypothesis or by treating them as an account of a post-sermon discussion in the Nazareth synagogue.

V

It is now time to draw together the main strands of our discussion.

(i) The pericope Luke iv 16-30, as it stands in the gospel, coheres without the linguistic reconstruction of verse 22. The reading of the Isaiah passage(s)—which Luke may be quoting freely or from memory—is followed by Jesus' affirmation that the year of God's favour has come: its announcement is virtually its realisation: this "message of grace" evokes an expectant and admiring response (verse 22): the people will desire immediate evidence of its ful-

---

[1]) M. BLACK, *An Aramaic Approach to the Gospels and Acts* (3rd ed.) p. 158 note 2.

[2]) FINKEL, *Abraham unser Vater*, p. 115.

filment in their midst: this Jesus refuses by asserting that the prophetic ministry which will win acceptance (primarily with God) has to transcend the limits of his own land and people, as the scripture attests in the cases of Elijah and Elisha: irritated at being denied what they want, the people react violently and hustle Jesus out of the town, with murderous intent.

(ii) This interpretative sequence—which makes for a consistent narrative—makes sense only from the point of view of Luke's theology as developed throughout his writings, *viz.* that because of the Jewish rejection of Jesus, the gospel turns to the Gentiles among whom it achieves "success". A *heilsgeschichtliche* pattern (similar to that of Paul in Romans) would then determine the theological meaning of the piece, Now, it is virtually impossible to imagine that Jesus actually asserted publicly (or even implied) that his ministry must—of divine necessity, almost—be among non-Israelites. Therefore, verses 24-28 probably represent an early Christian tradition formed around a logion like "A prophet is not without honour save in his own country" and used to offer an *apologia*, with dominical authority, for the mission to the Gentiles. Luke is responsible for its introduction into the record of Jesus' teaching.

(iii) The argument for the historical unity of the entire pericope (verses 16-30) which is based on the reconstruction of the lectionary system—itself very hypothetical—would collapse because of the utter unlikelihood of the situation envisaged.

(iv) That Jesus, in the course of his preaching and teaching ministry, visited Nazareth and its synagogue is inherently very probable and is well attested: that he received a less than enthusiastic response there is also strongly attested in the tradition; but that his appearance in Nazareth's synagogue was the first act of his public ministry—as Luke suggests—is quite unlikely. The position of the pericope is due to its character as an 'advance' notice of the essential message of Luke's theology, the victory of the gospel among the Gentiles.

(v) The possibility that at some time in his ministry Jesus applied to himself the words of Isa. lxi 1 f. cannot be excluded. The claim implied in the words quoted or read is that Jesus was a prophet [1]) engaged on the programme of service of the anointed

---

[1]) The Targum to "The spirit of the Lord is upon me" reads "The spirit of prophecy from before the Lord is upon me".

of God. "What Jesus proclaims and performs is possible because he has been anointed and possesses the Spirit of God" [1]. According to 11 Q Melch line 18 the "bringer of good tidings" (מְבַשֵּׂר) of Isa. lii 7 is "the anointed by the spirit (מְשִׁיחַ הרוח)" [2]. This is the first discovered instance in the Qumran literature of a single prophet being described as "anointed": CD ii 12 mentions prophets as "anointed with holy spirit" (cf. also CD vi 1 and 1 QM xi 7). The 11 Q Melch fragments are probably to be dated in the first half of the first Christian century [3]. That Jesus should have spoken of himself as the anointed, prophetic messenger of God, proclaiming God's salvation in terms of Isa. lxi, should not be regarded as utterly impossible in view of this newly-found Qumran document: as in 11 Q Melch, so in Luke iv, the emphasis lies on the proclamation rather than on the title or person of the herald, on the signs of God's salvation rather than on the fact that the opening words of Isa. lxi are open to a Messianic interpretation.

(vi) The suggestion that the Beatitudes represent a sermon, or the sermon delivered on the basis of Isa. lxi 1-5(7) is appealing. The number of allusions to the Isaiah passage in the blessings is striking. But even if we were to accept this view, our knowledge of the actual historical occasion or setting of the Beatitudes-sermon is not advanced. If the reading of the Isaiah passage is removed from its Lukan setting, as the first public act of Jesus' ministry, then its actual *Sitz im Leben* is impossible to determine. Perhaps Luke (for the theological reasons already adduced, and because

---

[1] W. C. VAN UNNIK, "Jesus the Christ", *NTS* VIII (1961-62), 113. He argues that the Messiahship of Jesus, in the view of the early Christians, was based on the fact that he was the person possessed by the Spirit.

[2] See M. DE JONGE and A. S. VAN DER WOUDE, "11Q Melchizedek and the New Testament", *NTS XII* (1965-66), 301-26. Originally VAN DER WOUDE thought that the "bringer of good tidings" was *the* Messiah (המשיח), *Oudtestamentische Studiën*, XIV (Leiden, 1965): but later he revised his opinion. Cf. also J. A. FITZMEYER, "Further Light on Melchizedek from Qumran Cave 11", *JBL* LXXXVI (1967), 25-41, who relates "*the* Messiah" of line 18 to Dan. ix 25. Among the many interesting points raised by 11Q Melch and other similar scrolls is the fact that they display a midrashic linking of Old Testament passages on the basis of word similarities, e.g. Lev. xxv and Isa. lxi are linked by דְּרוֹר, and Isa. lii 7 and Isa. lxi are linked by בשׂר. Here we have evidence of exegetical traditions being developed: there is no need to introduce here the hypothesis of linked *sedarim* and *haftaroth*. Is there such a need elsewhere?

[3] A. S. VAN DER WOUDE, 'Melchisedek als himmlische Erlösergestalt in den neugefundenen eschatologischen Midraschim aus Qumran Höhle XI', *Oudtestamentische Studiën*, XIV (1965), 357.

of his interest in the Spirit) has set at the commencement of Jesus' teaching the Isaiah passage of which the Beatitudes are a kind of *pesher*, whereas Matthew (in whose version of the blessings there are clearer allusions to Isa. lxi) has, for other reasons, set at the beginning of the teaching of Jesus in his gospel the Beatitudes themselves, without direct reference to their inspiration in the Isaiah chapter. The idea that the Lukan and Matthean passages put together form a single unit of dominical teaching remains attractive: but it is no more than a hypothesis.

JESUS' AUDIENCES, ACCORDING TO LUKE

VON

PAUL S. MINEAR

Guilford, Ct., U.S.A.

Professor J. ARTHUR BAIRD has called our attention to the care
with which the Synoptists identified the audiences of Jesus
(*Audience Criticism and the Historical Jesus*, Phila. 1969 pp. 32 f.).
In the light of this care it should be a fundamental responsibility
of Redaction Criticism to give special attention to the particular
audience indicated for each pericope. On the basis of the study
summarized herewith, I have concluded that a remarkable consistency exists in Luke's conception of Jesus' audiences and that
Luke's vocabulary in this respect is quite distinctive, i.e., different
from Mark and Matthew. I believe that proper regard for this
consistency and this distinctiveness may improve our grasp of
Luke's intention in his redaction of the tradition and in his understanding of successive episodes. We will try to justify this conclusion
by examining Luke's use of such words as λαός, ὄχλος, μαθηταί
and ἀπόστολοι, hoping that readers who are persuaded of the value
of such an analysis will consult the other two parts of this trilogy:
a study of the audiences of Jesus in Mark (cf. B. REICKE and
H. BALTENSWEILER, ed., *Neues Testament und Geschichte*, Tübingen
and Zurich, 1972, pp. 79-90) and a similar study of Matthew
(Anglican Theological Review, October 1973).

In what follows here we will first survey the normal connotations
of the key words; we will then explore a broad segment of Luke's
redactional work, and finally we will ask what light our study
may throw upon the exegesis of the Sermon on the Plain. Because a
verse-by-verse examination of all relevant texts would prove
too extensive and too tedious, we will summarize the lexico-
graphical data, looking first at Acts, where Luke may have been
freer to use his own diction, and then at the Gospel.

ὁ λαός—*"the people"*

It is notoriously difficult to find in English a precise equivalent
for λαός, a theological category which is far more central in Luke

than in Mark or Matthew. The difficulty in finding an equivalent corresponds to the ecclesiological importance of the term (cf. my *Images of the Church in the New Testament*, Phila., 1960, pp. 67 ff.). The RSV translation illustrates the problem. Without variation it renders ὁ λαός by the people. In instances where the Greek noun appears without the article, RSV varies the rendering: Acts v 37 "some of the people", referring to the followers of Judas the Galilean; Acts xv 14 "a people", referring to gentile converts; Acts xviii 10 "I have many people", referring to Gentile converts still to be gained. The difficulty with "the people" is this: the idiom in English does not connote a specific historical community which has been set apart by God from all other communities by the covenant which He has sealed with it the unique status of this community is indicated by the fact that God has called this nation "my people" (Acts vii 34); equivalent expressions are "men of Israel" (iii 12 and iv 10), "children of Abraham (xiii 26), dwelling of David (xv 16); whenever a person enters a synagogue or the temple in Jerusalem, he meets this particular people (v 20, 25; xiii 15, 17; xxi 30, 36). That to the RSV translators λαός denoted a vague and amorphous community is indicated by their use of the same phrase to render ὄχλος (Lk. iv 42; v 1,3; viii 42; ix 18; xi 14; xiii 14, 17). To correct this general vagueness one might often render ὁ λαός by the demonstrative: this people. Rarely, if ever, is the term used in any other sense in the Book of Acts. xv 14 and xviii 10 are apparent exceptions, though Conzelmann argues that here Luke assumes and accepts the identity of the church with Israel (*Theology of St. Luke*, London, Faber and Faber, 1960, p. 164 n. 1). There are, in fact, passages to suggest that to Luke there could be no salvation outside Israel (Acts iii 23). What prevents such a suggestion are two passages near the beginning and the end of the two-volume work where Luke, following scriptural prophecies, speaks of salvation coming to two groups: "the people" and "the Gentiles" (Lk. ii 32, 34; Acts xxvi 17, 23). Even these passages, however, support our basic observation, i.e., to Luke λαός, with the article, normally refers to Israel as the elect nation which forever retains the specific identity given to it by God.

It is this specific entity which Luke sees as the initial and ultimate audience for all God's messengers, whether John the Baptist (Acts xiii 24) or the apostles (iii 12 f.) It is before them that the

signs are performed (Acts vi 8). They see the signs, they hear
the Word, they are healed by power from the Most High—all this
as the intended first step toward repentance and faith (Acts v 12-16).
It is to them that the message of the resurrection is first addressed,
and they are the men whom Stephen provokes to anger or to faith
(vi 12 f.). Because Luke thinks of this entity as a whole, represented
by its members, his frequently used phrase πᾶς ὁ λαὸς should
probably be translated by "the whole people" rather than by
"all the people", which the RSV has preferred as being less awkward
(Acts ii 47; iii 9, 11; iv 10; v 34; x 41; xiii 24).

One significant exception is to be noted: whenever Luke wished
to draw a distinction between the leaders and the led he regularly
used "the people" for the larger group. The rulers (elders, priests,
Pharisees, scribes, etc.) fear the λαός (Acts iv 21) and also seek to
stir up in this same λαός hostility to the apostles (iv 27). The
context usually makes it quite clear that in these cases λαός equals
Israel minus these leaders. The apostles and these leaders openly
compete for the allegiance of the men of Israel (iii 9, 11, 12, 23).
Luke was not hostile to Israel, only to the rulers of this λαός.

The attitudes portrayed in the Gospel are virtually identical
with those of Acts. In Luke's gospel λαός appears 37 times, in
contrast to 3 in Mark and 14 in Matthew. ὁ λαὸς refers to the
house of David (i 68), Israel (i 17; ii 32) to God's elect community
(i 68, 77). It is especially at home in synagogue and temple (i 10;
xx 1). The events narrated depict God's promised visitation with
his covenanted nation (vii 16). In fact, the charge of perverting
the people is the same as the charge of perverting *this nation* (xxiii 2,
13). Whatever is said or done has been accomplished in the presence
of God and this people (xxiv 19). As in Acts, they represent the
prime audience for the message of John (i 17; iii 15, 18, 21),
Jesus and the apostles. The phrase πᾶς ὁ λαὸς is even more prominent
than in the Acts as defining the goal of preaching and healing.

As in Acts, however, there is also a pervasive distinction between
the rulers and the ruled (xix 47; xxii 2, 66; xxiii 5, 13). Unlike
Mark and Matthew, Luke does not describe the λαός as turning
against Jesus and demanding his crucifixion. There is a passing
conventional reference to God's wrath on this people (xxi 23),
but much more indicative of Luke's stance is the fact that at the
crucifixion the λαός is associated with the weeping women (xxiii 27)
in following the condemned to the place of execution and in behold-

ing the bestial mockery (xxiii 35). In Luke nothing comparable
to the horrible cry of Mt. xxvii 25 is attributed to the people,
nor does Luke preserve the Isaianic denunciation in Mark vii 6 or
Matthew xiii 14 f. The Pharisees and the rulers are assumed to
have moved beyond the range of repentance; for them doom
is sure. But the λαός is everywhere viewed as redeemable. Luke
did not minimize the guilt of Israel (e.g. iv 28 f.), but neither did
he charge the λαός with irretrievable and inherent guilt. For him
that septuagintal word retained its halo. As we will see, ὁ ὄχλος had
no such halo, a fact that is obscured whenever RSV translates the
two Greek words by the same English word—people. Especially
dubious is the term "all these people" in ix 13, which fails to suggest
the Lukan awareness that the five thousand who are fed in the
wilderness represent God's covenant nation as a whole. Luke's
concern for this specific nation does not, of course, exclude an
awareness that other peoples are addressed in the Gospel (ii 31),
but it reminds us of a type of collectivism in his thinking that
excludes a radical individualism. He is both consistent and distinctive in this concern for the people of God .. When μαθηταί and
λαός appear in the same context (vi 17; vii 1), the editor assumes
that Jesus is training the former to minister to the latter. This
is particularly clear in xx 45, where Luke replaces the Marcan
ὄχλος by λαός. His reliance on λαός increases during his account of
the passion (Ch. 20-24) in a suggestive way, inasmuch as salvation
is accomplished for the sake of this specific people. In line with this
emphasis is the remark of the two disciples at Emmaus: "a prophet
powerful in action and speech in the presence of God and the whole
λαός" (24:19). Fewer terms have greater ecclesiological resonance
in Luke's gospel; that the same feature is found in Acts corroborates
the conclusion that this attitude probably represents the editor
rather than his sources.

ὁ ὄχλος—"the crowd"

We may conveniently distinguish three ways in which this noun
is used in Acts. Least frequent is its use to indicate the size of a
group without any implication as to the character of that group.
The large number of followers (in i 15 it seems there were 120),
the similarly large number of priests (vi 7. RSV says "a great
many") and the group of converts made by Barnabas (xi 24.
Here ὄχλος ἱκανός seems to be equivalent to πολὺς ἀριθμός

in xi 21). In the second use, where the noun appears with the article but without a qualifying genitival phrase (e.g. of believers) the number of persons seems less significant that does their role. They represent a fairly constant element in apostolic work as an audience, whether of Philip (viii 6), of Paul and Barnabas (xiii 42-45), or of Paul alone (xiv 11-19) They come to the apostles to hear the word and to see the signs; thus they represent potential believers (xi 21). In Jewish regions they are synagogue attendants, in Gentile regions pagan worshipers, but in neither case is there an effort to describe their character. They usually speak as a chorus; although they can take decisive action, their profile remains vague.

A third role emerges in situations of tension when enemies of the apostles prompt the crowds to become agents of their violence. The ὄχλος which at one moment is bent on worshiping the apostles turns into a mob that stones them. (xiv 18, 19. The similarity with the crowd in the Nazareth synagogue in Luke 4 is surely more than coincidental.) In Philippi the magistrates enlist the Gentile crowds in savage brutality (xvi 22). Their behavior is similar in Berea (xvii 8, 13) and in the temple in Jerusalem (xxi 27) where their help as "men of Israel" is commandeered. In this third role, as crowds used to oppose the mission, the word comes to connote "an unruly mob". Where a riot breaks out, a crowd is found which has come under the power of apostolic enemies (xix 33, 35; xxi 34-36; xxiv 12, 18). Paul and his foes can each charge the other with fomenting the strife.

In Acts ὄχλος, unlike λαός, does not seem to have a technical meaning with more or less fixed content. It is not an ecclesiological term. Normally its numerical value remains extremely vague; i.e., only rarely can the actual size of the group be determined. The role of the crowds is less vague and somewhat contingent upon the missionary situation; they are potential believers or enemies of the apostles. It would in fact be hard to imagine a mission being conducted without this double feature. Everywhere the ὄχλοι come out, hear the message, see the signs and react to the apostles' call to repent in the face of their enemies' charge of blasphemy/treason. The crowds either become disciples themselves or turn into an unruly mob under the influence of "the establishment". Luke depicts this situation as a recurring aspect of apostolic work.

The picture of the crowds in the Gospel is very similar. On rare occasions the noun is used with a qualifying phrase as an estimate of numerical size: a great crowds of disciples (vi 17) or of tax collectors (v 29). Much more frequently the noun is used without such a phrase to refer to groups who come to John (iii 7, 10) or to Jesus. Their primary role is to hear the word and to see the signs. Quite typical is v 15: "Great multitudes gathered to hear and to be healed of their infirmities." Often they come from synagogue or the temple (iv 42; v 1 f.; vii 9). At times they follow John or Jesus to the wilderness (vii 24; ix 11 f.). Often they press around Jesus, trying to touch him (v 1, 19; vi 19; viii 19; viii 42, 45). They appear to be eager to learn what they must do to be saved (iii 7, 10). The statistics of Luke's use of ὄχλος are evidence of his freedom vis-a-vis his sources. Of the 38 times that this word appears in Mark, Luke uses without change 9. In 9 cases the Markan section has no parallel in Luke. On 7 occasions Luke includes the section but omits the word. Some 10 times Luke changes the word to λαός (vii 29; viii 47; ix 33; xix 48; xx 6, 19, 45; xxiii 13, 14) and in several other cases he uses ὄχλος but with changed significance (v 29; vi 19; viii 19). He uses the word in verses or passages which have no parallel some 22 times; most of these cases are in editorial introductions to pericopes. Generally this editor takes care to assign to an episode or teaching an audience which he feels is most appropriate. In at least three passages Luke alternated between ὄχλος and λαός where his sources, MK and Q, had used only the former term. From this fact Conzelmann infers that to LK the two terms were interchangeable (*op. cit.*, p. 164). I prefer to say that in these cases the sources had given to ὄχλος a positive weight which in LK's mind was more appropriate to λαός. In vii 24, 29 the referent is the community baptized by John; in ix 12, 33 the community which Jesus fed in the wilderness; in viii 42, 45, 47 the community to which a cured woman gave her testimony. These instances do indicate the kinship of the two terms in Luke's thought, but not, I think, their identity.

Luke frequently distinguished ὄχλοι from λαός, but the former are usually drawn from the latter and represent them. RSV often blurs this distinction by translating ὄχλος as the people (iv 42; v 1, 3; viii 42; ix 18; xi 14; xiii 14, 17). This obviously presupposes a stronger sense of ὄχλος than is characteristic of Luke. Luke also distinguishes crowds from disciples; the former are potential disciples. Summoned to repent, their action will depend on how they hear (viii 8). Their coming out to hear Jesus indicates a generally favorable disposition toward his work, but Jesus takes every opportunity to make it clear what they must still do to become his disciples. Thus the distinction is maintained between crowds and disciples (ix 10 f., 18 f., 37 f.,; xii 1) The difference in this regard from Mark is illustrated in Luke viii 19-21. According to the Markan tradition Jesus identified the ὄχλος as his true family, replacing his natural kinsfolk, because they have done God's will. Not so in Luke. By gathering about Jesus the crowd prevented access by his natural family and occasioned the teaching, but the crowd is definitely not identified with those who have done God's will.

Less than in Mark and Matthew are the crowds seen as guilty of Jesus' death. Only in two verses are they associated with the betrayal and execution (xxii 47; xxiii 4) and this association is more tenuous than in the other Gospels. According to Luke neither λαός nor ὄχλος bear a primary responsibility for the crucifixion. Both the rulers of the λαός and the twelve apostles are more culpable than they. The term ὄχλος has no theological significance of its own; its significance derives from the mission: the crowds represent the λαός as the group from whom disciples are enlisted. That the relationship is close is demonstrated by the ease with which Luke uses both terms to refer to the same group (iii 7-21; vii 24, 29; viii 47; ix 10-17). That there are subtle distinctions is indicated by the special relations of λαὸς to temple. Of the 37 uses of λαός, 26 are in connection with the temple, 8 in Chapter 1, 2 and 18 in Chapters 19-24. ὄχλος appears first in iii 7 and only rarely (6 times) after xix 41 at which point the function of the word shifts noticeably.

In Luke, then, the crowds have much less positive significance than in Mark or Matthew, where they are the followers of Jesus. In Luke they constitute a neutral, anonymous, undifferentiated entity, a necessary but indistinct part of the stage setting, roughly equivalent to *many* (πολλοί, v 29 par; vi 19 par.) or to *men* (ἄνθρωποι, ix 18 par.). The group lacks internal cohesion and external boundaries, so that the English term crowd is more accurate here than in the other synoptics.

οἱ μαθηταί—*the disciples*

Acts is the only New Testament writing outside the Gospels which uses this Greek word. It is also the only book in the New

Testament which clearly uses this word to refer to all believers, and in this respect it has determined later Christian practice. In Acts a clear distinction is drawn between the Twelve, or the apostles, and the whole multitude (πλῆθος) of disciples (vi 1). Μαθηταί is never used to apply simply to the smaller group. Pentecost marks a rapid increase in the number of disciples (vi 7). Included under this term are members of the Way in Damascus (ix 1, 19, 25), Jerusalem (ix 26), Joppa (ix 36, 38) Antioch (xi 29) or the other cities (xiii 52; xiv 20, 22, 28; xv 10; xix 1, 9, 30). According to Acts this term antedated the title Christian for all believers (xi 26) and it remained the most common term, at least in internal use, to apply to all who followed Christ. In this case the RSV translators had no difficulty in adopting a single equivalent: μαθητής = disciple. Modern idiom in this case, as with ὄχλος, coincides with Luke's.

Almost the same picture pertains to the use of this term in the Gospel of Luke. With few exceptions all who believe and follow Jesus are called disciples. All are invited to become disciples, and anyone can do so who makes the requisite sacrifices (xiv 26-33). The group around Jesus is compared to similar groups around John or the Pharisees (vii 18; xi 1), and in none of these cases is the size of the group limited to a certain number. In fact, when Jesus chooses 12 and later 72, Luke says quite clearly that he chooses them from a larger number of disciples (vi 1, 13, 17; x 22, 23; xix 37-39). Luke even appears to include various women in the group (xxiv 6). Only in two instances does the number of μαθηταί become 12. The first case (ix 10-17) is the feeding of the 5,000. Here both the well-established Markan tradition and the symbolic weight of 12 dictated this number of disciples. Again in the narrative of the Last Supper (xxii 11, 39, 45) neither the tradition nor the symbolic values would permit a larger number. In this latter text Luke explicitly identifies the disciples present with the apostles. In neither of these texts is there a clear implication that Jesus had no more than twelve disciples. Not only is Luke consistent in calling all believers and followers μαθηταί; he is also the only one of the Synoptists to do so. In Mark and Matthew, as we have shown in the essays mentioned above, μαθηταί is almost always limited to the Twelve whom Jesus chose for special duty. Not so in Luke, who keeps a much larger group in mind. Luke's special interest in the office and role of the twelve *apostles* has been much studied, and we need not pursue that topic here.

To summarize: the most frequent and important audiences of Jesus, as seen by Luke, are as follows:

— the people (λαός); the largest, most inclusive audience. With few exceptions this term refers to Israel as God's covenant community, as represented by Jerusalem or by the crowds which come to hear Jesus, God's appointed messenger to them. This term bulks largest in the accounts of Jesus' birth and Passion.
— the crowds (ὄχλοι): the usual links between prophets and the people. They come out from synagogue and temple to see and to hear, to be healed, to decide whether or not to repent and believe. They are the major source of disciples.
— the disciples (μαθηταί): all who hear and obey, who after counting the cost determine to enlist with a particular teacher or prophet; the band includes men and women, rich and poor.
— the Twelve and the Seventy-two: men chosen from the larger number of disciples to whom Jesus gives special authority to preach and to heal, and whom he sends out to minister to the crowds and to the people.
— the rulers of the people: priests, elders, scribes, Pharisees, who normally reject the message of Jesus, refuse to repent, and form a coalition of enemies, rivals of the Twelve and of the 72. They seek, though with little success, to dissuade disciples and to restrain the interest of the ὄχλοι.

The Redactor at Work

Selecting as a broad base of study the Travel Narrative (ix 51-xviii 30) we will now assess the influence of Luke's conception of these audiences upon his editorial selection, arrangement and adaptation of the diverse traditions available to him. We will rather arbitrarily break up his narrative into units marked by shifts in the audience, shifts which are typically indicated in the transitional sentences.

ix 51-62. Many interpreters have detected the editor's hand in the introductory sentence of v. 51, in the transitional sentence of v. 52, and in the setting described in v. 57a. Verse 51 accents Jesus' concern with the culmination of his mission in Jerusalem, i.e., with the climactic address to the people of God in its heartland. This planned visitation dominates the narrative much more than in Mark x 1 or Matthew xix 1. To Luke it is "the face set to go to Jerusalem" which provokes Samaritan hostility to Jesus and his messengers. Moreover, whereas both Mark and Matthew picture the crowds (ὄχλοι) as his constant companions, Luke omits such a reference in telling of this trip to the Holy City. To the other Synoptists these ὄχλοι were genuine followers and believers.

Not so to Luke, who visualized a sharp distinction between ὄχλοι and μαθηταί, a distinction measured by acceptance of the require-ments in v. 57-62. For him Jesus and his μαθηταί alone were members of the Way (vs. 57), a term which for Luke had become a designation of the Church (Acts viii 36, 39; ix 2; xviii 25 f.; xix 9, 23; xxii 4; xxiv 14, 22; xxv 3; cf. my *Images of the Church*, Phila., 1960, pp. 148 ff.). To Luke the decision to follow Jesus had not as yet been made by the interlocutors of v. 57-62, inasmuch as following entailed joining Jesus on this very dangerous *Way* to Jerusalem. To Luke the question is this: who is worthy of entering the kingdom of God? The presumption is this: everyone who enters becomes a messenger who goes before Jesus announcing that kingdom (v. 52a, 60) and encountering the inevitable opposition to the *Way*. Matthew and Mark used μαθηταί to refer to the smaller group and ὄχλοι to the larger group of followers; Luke used μαθηταί to refer to all followers and he pictured all others as separated from the *Way* by the costly decisions outlined in v. 57-62. (Cf. the companion essays referred to in note 1).

Incidentally the RSV insertion of *the people* as the subject in v. 53 is quite misleading, inasmuch as for Luke that category, the usual rendering for ὁ λαός, had a strong theological nuance suggesting Israel, whereas on this occasion the subject is Samaritans who resented the mission to Jerusalem.

x 1-24. Here Luke turns to the disciples (vs. 23) who have made that commitment demanded in the previous verses. But whereas Matthew thinks of this group in terms of Twelve (Mt. ix 37-x 1), Luke specifies seventy-two (or seventy). Moreover, where Matthew implies that the Twelve embraces all μαθηταί, Luke encourages the reader to assume that the seventy-two have been chosen from a larger number of disciples. Both editions stress the character of the disciples as workers, harvesters, preachers and exorcists. They are recipients of Christ's authority to the degree that the response of men to them determines their response to him. Luke visualizes a much more thorough and extensive campaign than Matthew, as he also visualizes a sharper distinction between μαθηταί and ὄχλοι. It may be that this affects the location of the pericope in Luke x 21-24 and Matthew xi 25-27. To Luke, the mention of exclusive revelation makes necessary an explicit limitation of the audience to disciples; to Matthew God's gracious intention to reveal

these things *to the babes* suggests instead an address to the crowds
(xi 7 f.).

x 25-37. The lawyer here appears to represent the larger group
of "rulers", who have a penchant for putting Jesus on trial (vs. 25)
and for self-justification (vs. 29). His behavior distinguishes him
sharply from the disciples of v. 23, 38 and xi 1. The answers to
his two questions are especially appropriate to rulers; that is,
they are based upon their knowledge of the Law and upon the
customary failure of the priest and Levite to obey that Law.
It is worth noting that Luke omits the commendation of Jesus
by the lawyer (Mk. xii 32) and he weakens Jesus' praise of the
lawyer (Mk. xii 34). Luke takes it for granted that such lawyers
whom he usually associates with the Pharisees (xi 45 f.; xiv 3)
have already rejected the demand of Jesus (cp. vii 30). He also
gives no indication that Jesus would invite such questioners to
become disciples. Neither does the Evangelist associate this
lawyer with the ὄχλοι. He is not considering discipleship as a
genuine option for himself.

x 38-xi 13. Would Luke classify Martha and Mary with the
ὄχλοι or the μαθηταί? As it stands the pericope leaves both options
open. The introduction in vs. 38 links this episode to the journey
of the 72 on the Way toward Jerusalem and to the responses by
successive villages and homes to the messengers (x 5-7). The
hospitality offered by the sisters and Mary's eagerness to listen
to the Word are features which link them to Luke's conception
of the ὄχλοι (v 1, 15; vi 17; viii 8, 21; xiv 35; xv 1). On the other
hand, there are features suggestive of μαθηταί: e.g. the concern
with διακονία, the rôle of the sisters (ἀδελφαί is a christianized
term here) in caring for the needs of the Lord together with his
apostles (xvii 8; xxii 26; xxiii 49, 55, 56; xxiv 10). It is unlikely
that female disciples would have been required to adopt the nomadic
and mendicant manner of life of the 72. Moreover, the rebuke of
Martha should not be interpreted as a flat repudiation of her
διακονία as one legitimate form of discipleship. Jesus' rebuke
was a protest against her petulance and narrowness more than
against her διακονία. Certainly Christian audiences have from
the beginning felt themselves addressed through both sisters.
On the authority of Jesus, the good duty of listening to his word
will not be taken away from any female disciple because of the
pressure of her more domestic duties.

Whether or not the sisters were disciples, there is no doubt about the audience in the following unit: the disciples. Although one of them makes the request, all are addressed—αὐτοῖς in v. 2, αὐτούς in v. 5. Presumably the audience includes the 72 of Chapter x, for the prayer implicitly includes their daily needs for bread. It also visualizes the situation of their hosts (x 7), for the parable in v. 6 speaks of the sudden visit at night by a "friend" coming from the "Way", one who thus has urgent need for food. The situation is similar to that faced by Martha. Recognition of the importunity of both the guest and his host links the "which one of you" in vs. 5 to the God of Vss. 9-13 who is addressed in the prayer. The whole teaching in Luke is addressed solely to the disciples (v. 1), a group which in size and character is similar not to the μαθηταί of Mt. v 1 but to the ὄχλοι of Mt. vii 28.

This concept of audience makes a bit more intelligible certain distinctive accents in the Lukan version. For example, the assurance of the gift of the Holy Spirit from heaven (vs. 13) is appropriate to the 72 disciples of Chapter x who, because of the rigors of this missionary campaign en route to Jerusalem, have special needs for that gift (x 17-23), especially in the exorcism of demons, an instance of which immediately follows. The contrast between the Holy Spirit and the serpent and scorpions of xi 11, 12, is surely not unrelated to the power which Jesus granted over such demonic forces in x 19. In this teaching concerning prayer, then, Luke as editor remained keenly aware of the distinctive duties and dangers of the disciples.

A second instance would be provided by the variant text in vi 2: "May thy Holy Spirit come upon us and cleanse us." This reading has had several staunch supporters, including Harnack, Streeter, Lampe and Leaney (cf. A. R. C. LEANY, *The Gospel According to Luke*, N.Y., Harper, 1958, pp. 60 ff.). The disciples who had so recently been dispatched on a dangerous mission which included healings (x 9) and exorcisms (x 19) needed the Spirit above all else. It would be entirely pertinent to have a communal prayer in which such a plea constituted the first petition, along with a binding assurance that the Father would grant that request (xi 13) and not give them serpents or scorpions. Such a gift was more than ever pertinent in view of the fact that it became immediately clear that exorcisms, whether by Jesus or by his emissaries, were likely to be explained as due to the power of Beelzebub. Although the disciples would know better, Luke realized that the sign-hungry crowds would not, a distinction which the next pericope makes clear.

xi 14-36. Here the audience is immediately introduced as the crowds. (The RSV translation of ὄχλοι in v. 14 as *the people* is highly dubious). Their perspective on exorcisms is immediately shown to be different from that of Jesus and the disciples. In choosing this audience Luke differs from Mark and Matthew, who attribute this accusation to scribes (Mk. iii 22) or to Pharisees (Mt. xii 24). Why this change? In the other Gospels the ὄχλοι are treated as being already followers. In Matthew they virtually identify Jesus with the messianic figure: Son of David; in Mark these crowds are accepted as members of his true family, i.e., they do the will of God (iii 34). Not so in Luke, where, as we have seen, the ὄχλοι are only potential disciples who come out to hear Jesus, to see his signs and to be healed. They are capable of deciding *pro* or *con* on the issue of believing. In short, their questions (v. 15, 16) are viewed by Luke as genuine queries, not to be compared to the loaded questions of the rulers. In the other Synoptists the charge of devil-power leads to forthright condemnation of those rulers by Jesus; here in Luke that same charge by the crowds leads to a proclamation of the kingdom (vs. 20), a call to take their stand with Jesus (vs. 23), and an explicit invitation to repent (vs. 30 ff.). Jesus views the desire for signs, so typical of the uncommitted crowds in Luke, as a mark of an evil generation and as a threat that his own exorcisms may not be permanent; but he also uses it as an opportunity to warn the crowds "lest the light in you be darkness" (vs. 33-36). This cluster of axioms receives quite different accents when addressed to Luke's ὄχλοι rather than to Matthew's disciples (Mt. vi 22, 23). The desire for signs may itself become a source of enlightenment as a result of Jesus' teaching. The Lukan view of the crowds is reflected both in the fact that they constantly increase (vs. 29; xii 1) and that they are capable of words of praise, however ill-considered (vs. 27). The reply of Jesus to the woman in v. 28 is also typical of Luke's thinking: members of the ὄχλοι hear the word of God; by keeping that word they would be enabled to become *disciples*. They come out to hear him; let them hear *and obey*. They come out to be healed; let them beware of the dangers following an exorcism. They come out to see signs; let them not avoid the true issue of whether to repent

like the men of Nineveh. What will they do with the light that is in
them? This is the question raised of the crowds by the exorcisms
which had attracted them. The questions raised of the disciples by
those same exorcisms were different and had, in fact, already been
answered (x 17-24). The problem faced by the rulers was very
different still. In each case the character of the audience determined
the shape of the problem and of its treatment.

xi 37-54. Here there is no uncertainty about audience or about
attitudes; a verbal battle is drawn between Jesus and the Pharisees,
with whom the lawyers are included (v. 45). They are out to trap
him; he condemns them without qualification. There is no prospect
of either side modifying its behavior. When the reader inquires
as to the reason for Jesus' bitter attack, one can point to his concern
for the laymen who are made unclean by the Pharisaic uncleanness
(v. 44), and for those who, seeking to enter the kingdom, are
hindered by the requirements laid on them by the lawyers (v. 46)
or by violent persecution (v. 52). Another answer is Jesus' concern
that his μαθηταί should avoid their leaven (xii 1). In these respects
Luke is not far from the position of Matthew (xxiii 1-36). It is
noteworthy, however, that he reduces the triple audience in
Mark ix 1-23 and Matthew xxiii 1-36 (enemies, crowds, disciples)
to a single audience of enemies.

xii 1-12. This set of warnings to the disciples presupposes the
preceding picture of hypocrisy. It also presupposes a radical self-
commitment on the part of Jesus' followers. The expectation of
Pharisaic violence (xi 48 f.) is matched by the call to disciplic
fearlessness (xii 4 f.). The dangers of Pharisaic duplicity and
secrecy (xi 40 f.) is to be matched by the disciplic openness, integrity
and publicity (xii 2, 3). The issue faced by the disciples is whether,
under pressure, to acknowledge or to deny the Son of man; whether
to blaspheme the Holy Spirit or to rely on its guidance (xii 10 f.).
It is the gift of the Spirit (x 17-23) which distinguishes this audience
from both Pharisees and multitudes (xii 1-13). So, too, it is distinguished by the specific set of dangers: fear and despair that induce
dishonesty, equivocation, silence when the Word should be spoken,
and distrust of the Holy Spirit in times of crisis.

Luke's interpretation of these sayings differs to a degree from
the other Synoptists because of their different concepts of audience.
The warning against hypocrisy is addressed in all three Gospels to
the disciples; but in Matthew and Mark this is the smaller group

of selected leaders, as symbolized by their withdrawal with Jesus in the boat (Mk. viii 14 f.; Mt. xvi 5 f.). Again the injunctions against fear are directed in Mt. x 26 f. primarily to the Twelve on their apostolic journey, and not as in Luke to the larger group of all followers. More significantly, in Luke the danger of blasphemy may confront especially the *disciples* as they face persecution, whereas in Mark (iii 28-30) and Matthew (xii 31, 32) it is more likely part of the attack on hostile Pharisees and scribes. This contrast is not unimportant.

xii 13-21. From these verses to xiii 30 the various traditions are organized around two audiences—the crowds and the disciples. For some purposes the second address to the crowds (xii 54-xiii 30) should be treated as a continuation of the first, as we shall see. There are, however, certain contrasts to be observed between the first address to the crowds and the address to the disciples (xii 22-53). Thus we will hold to the pattern of the Lukan alternation from one group to the other.

In xii 13 a man from the crowd (a typical Lukan introduction, cp. ix 38, xi 27) poses a problem and is rebuffed by Jesus. For one thing, his question implies that Jesus is a potential surrogate for the lawyers, who elsewhere have proved so blind and hostile (cp. xi 46 f.). Jesus refuses to accept such a role. (xii 57 f. may be another answer to this request). For another thing, the query implies on the part of the crowd a general covetousness which breaks the tenth commandment. To this aspect of the request the parable of the rich fool is an answer. We note that the parable does not presuppose the unique commitment which disciples were expected to make, but only that desire for heavenly treasure which could be assumed on the part of Jews. It does, however, attack the desire for economic security which would prevent a man from deciding to become a disciple. Moreover, it pictures the crowd confronting "the night" of an accounting, thus calling for an insight into the peculiar significance of "the present time" (cf. xii 54-56). Therefore this query, together with its answer, constitutes an implicit call to repentance—a call which becomes explicit in xiii 1-5. Luke sees Jesus using this occasion to call the crowds to lay up treasure with God.

xii 22-53. The change in audience here is based on the assumption that this initial step has already been taken by the disciples. Their anxiety is not the same as that of the rich man or of the questioner of v. 13; it is due rather to the apparent helplessness and insecurity of a poverty accepted by all disciples (cf. vi 20-23). They, as the little flock for whom the danger is a lack of trust in God's love, must put their hearts where their treasure is. Even though their lives prove to be as short as that of the grass (v. 28) and as cheap and insecure as that of the birds, they must rely on special care by their father. As the parable of the rich fool pre-supposed the stance of the crowd, so the parable of the absent lord presupposed the stance of the disciples (vs. 35-40. Cf. my *Commands of Christ*, New York, 1972, pp. 132-152).

Luke makes it quite clear that the question of audience here is a vital one. He adds to the tradition Peter's question "Lord, are you telling this parable for us or for all?" (v. 41). By other remarks (vs. 22, 54) Luke shows that Jesus did not intend this teaching for all men or for all members of the crowd, but for all servants. Therefore the two parables raise the question for him—"Who is the faithful and wise steward?" The parables also answer that question in terms of obedience to the *master's* will. This answer involves sharing with the master in his work of casting fire, in his baptism, in a vocation that provokes universal conflict. Failure to be ready for this master's return will be punished by a rejection which places the servant with the unfaithful (v. 46. ἀπίστων—the unbelievers? the crowds?) As Matthew relays these teachings, they are addressed primarily to the Twelve in Ch. 6 and 24 in view of their special missionary assignment in Ch. 10 Luke has in mind a larger number of slaves, stewards and deacons. In fact, he anticipates a baptism by fire for every believer and follower—the entire Pentecostal company of Acts. ii, iii.

xii 54-xiii 30. Although there is a passing reference to the synagogue ruler (xiii 14), the focus of interest falls on the ὄχλοι as the audience (xii 54; xiii 14, 17). In the RSV the last two texts are unwisely translated as "the people". As we have noted, Luke treats the problem of interpreting the signs of the times as a matter for the crowds, whereas the other synoptists view it as proof of Pharisaic blindness and hostility (Mk. viii 11 f.; Mt. xvi 1 f.; xii 38 f.). Moreover, Luke assumes that these crowds know how to judge what is right (v. 57). He therefore can appeal to them to prepare for the final court session (v. 58) and can address them with a command which in Matthew reinforced the special duties of disciples (Mt. v 25 f.). The epitome of all Jesus' messages to the crowds is found in the analogies in xiii 1-5. "Unless you repent you will all likewise perish". (Disciples have already repented; the rulers are unable to do so xvi 31). Repentance is the door leading to discipleship/salvation, a door still open to Israel, as the parable of the fig tree proves. If, as many exegetes hold, this parable is the Lukan version of Mark xi 12-14 and Matthew xxi 18, 19, it is significant that in those other Gospels the time for repentance had already expired when Jesus approached the temple.

The belief that this very liberation was still accessible to Israel, although closed to the rulers of Israel, is then documented by the story of sabbath healing (xiii 10-17). Satan's eighteen year bondage for Abraham's daughter has been broken. This act of liberation marked defeat for Jesus' adversaries, but for the crowds it produced joy over the spread of the power of the Kingdom (v. 17). To Luke this release from Satan's bonds had become a fitting occasion for the twin parables of the seed and the leaven. There was no need here for a complex theory of parables, as in Mark iv and Matthew xiii. The cure of the woman illustrated in itself the inconspicuous and hidden character of the kingdom in such a way that the crowds could grasp the sense of these analogies.

Although the ὄχλοι are not mentioned in xiii 22-30, we may safely assume that the questioner of v. 23 belonged to them. His problem is quite general, and the answer he receives is entirely intelligible to non-disciples. In fact, the pericope is a direct plea for non-disciples to become disciples while there is yet time. The alibi of those who postpone decision too long clearly applies to the ὄχλοι. In Matthew vii 22 f. a different alibi is formulated, one more appropriate to prophets and exorcists. As Israelites, unrepentant ὄχλοι will see non-Israelites join patriarchs and prophets in God's kingdom. In this context the first-who-will-be-last probably represent these Israelite crowds, and the last-who-will-be-first represent later Gentile crowds (e.g. Acts xi 18. For a more detailed study of how different audiences affect the meaning of this proverb, c.f. *Commands of Christ*, p. 83-97). Even so, the function of the prophecy in Luke is to induce the crowds (as the sons of Abraham) to repent while it is still possible.

xiii 31-xv 32. Two things characterize the audience here: the absence of the disciples and the double presence of crowds and rulers. The presence of the two groups offers the editor excellent opportunity to focus on Jesus' message to both and to make clear their opposite responses.

xiii 31-35. The report concerning Herod's plot provides the occasion for Jesus to speak of the fate of Jerusalem as determined by the rulers' violence and to stress his love for the children of Jerusalem. To the rulers he can only say "Your house is forsaken"; to the children he offers a more propitious fate. The rulers are incurable, the sick from among the crowds prove curable (xiv 1-6).

The table-talk provides an apt location for three Lukan parables; two center in the guests, one in the host. The acceptance of an invitation (marking a member of the ὄχλοι) to a wedding feast denotes a call for guests to humble themselves, an implicit call to repentance (xiv 7-11). Similarly, the issuing of invitations by hosts provides them with the opportunity of securing rewards at the resurrection of the just. To enter the kingdom one must befriend those who cannot repay (xiv 12-14. cp. Lk. vi 27-38). The third parable suggests how the blessedness of a feast in the kingdom depends on foregoing the excuses which are always at hand. By implication, none of the rulers of the people will taste of the banquet (v. 24); yet the tables will be filled with "poor, maimed, blind, lame", members of the ὄχλοι. This, it seems to me, is the reasoning expressed by Luke's arrangement of these episodes. The two succeeding sections (xiv 25-35 and xv 1-32) support this idea.

xiv 25-35. The Lukan introduction is clear: many crowds were going with him, indicating at least partial acceptance of the parabolic invitation of v. 21. For the moment they constitute his sole audience and he takes the opportunity to indicate to them what is essential should they decide to become his disciples. According to his answer the maximum sacrifice becomes the minimum demand. Self-renunciation must be nothing less than total. Before they begin this war they should know its full cost. The proverb of the salt (v. 34, 35) derives its force from this context; i.e., saltiness is dependent on such total renunciation. Ability to season food indicates the divine vocation of Israel in the world, to be accomplished only by representatives of the λαός who come out to hear Jesus and who are then enabled to understand and to obey his demands.

In their respective editions of a teaching from Q there is a striking difference between Luke and Matthew. Three times

Luke repeats "he cannot be my disciple" (xiv 26, 27, 33); thrice
Matthew repeats "he is not worthy of me" (x 37, 38). The different
expressions are naturally explained by reference to the difference
in audience. In Matthew the question is how the itinerant apostles
may become worthy of the one whose authority has been given to
them; in Luke it is how a member of the uncommitted crowd
should calculate in advance the cost of discipleship. It is strange
that the great exegete T. W. Manson, who made so much of audience
criticism, should in this case have looked for an explanation to
divergent translations by the two evangelists of an hypothetical
Aramaic original. (*The Teaching of Jesus*, Cambridge, 1953, pp.
237 f.)

xv 1-32. This setting focuses upon two groups, described in
characteristic fashion. Tax collectors and sinners have chosen
to *hear him*. (The link to xiv 35b is clear). His welcome and his
readiness to eat with them signifies the fact of their repentance
(v. 7, 10, 18 f.). In them the quest for the lost sheep of the house
of Israel proves successful and there is joy in heaven. But the rulers
reject this whole process of invitation to the heavenly banquet.
Not only does the joy in heaven throw their hostility into the
spotlight; the third parable, with its long climactic description
of the elder brother, offers an appropriate rebuke. How different
Luke's conception is from Matthew's is shown by the fact that
Matthew used only the first of the three parables (xviii 10-14)
in an address to the Twelve as rulers of the church, to counter
their tendency to despise the little ones within the church. In Luke
this block of tradition serves instead to make clear what repentance
and discipleship entail, and to accent God's joy over the response
of the ὄχλοι and his anger at the impenitence of the rulers. (xv 1
is a sequel to xiv 24).

xvi 1-13. It is not difficult to see why Luke thinks that these
teachings should be addressed to the disciples. They all deal
with the master/servant relationship and with the tests of a steward's
faithfulness during the short interim before the final accounting.
Although various interpretations of the parable have been added
to it, and it is difficult to determine the original focus or even
Luke's own conception, the least common denominator in the
congeries of sayings deals with the degrees of faithfulness on the
part of "sons of light" who have become stewards of a master
who fully knows their doings. It is perhaps significant that each

of the major audiences—crowds, disciples, rulers-heard from Jesus a rich-man parable appropriate to its own situation (xii 15-21; xvi 1-13; 19-31).

xvi 14-31. Although four units of tradition are here addressed to the Pharisees, Luke has not fully absorbed them into a single continuous line of thought. Probably various traits of these enemies furnish a loose connection. They are money-lovers, scoffers, self-justifiers and proud, violent antagonists of the kingdom, strict legalists. Curiously enough, the same sayings find different audiences in the other gospels: either the crowds (Mt. xi 12 f.) or the disciples (Mt. v 18, 32). Luke's chief interest, however, falls on the parable, and in the parable the accent falls on the pattern of Pharisaic deafness. On the word of Father Abraham himself, the rich Pharisee (v. 14, 19) who has not obeyed Moses or the prophets would not "be convinced if someone should rise from the dead". There could be no stronger evidence of the editor's conviction of the hopelessness of appeal to the rulers of Israel. They remain as jealous as the elder son in Luke xv. They neither enter the kingdom nor allow others to enter xi (52).

xvii 1-xviii 30. At xvii 1 the editor turns from an audience of Pharisees to one of disciples, and there is good reason for his doing so. As Luke sees it, the σκάνδαλα are specially appropriate to believers in their treatment of brothers, i.e., other believers. Moreover, at xvii 5 there is reason for turning from the disciples (all believers) to their leaders, the apostles, among whom an increase of faith was especially necessary and especially difficult. From apostles Luke expected signs of their faith and authority which could be compared to the shifting of the sycamine tree. I am also convinced that the parable of the slave derives unusual resonance when the duties of the slave are seen as analogous to the vocation of the apostles rather than to the "ordinary duties of the Christian life" (PLUMMER). The three commands are those which elsewhere are the mark of apostleship: shepherding (Mk. vi 34; Lk. xii 32; Jn. xxi 16; Acts xx 28; 1 Cor. ix 7; Eph. iv 11; 1 P. v 2); plowing (Lk. ix 62; 1 Cor. iii 6-9; ix 10); waiting on tables (Mt. xxv 44; Lk. xxii 26; Jn. xii 26; Acts i 17, 25; Rom. xi 13). The idioms used to describe the waiting on table had elsewhere been applied to apostolic διακονία: "prepare supper . . . gird yourself, . . serve, . . eat and drink". In one other passage addressed to the apostles, their field work had immediately been followed by their waiting on tables: ix 1-17. In still another passage in which they were the audience, Jesus' own field work had been followed by his service at table (xxii 14 ff.) The parable itself suggests the distinction between field work and house work, and the likelihood that this particular slave might do the first but hesitate to do the second. This feature echoes teachings in which apostles had been assured of their right to receive wages in the form of meals (Luke ix 3 f.; x 7 f.). Luke knew of situations in which table service had been neglected by apostles who had excelled in preaching the word, their "fieldservice" (Acts vi 1-6). He probably knew of difficulties like those in Corinth (1 Cor. ix) in which quarrels among apostles had been provoked by their right to food and drink. Some claimed the privilege of being fed as a mark of superiority; others claimed that their refusal to use this privilege indicated their superiority. The parable in Luke xvii was relevant to all such disputes, especially when the question of vs. 9 is taken to be its original ending. In locating the parable where he does, in material addressed to the apostles on the way to Jerusalem, Luke under-scores that relevance.

xvii 11-19. The episode of the lepers is unusual in that the basic audience remains unclear. Jesus first addresses the ten (v. 14), then unspecified listeners (v. 17, 18) and finally the grateful leper (v. 19). Internally, the pericope is pertinent to several different audiences. The crowds had been with him and had frequently been represented by sick men who came to be healed and were in fact healed (vi 17). The gratitude of the tenth leper provides a model for them. But it was the apostles who had been addressed in the previous teaching, and this story continues the discussion of faith (v. 6, 19). Moreover, it was relevant to their mission of healing (x 1-9), to their journey with him to Jerusalem (v. 11), and to their debates with the Pharisees. It is they who are the likely recipients of Jesus' query in v. 17, 18.

The healing of the leper may have suggested to Luke the question of the Pharisees in xvii 20. For Luke, such faith and gratitude as were exemplified in the cleansing of the leper may have been tantamount to saying "The kingdom of God has come near to you". (x 9) If so, the question of the Pharisees simply disclosed their inveterate blindness. If they had had eyes to see, they would have seen in their midst the signs of that kingdom. Luke spends so few words on this interchange, however, that its interpretation has always baffled scholars. Perhaps the brevity is due to the fact that at this point in his editorial work he is more interested in the disciples, since he turns immediately to them in v. 22 and takes up a problem similar to that of the Pharisees, but seen from the standpoint of followers, neither enemies nor crowds.

Their problem is not inability to see evidences of the kingdom in their midst (x 23, 24), but an acute desire to see one of the days of the son of man. They face the danger of impatience and despondency, dangers which would become all the graver after Jesus' death (xvii 25). They should not desire such days, since they will be days like the flood or the deadly rain on Sodom, destroying all (v. 27, 29). They should fear being caught unprepared. Will the son of man find faith in *them*? The only proper stance for them is "always to pray and not lose heart". In editing these materials Luke agrees with Matthew and Mark that they are especially appropriate to the disciples of Jesus during the period after his death, when their faith would be subjected to maximum strain. It is of course possible that in an earlier edition the parable of the patient widow had a different audience, but Luke's introduction and conclusion (xviii 1, 8) clearly adapt the parable to the later situation of the disciples.

It is possible that the parable of the two prayers (xviii 9-14) was addressed to a wider audience than the disciples, inasmuch as the words are so vague: "He told this parable to some who trusted in themselves that they were righteous and despised others". This context might prompt the reader to visualize a quite general audience. But several features strengthen the hypothesis that even here Luke had the *mathetai* in mind. (1) The problem is how to pray, as it had been in the earlier verses. (2) The sin of despising others is in the following story assigned to the disciples (v. 15). (3) The term 'righteous' (v. 9) early came to be used to describe members of the church. (cf. *Images of the Church*, p. 143 f.) (4) The use of Pharisee and tax-collector as antithetical models would exert maximum appeal to leaders who had suffered much from one and had been helped much by the other. We conclude therefore that Luke used this parable as a warning to his fellow Christian leaders, though in other contexts it no doubt could speak to a larger audience. Luke was aware that self-exaltation was a special plague of leaders and that one expression of it was a tendency to despise children (v. 15 ff.). The children are explicitly used here as models for adults.

Having followed the sequence of audiences in Luke's redaction
of these diverse materials, we may now be able to detect the presence
of several of those audiences in the last episode before Jesus' ascent
to Jerusalem (xviii 18-30). Jerusalem is the goal, for the holy city
and the temple represent God's λαός. First is introduced the ruler,
representative of the present leaders of that λαός, the Pharisees and
scribes. Characteristic of the interchange with this entire group
is (1) the issue of the role of the Law in securing eternal life, (2) the
demands of Jesus for total self-denial and discipleship, (3) the
refusal of the rulers to accept those demands. This group is very
near to the kingdom, yet the one thing lacking proves to be an
insuperable obstacle.

Who is it who speaks in xviii 26—"Then who can be saved?"
οἱ ἀκούσαντες, "those who heard it". The reference, I suggest, is
neither to the Pharisees nor to the disciples (who have already
demonstrated such self-denial, as v. 28 shows), but to the crowds.
From the beginning they have been described as those who came
out to hear Jesus. It is to them that v. 27 is addressed. This is the
miracle which they themselves have seen and have heard. "What
is impossible with men is possible with God". Whenever the kingdom
has come near to them, it has illustrated this possibility. (Mark and
Matthew assign this axiom to Jesus' discussion with the disciples.)
It is this miracle which Luke describes at length in the Passion
Story and in Acts. The ruler here stands as the measure of im-
possibility, Jesus and the disciples as the measure of possibility,
the *crowds* as those who, by witnessing both, face the crucial issue
of salvation. Luke's central interest falls on the disciples as represented by Peter and on the promise given to them. But he sees
the life of self-denial and the promise attending it as a valid option
for "those who heard". It is probable that in Luke's mind Peter
is seen here as spokesman for all followers, since in v. 31 the Twelve
are introduced as a distinct inner group. If this is so, the Evangelist
brings within the compass of this single episode, either explicitly
or implicitly, all the audiences we have noticed: λαός, rulers,
ὄχλοι, μαθηταί, twelve; and each plays a distinct role in the story.

An exegetical detail

Does this study of Luke's audiences improve our understanding
of specific episodes and of their function in his redactional work?
As a test case, we may choose the so-called Sermon on the Plain

in Chapter 6. Within this chapter all five of the audiences appear.

(1) In the first two stories in the chapter (vss. 1-11), the scribes and Pharisees are identified as enemies, their plot against Jesus is initiated, and then they disappear from the stage until vii 29.

(2) Next Luke tells of the choice of the twelve apostles, though curiously they do not appear again as a distinct group until viii 1. In vi 13 the twelve are distinguished from the entire group of μαθηταί; presumably they are included in the great crowd of disciples mentioned in vi 17, whom he singles out for a special word in vi 20. Thereafter, apart from a very general word in vi 40, the term μαθηταί does not appear again until vii 11.

(3) The λαός is mentioned explicitly at the beginning and at the end of the address, which has been given in their "hearing" (vii 1). They are well represented by a great multitude (πλῆθος πολύ) from Judea, Jerusalem, Tyre and Sidon. (Does Luke intend to cover the Dispersion as well as those at home?) This is the more promising "remnant" of Israel because they come "to hear him and to be healed of their diseases". After this introduction, this audience is represented by the ὄχλος (v. 19).

(4) In vi 17 Luke carefully divides the immediate audience into two segments, the disciples and the crowd which represented the λαός. Μαθηταί here appears to represent many more than the Twelve, covering all who have decided to become followers of Jesus. This group corresponds, I think, to the ὄχλοι of Mark iii 7-12 and Matthew iv 25-v 1. First mentioned in the double audience, they are addressed in the beatitudes (vi 20-23). These beatitudes, with their stress on the present tense *now*, imply that these men have already fulfilled the demands levied against all disciples; they have renounced everything and have become poor, hungry, deprived and reviled. They have proved to have ears that hear, they have obeyed his commands and have determined at all cost to seek first the Kingdom of God (cf. xviii 29).

(5) Where do the crowds appear as an audience in the Sermon? If we assume no change in the audience at vi 27, we would conclude that they do not appear at all as an audience, in spite of the explicit introduction in vi 17 and the conclusion in vii 1, and in spite of the repeated earlier description of the crowds as wanting to hear the Word (v 1, 15). However, I believe that they do appear in the awkward introduction in v. 27—"But I say to *you who hear*". We should note first the sequence of references in which this

identity emerges. Vs. 17 refers to the crowd of the λαός who had
come *to hear him*. As we have seen elsewhere Luke often refers to
this crowd in this way (vii 29; viii 4ff., xi 28; xv 1; xix 48; xxi 38).
vii 1 speaks of the series of teachings as having been given *in the
hearing* of the λαός. (cp. xx 45) Moreover, the concluding parable
of the two houses stresses the significance and the incompleteness
of the act of hearing. This parable is most pertinent to those
who come "to me" and hear "my words". All members of the
crowd are surely embraced by that condition. The decision which
confronts them is whether or not they will go further and *do* those
words, i.e., obey him as Lord, as one having final authority to
disclose the will of God for them. Once we have made this distinction
in audience, we should notice that the teachings of vss. 27-49
are in the main conditional, unlike the beatitudes where disciples
have already met the requirement of poverty etc. Luke took the
"ifs" in vss. 32-34 seriously, as indicating genuine options on the
part of uncommitted men. The demands of vss. 35-38 have not
as yet been met by this audience. One could say of these teachings
that they are tantamount to saying "If any of you wishes to
become a disciple, this is the kind of behavior which will be required". (A parallel passage with similar function is xiv 25-34).
This, I think, is the probable force of that clumsy phrase in vi 17:
"But I say to you who hear", i.e., "Now I am no longer speaking
primarily to the disciples, but to you crowds who have come out
to hear me, as representatives of the λαός." Unlike Mark and
Matthew, Luke does not say that these crowds followed Jesus,
but only that they had come to hear and to be healed. According
to vi 18 and vii 1-23, they *were healed*; according to vi 27-49,
they *heard* these demands which answered the very question,
presumably, which the same crowds had asked of John: "What
then shall we do?" When such an interpretation is accepted it
conditions our understanding of Luke's message in the Sermon
on the Plain.

I believe that it also solves the riddle of vi 27a, on the solution
of which exegetes have long been at odds. The riddle is this:
why do we find in v. 27a this adversative clause which is "in-
contestibly clumsy and awkward?" (J. DUPONT, *Les Beatitudes*,
Louvain, 1958 I, p. 314. In what follows here I have made use of
an unpublished essay by Jack SUGGS, even though my solution
differs from his.) Why this *but*? Why is any such clause needed

between vs. 26 and 27 f.? Several explanations have been offered. One solution is to trace this antithesis to a hypothetical source in which a contrasting command had been stated—e.g., "It has been said of old 'Thou shalt hate your enemies', but ...." On this reading of the matter we would find in this source, usually called Q, at least some of the six antitheses in Matthew 5. (W. D. DAVIES, *The Setting of the Sermon on the Mount*, Cambridge, 1964, p. 388) Pere M. -J. La Grange preferred another solution, in which this adversative should be set over against vi 23, as if to say "You disciples will have many enemies; but ... love your enemies." (Evangile selon S. Luc., Paris, 1948, p. 192). Victor Furnish believes that the clause is intended to accent the contrast between the woes as prohibited actions and the works of mercy as commanded actions. (*The Love Commandment in the New Testament*, Nashville, 1972 p. 55). J. JEREMIAS argues for still another solution. He assigns the four beatitudes (vi 20-23) to an audience of disciples; everything that follows beginning with the four woes he assigns to an audience of crowds (vi 24-49). This overlooks several facts: The absence of a separate address in v. 24 and the inclusion of such an address in v. 27; the tightly knit balance between beatitudes and woes which argue against separate audiences; the awkwardness of assigning the fourth woe (the danger of *becoming* false prophets) to an audience of uncommitted crowds. (cf. J. JEREMIAS, *The Parables of Jesus*, N. Y. Scribners, 1963, p. 42 n.)

All these efforts to solve the riddle focus upon the contrast between the behavior commanded and an opposite kind of behavior, in either Luke or his source. They all ignore the tell-tale participle "you who hear" and the indicated contrast between two audiences. When the exegete accepts that contrast as the most likely option, then he may also suppose that this awkward clause served in Luke's mind as an introduction not simply to the command which immediately followed (v. 27, 28), but rather to the entire collection of subsequent teachings which determine whether those who hear will also obey. On this point I gladly accept J. SUGGS' idea that 27a should be viewed as the introduction to this whole block of teachings. As of the time of the Sermon, the disciples are blessed but it remains to be seen where the crowds (the second half of the audience in v. 17) will decide to build their house. The Pharisees have determined not to hear and are therefore quite unable to hear (vii 29, 30; xvi 29-31). The μαθηταί both hear and comprehend (viii 8; xiv 35), both hear and obey (viii 21; xi 28); they take heed how they hear, therefore to them more will be given (viii 18). But the ὄχλοι as representatives of the λαός, having once heard the word, have yet to decide whether to hold the word fast "in an honest and good heart" (viii 15) or whether the devil will prevent them from believing (viii 12). In repentance, i.e., in guarding the word, they would cease being ὄχλοι and would become disciples (xi 28).

The difficulty in identifying the audience stems in large part from the inclusion of the woes in this context. At first sight they appear to be addressed neither to the disciples of vi 20a nor to the crowds of vi 27a, but to an absent group of rich and happy Jews. Thus the four woes seem quite alien to the present context in Luke, a factor often attributed to a pre-Lukan source in which Jesus addressed two separate groups, the poor and the rich. When, however, we examine closely the structure of the beatitudes and woes, another option emerges.

It is altogether probable that the four beatitudes envisage a single group, all the while specifying different attributes of that group. The same is true of the four woes. It is also probable that, in the present formulation of the complex, the accent falls upon the fourth beatitude and the fourth woe, which by reason of their fullness of detail give the clearest pictures of the contrast between the two groups. Wherein, then, lies the basic antithesis between this fourth beatitude and the fourth woe? We do *not* find the opposites stated in terms of the persecuted vs. the persecutors. No, the contrast falls between two potential choices which will be made by the same group, addressed throughout as *you* and distinguished from the same group, ἄνθρωποι (v. 22, 26). "You will be either persecuted or praised, will be the sons either of true or of false prophets. If you choose to be praised, you will be a rich, well-fed and happy company; but you will betray your calling as prophets." In Luke's edition, therefore, the woes are rightly addressed to the μαθηταί and not to the crowds or to the enemy scribes, since only the μαθηταί were called by Jesus to serve as prophets and sons of the prophets. They alone are threatened with the fate of becoming false prophets through the fear of persecution (v. 22) and the desire for popular response. If they seek prestige and security they will become accursed. Luke is not here concerned with the fate of the persecutors or "their fathers". The woes and the beatitudes are in his mind addressed to a single group—the disciples—and not to the more general audience of those "who hear" but who have not yet determined to obey Jesus (v. 27a, 46-49). J. REILING and J. L. SWELLENGREBEL, along with most interpreters, are mistaken in instructing translators that the woes are not addressed to disciples and that the teachings of vi 27 f. are so addressed (*A Translator's Handbook on the Gospel of Luke*, Leiden, Brill, 1971, p. 273 f.)

Interpreted in this way, Luke's Sermon is freed from one of the ambiguities of Matthew's Sermon. In the latter the double audience is divided at the beginning (v 1 f.) so that Jesus addressed only the disciples (the Twelve), but is united at the end (vii 28); it is difficult to tell at what point the crowds have begun to hear what Jesus teaches. It is virtually impossible to be sure which teachings are addressed to the smaller and which to the larger group. On our reading of Luke vi 17, 27, this ambiguity dissolves. Both groups were present throughout; the smaller group is the primary audience of vi 20-26, the larger group is the primary audience of the rest. In Luke also there is a sharper contrast between the degree of commitment of the two groups. Both of these contrasts, I believe, are expressed in the baffling introduction in vi 27.

Behind what seems to be a trivial matter of editorial language there often lurk more important matters of substance. Matthew's Sermon, for example, is far more ecclesiastical and catechetical in function; Jesus the teacher is providing the basic definition of duties for the Twelve as future prophets and teachers of the Church. Luke's Sermon, in contrast, marks an important early stage in Jesus' mission to Israel, as he makes clear to the non-believing but interested crowds the kind of behavior that is incumbent on all who would enter God's kingdom. When we keep the function of these teachings in mind, the thrust of the teachings is subtly altered. For example, the love of enemies becomes not the final test of a disciple's obedience, marking his progress toward perfection (Mt. v 48), but the initial test of whether a man is willing to make the sacrifices expected of even the least disciple. Their future relation to the brothers is determined at the outset by concern for the 'log' in their own eye. All their hopes for salvation must be seen as conditional upon obedience to the demands of Jesus; the blessedness of the poor awaits their willingness to enter the narrow door (xiii 22-30). This interpretation makes Luke's understanding of discipleship even more rigorous than Matthew's. Like the parable of the man building a tower (xiv 28), the parable of the two houses epitomizes the need for every Israelite member of the crowds to calculate the cost of discipleship in advance, before he decides to obey the commands given to *those who hear*.

We conclude, therefore, as we began, with the conviction that Luke was highly consistent and quite distinctive in his editorial treatment of the five major audiences of Jesus, and that to recognize this editorial attitude enhances our understanding of his organization of the traditions, along with our grasp of his intention in such specific segments as the Sermon on the Plain. Whether or not a reader agrees with my analysis of each term and each pericope, I hope he will agree that a careful examination of audiences constitutes a valid and valuable tool of redaction criticism. Whether or not Luke's conception of these audiences accurately preserves an original and authentic feature of each pericope is a problem into which we cannot venture here. Suffice it to observe that there is no antecedent reason why we should doubt that Jesus constantly encountered all five of these groups in the Lukan *dramatis personae*. In fact we could mount a rather impressive defense for the thesis that a basic continuity linked those groups in the days of Jesus' mission to similar groups in the days of the apostolic mission as remembered by this Evangelist. When we ask why the Synoptists should have so carefully described the audiences of Jesus, as well as those of the apostles in Acts, one answer, seldom noted, lies near at hand. Recipients of charismatic gifts, especially the gift of prophecy with its vision and audition of heavenly things, normally were sent by the heavenly dispatcher (word of God, angels, Holy Spirit) to a specific group. God's message was rarely addressed to all and sundry, but was usually designed for a target chosen in in advance. Prophets paid attention to such instructions, whether they envisaged such limited terms as Agabus (Acts xi 28) or such inclusive terms as the prophet John in the Apocalypse (x 11). It is not strange, therefore, that editors should pay similar attention to such matters.

THE LUKAN KINGSHIP PARABLE (LK. 19:11-27)

by

LUKE TIMOTHY JOHNSON
Yale Divinity School

In a season when the parables of Jesus generally are subject to tireless investigation, the Lukan Parable of the Pounds (19:11-27) stands strangely neglected.[1] Perhaps the apparently conflated and secondary condition of the parable makes it less interesting to those seeking the literary persona of Jesus.[2] Or perhaps the conventional wisdom on the parable in its present context is so consistent and so strong that, in spite of all the talk about paradox and polyvalence elsewhere, here there seems to be no mystery. Scholars debate the process of the parable's formation.[3] Does it combine two smaller parables (the "throne-pretender" and "the pounds")? Has Luke simply allegorized (with an eye to recent history) a story shared at some point in the tradition, with Matt. 25:14-30?[4] These questions

---

[1] In the spate of studies devoted to the parables as literary artifacts, no one has looked hard at this one. There is nothing at all in E. Linnemann, *Parables of Jesus* (London: SPCK, 1966) or M. A. Tolbert, *Perspectives on the Parables* (Phil.: Fortress, 1979), or in the volume from the Entrevernes Group, *Signs and Parables* (Pittsburgh: Pickwick Press, 1978), or in that edited by D. Patte, *Semiology and Parables* (Pittsburgh: Pickwick Press, 1976). Only passing reference is made in J. D. Crossan, *In Parables* (N.Y.: Harper and Row, 1973), M. Boucher, *The Mysterious Parable, A Literary Study* (CBQMS 6; Washington: CBA, 1977), D. O. Via, *The Parables* (Phil.: Fortress, 1967), and K. Bailey, *Poet and Peasant* (Grand Rapids: Eerdmans, 1976). J. D. Crossan has given a bit more attention to it in "The Servant Parables of Jesus," *Semeia* I (1974) 22-25.

[2] This quest is made most explicit by Crossan, as in his *Raid on the Articulate* (N.Y.: Harper and Row, 1976) 165-182.

[3] Some older studies simply assert that Jesus spoke two similar but different parables at different points in his ministry, as M. J. Ollivier, "Etude sur la physionomie intellectuelle de N.S.J.C.: la parabole des mines (Luc xix 1-27)," *RB* 1 (1892) 589-601; H. Thiessen, "The Parable of the Nobleman and the Earthly Kingdom, Luke 19:11-27," *Bibliotheca Sacra* 91 (1937) 180-190; P. Joüon, "La parabole des mines (Luc 19:13-27) et la parabole des talents (Matthieu 25, 14-30)," *RSR* 29 (1939) 489-94.

[4] For a full discussion of the options, cf. esp. M. Zerwick, "Die Parabel vom Thronanwaerter," *Bib* 40 (1959) 654-674, in which the Archelaus connection is extensively displayed, 660ff; and, J. Dupont, "La parabole des Talents (Matt. 25, 14-30) ou des Mines (Luc 19:12-27)," *RTP* ser. 3 19 (1969) 376-391; for shorter

disappear when it comes to Luke's redactional introduction to the parable in 19:11: all agree that this makes *his* understanding of the parable absolutely clear.[5] 19:11 reads, ἀκουόντων δὲ αὐτῶν ταῦτα προσθεὶς εἶπεν παραβολὴν διὰ τὸ ἐγγὺς εἶναι Ἰερουσαλήμ αὐτὸν καὶ δοκεῖν αὐτοὺς ὅτι παραχρῆμα μέλλει ἡ βασιλεία τοῦ θεοῦ ἀναφαίνεσθαι. In the light of this introduction, the parable (which speaks of a nobleman going off to get a kingdom) must refer allegorically to the ascension of Jesus and his return at the parousia for judgment.[6] Luke has Jesus tell the story here to counter any misunderstanding about the entry of Jesus as a messianic enthronement,[7] and, for his Christian readers, to show that Jesus himself predicted the delay of the parousia.[8] The business of the pounds and servants points to a

discussions, cf. J. Jeremias, *The Parables of Jesus* Rev. Ed. Trans. S. Hook (N.Y.: Charles Scribner's Sons, 1963) 59; Crossan, "Servant Parables," 22-25, and F. D. Weinert, "The Parable of the Throne Claimant (Luke 19:12, 14-15a, 27) Reconsidered," *CBQ* 39 (1977) 505ff.

[5] The decisive role of 19:11 is especially emphasized by Jeremias, *Parables*, 59; H. Conzelmann, *The Theology of St. Luke* tr. G. Buswell (N.Y.: Harper and Row, 1961) 113; A. Plummer, *A Critical and Exegetical Commentary on the Gospel According to Saint Luke* (ICC; N.Y.: Charles Scribner's Sons, 1903) 439; and, G. Schneider, *Parusiegleichnisse im Lukas-Evangelium* (Stuttgart: KBW Verlag, 1975) 38-42.

[6] The consistent view of the commentaries is expressed by B. S. Easton, *The Gospel According to St. Luke* (N.Y.: Charles Scribner's Sons, 1926), 200: "To Luke this whole narrative was a transparent allegory of the church during the absence of Christ." With some variations, the same is advanced by A. Loisy, *L'Evangile selon Luc* (Paris, 1924) 458; I. H. Marshall, *The Gospel of Luke* (Exeter: Paternoster Press, 1978) 700-701; E. E. Ellis, *The Gospel of Luke* (London: Nelson, 1966) 223; J. M. Creed, *The Gospel According to St. Luke* (London: Macmillan and Co., 1930) 232; W. Grundmann, *Das Evangelium nach Lukas* (THNT III; Berlin: Evangelische Verlaganstalt, 1963) 363; E. Klostermann, *Das Lukasevangelium* (HNT II, I; Tübingen: JCB Mohr, 1919) 549-550. Cf. also M. D. Goulder, "Characteristics of the Parables in the Several Gospels," *JTS* n.s. 19 (1968) 55; E. Kamlah, "Kritik und Interpretation der Parabel der Anvertrauten Geldern, Mt 25:14ff, Lk 19:12ff," *Kerygma und Dogma* 14 (1968) 30; J. D. Kaestli, *L'Eschatologie dans l'Oeuvre de Luc* (Geneva: Labor et Fides, 1969) 39; H. Flender, *Heil und Geschichte in der Theologie des Lukas* (München: Chr. Kaiser Verlag, 1965) 73.

[7] This is stressed by M. J. Lagrange, *Evangile selon Saint Luc* (EB; Paris: J. Gabalda, 1948) 492, who sees it as addressed, not to Luke's contemporaries, but to the disciples. Cf. also Marshall, 700, and E. Franklin, *Christ the Lord* (Phil.: Westminster, 1975) 26.

[8] "The parable is made explicitly to teach a lesson concerning the delay of the second advent," C. H. Dodd, *The Parables of the Kingdom* (London: Nisbet and Co., Ltd, 1935) 147 (cf. also p. 153). Not everyone is so confident as that, but this function of the parable is the standard view, as in Goulder, "Characteristics," 62; Kaestli, *L'Eschatologie*, 38; Schneider, *Parusiegleichnisse*, 38-40; Kamlah, "Kritik," 29; Jeremias, *Parables* 59; Conzelmann, *Theology*, 113; Dupont, "parabole," 382; F. Bovon, *Luc le Théologien* (Paris: Delachaux et Niestle, 1978) 58; Marshall, 702; R. Hiers, "The Problem of the Delay of the Parousia in Luke-Acts," *NTS* 20 (1974) 148.

secondary teaching, the need to deal with material possessions creatively and responsibly in the interim between ascension and parousia.[9]

Some have raised objections to one or the other aspect of this interpretation. In his recent article, for example, Weinert notes that two key elements of the story (the hostile mission of the opposition, and the account of the revenge by the king) do not fit comfortably within Luke's supposed interpretative framework.[10] But he does not question the conventional understanding of Luke's intention.[11] David Tiede, on the other hand, has broken with the accepted interpretation of this parable. He says that it does *not* refer to the delay of the parousia, but is best understood as an interpretation of the larger Lukan story at that point: "Whether the dominion of the king actually comes with his acclamation or his return in power, Luke warns that those who refuse to acknowledge such a king are playing a deadly game and, in effect, are already judged."[12] Tiede suggests that this judgment is pronounced by Jesus's words over the city in Lk. 19:42-44.[13] Although Tiede is certainly correct in his view, he could not, within the framework of his book, adequately support this position,[14] as I could not when I first made a similar proposal.[15] Since this way of reading the parable involves as well a shift in perception regarding the way Luke works, it may be appropriate to place the discussion of the passage firmly within that perception by means of a longer treatment.

Some Preliminary Remarks

The interpretation of the parable here being advanced depends on three principles concerning Luke's literary method which meet with wide approbation in theory but less application in practice. The first is that Luke-Acts is a single, though two-volumed, literary

---

[9] Cf. Flender, *Heil und Geschichte*, 73-74; S. Brown, *Apostasy and Perseverence in the Theology of Luke* (AB 36; Rome: Pontifical Biblical Institute, 1969) 104; Kaestli, *L'Eschatologie*, 40; Marshall, 701; Grundmann, 363; Plummer, 438.

[10] Weinert, "Throne-Claimant," 507.

[11] Weinert, "Throne-Claimant," 506.

[12] D. L. Tiede, *Prophecy and History in Luke-Acts* (Phil.: Fortress, 1980) 79.

[13] Tiede, *Prophecy and History*, 80.

[14] His discussion of the parable falls within a presentation of conflict and judgment in Luke-Acts. Tiede does a good job of showing the thematic connection of this passage to the opening of Luke's journey narrative, Lk 9:51 ff (cf. p. 57).

[15] Cf. L. T. Johnson, *The Literary Function of Possessions in Luke-Acts* (SBLDS 39; Missoula: Scholars Press, 1977) 168-170.

work. The story of Acts not only continues, but interprets Luke's version of the Gospel. The exegetical implication is that one must reckon with all of Luke's story to adequately assess his purposes. An interpretation of any passage which fails to take into account Luke's later development of the narrative is insufficient.[16]

The second principle is that Luke intends to give his audience ἀσφάλεια by writing his story καθεξῆς (Lk. 1:3). I take this to mean that it is precisely the sequence (ordering) of the narrative which is significant.[17] The use of this term in Acts 11:4 shows Luke's aim clearly: by reciting the events of Cornelius's conversion *in order* (and with interpretation), Peter convinces his listeners.[18] So Luke intends his story to give ἀσφάλεια to Theophilus. The exegetical implication is that, in Luke, we need attend not only to *what* Luke says but also to *where* in the story he says it. Losing the thread of the story in Luke-Acts means losing the thread of meaning.

The third principle is that within his larger story, Luke uses sayings material to interpret the narrative for his reader. The interpretative function of the speeches in Acts has received considerable attention,[19] and an increasing amount of work is also being done on the Gospel sayings material from this perspective.[20] I have called some of these interpretative sayings "programmatic prophecies," which is a rough and ready characterization.[21] Sometimes Luke's sayings material points forward, and sometimes backward.[22] At

---

[16] For example, a study of "the poor" which does not take into account the complete cessation of this theme in Acts would be skewed, as in R. J. Karris, "Rich and Poor: The Lukan Sitz-im-leben," *Perspectives on Luke-Acts* ed. C. H. Talbert (Danville: Assoc. of Baptist Professors of Religion, 1978) 112-125.

[17] For recent discussion of this, cf. G. Schneider, "Zur Bedeutung von *kathexēs* im lukanischen Doppelwerk, *ZNW* 68 (1977) 128-131, and, R. J. Dillon, "Previewing Luke's Project from his Prologue (Luke 1:1-4)," *CBQ* 43 (1981) 205-227, esp. 217-223.

[18] Cf. also Dillon, "Previewing," 220, n. 43.

[19] Cf., e.g., U. Wilckens, *Die Missionsreden der Apostelgeschichte* (Neukirchen: Neukirchen Verlag, 1961) 7-31; F. Prast, *Presbyter und Evangelium in nachapostolischer Zeit* (Stuttgart: Katholisches Bibelwerk, 1979) 17-28; D. Hamm, *This Sign of Healing: Acts 3:1-10, A Study in Lukan Theology* (PhD Dissertation: St. Louis University, 1975); Johnson, *Literary Function*, 16-19.

[20] Cf., e.g., P. Schubert, "The Structure and Significance of Luke 24," *Neutestamentliche Studien für Rudolf Bultmann* (Berlin: A. Toepelmann, 1959) 165-186; P. Minear, "Luke's Use of the Birth Stories," *Studies in Luke-Acts*, ed. L. Keck and L. Martyn (Nashville: Abingdon, 1966) 111-130; Tiede, *Prophecy and History in Luke-Acts*, passim.

[21] Johnson, *Literary Function* 18.

[22] Cf. esp. R. J. Dillon, *From Eye-Witnesses to Ministers of the Word* (AB 82: Rome: Pontifical Biblical Institute, 1978) 50, 116ff.

other times, he uses sayings to illustrate what is happening in his larger narrative.

Taken together, these three principles demand that the exegete take seriously the function of individual pericopae within the larger Lukan plot. Luke has a literary-theological goal which is connected to the way the story is told as a whole, and the way it unfolds in sequence. Before looking to what Luke may have wanted to teach a (putative) community by a single pericope, therefore, the exegete needs to look first to the role that passage plays in the literary composition as a whole.[23] The two perspectives need not conflict. Luke can use material both to advance his story and edify his readers. The exegete's first task, however, is to check on its function within the whole, for it is in that whole where the purpose of Luke is most certainly to be found. Before applying these principles to the Parable of the Pounds, it will be helpful to clear the way by raising some specific questions concerning the usual understanding of the passage in its Lukan context.

Problems of the Traditional Interpretation

I. There is little in the parable itself which demands considering it an allegorical tale about the ascension-parousia. In particular, there is nothing in Luke's version to indicate a temporal delay. Matthew's Parable of the Talents appears to have affected the reading of Luke's story. By the way hc has clustered 25:14-30 with the "Ten Maidens" (25:1-23) and "The Judgment of the Nations" (25:14-30) within his eschatological discourse (24:1-51), Matthew has made his parable one of eschatological judgment, Matthew alone has any indication that the man was gone πολὺν χρόνον (Mt. 25:19).[24] In Matthew, the reward is for the future (25:21, 23) and is connected to τὴν χαρὰν τοῦ κυρίου σου. These notes point to an eschatological dominion for the faithful ones. This picture accords with Matt. 19:28, in which the rule of the Twelve over Israel is seen in strictly eschatological terms (in contrast, as we shall see, to Luke). Luke's version of the parable has no significant delay in the

---

[23] Cf. L. T. Johnson, "On Finding the Lukan Community: A Cautious Cautionary Essay," *1979 SBL Seminar Papers* ed. P. Achtemeier (Missoula: Scholars Press, 1979) 87-100.

[24] Against Creed, 232; Klostermann, 549; Dupont, "parabole," 382; Kaestli, *L'Eschatologie*, 39-40, one cannot take Luke's "far country" as indicating a significant temporal delay. Travel was not so bad, then.

nobleman's return as king. Everything gets carried out with dispatch. The "getting of the kingdom" is not an unrealized event of the future, but one already accomplished in the story (Lk. 19:15).[25] The reward to those who have handled their charge well does not consist in some future overseeing of possessions, but is present (ἴσθι, γίνου), and consists in power (ἐξουσία) over cities within the King's realm (Lk. 19:17, 19). They play a present leadership role within the kingdom gained by the nobleman. This political reward for the faithful use of possessions integrates the two parts of the story, and indicates as well that the "political" aspect of the parable is not secondary but, in its present version, primary.

Other parts of the story do not fit the usual interpretation of the parable as a parousia-allegory. If the "going away" refers to the ascension of Jesus, what are we to make of his fellow "citizens" (19:14)—who are they? When and how do they voice their protest?[26] The slaughter of the opponents is even more difficult. Is there any indication elsewhere in Luke-Acts that there will be a final judgment looking like this?[27] The usual view of the parable also leaves hanging the fate of the third servant. In Matthew the profitless one is thrown into the outer darkness (Matt. 25:30). Again, this is a recognizably eschatological element in Matthew (cf. Matt. 8:12; 13:50; 22:13; 24:51). But although Luke knows this stereotype for eschatological judgment (cf. Luk. 13:28), he does not use it here. Indeed, this man is simply deprived of his pound (and his potential leadership). He is not utterly rejected; only "the enemies" are eliminated. If the story is about judgment for stewardship in the period of the Church, therefore, it limps at this point.

Since there is nothing in the story itself which compels its being read as a parousia parable, and since some parts of the story militate against this reading, even more weight falls on the introduction in 19:11. The conventional reading is saved in this fashion: no matter how poorly the parable itself fits the setting, Luke sees it that way. But does he? Is 19:11 really so clear? If the

---

[25] Cf. Tiede, *Prophecy and History*, 79.

[26] To identify the opponents simply as "the Jews," without any qualification (as in Plummer 438, Marshall 701), is to miss the careful presentation of Luke concerning "the divided people of God." cf. J. Jervell, *Luke and the People of God* (Minneapolis: Augsburg, 1971) 41-74.

[27] Weinert, "Throne-Claimant," 507.

introduction and parable go together so feebly, must we regard Luke as a sloppy workman? No, because we can ask whether this introduction means what it is usually taken to mean. Perhaps Luke's parable accords very well with another understanding of the introduction.

II. The Introduction, 19:11. This single verse seems to be straightforward, but is not. Each part of the verse presents multiple possibilities for interpretation.

A. To whom is the parable spoken? 19:11 links the parable to the story of Zaccheus and its concluding sayings (19:1-10) by a genitive absolute, ἀκουόντων δὲ αὐτῶν ταῦτα. Who are the αὐτοί? The strict grammatical antecedent would be the πάντες of verse 7, who grumbled because Jesus entered the house of Zaccheus.[28] They fit Luke's usual way of presenting the hostile leaders of the people, and the content of their complaint (cf. e.g. 15:1-3).[29] If the parable is told specifically to opponents, the harsh ending would surely be the point. It is possible, however, that the αὐτοί refers generally to either the ὄχλοι or μαθηταί who make up the other parts of Jesus's entourage as he goes toward Jerusalem. We last saw the ὄχλος in 18:36 (designated as λαός in 18:43) at the healing of the blind man who proclaimed Jesus as Son of David (18:37-39). The μαθηταί last appeared as represented by the Twelve in 19:31, the audience for the third passion prediction (18:31-34).

There are, then, three possible audiences for the parable: the crowd, the disciples, or the opponents. In the journey narrative, Luke is generally careful to specify Jesus's audiences, and purposefully.[30] To the disciples, he has Jesus address teachings on discipleship; to the crowd, calls for repentance, and warnings; to the opponents, sayings of rejection and judgment.[31] His failure to make *this* audience clearer to his reader leads one to think that the group to whom the parable was spoken was meant to consist in all those with Jesus on the way to Jerusalem, with the parable addressing each segment in diverse ways, and Luke's readers most of all.

B. Is the story told to confute the audience's expectations, or confirm them? This is the critical issue posed by 19:11, and one not

---

[28] Cf. Joüon, 489, who then sees this as a parable told to opponents, 493.

[29] Johnson, *Literary Function*, 109-113.

[30] Cf. A. Mosely, "Jesus' Audiences in the Gospels of St. Mark and St. Luke," *NTS* 10 (1963) 139-149.

[31] Johnson, *Literary Function*, 107-108.

easily resolved. The usual understanding is, of course, that the parable is told to refute the expectation.[32] But is there anything in the introduction itself which leads to this conclusion? Luke says that the parable was told because of two circumstances: he was near Jerusalem, and "they" considered ὅτι παραχρῆμα μέλλει ἡ βασιλεία τοῦ θεοῦ ἀναφαίνεσθαι. That he was near to Jerusalem is not in doubt (18:31). If Luke wanted the parable to serve as a rebuttal, then it must have been addressed to their expectation.

Before looking at the content of that expectation, we should note that neither Luke's language here, nor his accustomed usage, demands that we see the introduction as setting up a reversal of their expectations. The language: The verb δοκέω is used by Luke in its full range. Sometimes it appears in sentences containing false suppositions which are either implicitly or explicitly refuted.[33] Just as often, though, Luke uses it in a neutral sense.[34] It depends on the content whether it is a mere "supposition", or a "consideration." Nor does Luke's customary way of introducing parables help us determine whether this one is meant to support or deny the audience's expectations. He takes care to indicate the setting of the parables in Jesus's ministry, and we are able sometimes to determine the audience because of his consistency in stereotyping his characters.[35] He can even explicitly state the purpose of a parable, as in the Woman and the Judge. This was told to the disciples πρὸς τὸ δεῖν πάντοτε προσεύχεσθαι αὐτοὺς καὶ μὴ ἐγκακεῖν (Lk. 18:1). The structure of this introduction is similar to that of 19:11, but it is much more explicit in its intention. Only once in Luke do we find Jesus telling a parable explicitly to refute an understanding of his audience. This is the parable of the Pharisee and Tax-Collector, told πρός τινας τοὺς πεποιθότας ἐφ' ἑαυτοῖς ὅτι εἰσὶν δίκαιοι καὶ ἐξουθενοῦντας τοὺς λοιπούς (18:9). In that case, however, it is not a specific expectation, but an entire viewpoint which is countered. The parable of Lazarus and Dives (16:19-31) is likewise told to those we recognize as opponents of Jesus (16:14-15), and is an implicit rebuff to their attitude of φιλαργυρία (16:15), but the point is made subtly.

---

[32] Cf. esp. Conzelmann, *Theology* 113; Jeremias, *Parables* 59; Dodd, *Parables* 153.
[33] Luke 8:18; 12:40, 51; 13:2, 4; 24:37; Acts 12:9; 17:18.
[34] Luke 1:3; 10:36; 22:24; Acts 15:22ff; 25:27; 26:9; 27:13.
[35] As in Luke 16:14-15 and 18:9.

The parable of the Good Samaritan (10:30-35) is told in response to a question, and while it may subvert the implicit understanding of the questioner,[36] is not strictly a refutation of it (cf. 10:28, 36-37). The parable of the Rich Fool (12:16-21) is told to the crowd (12:13, 16) in response to an inappropriate request (12:13), but does not function as a rebuttal of the request. The fascinating question of Peter in 12:41 makes the intended audience for Jesus's parable of the Household Manager in 12:42-48 the Twelve,[37] but once more, the parable does not overturn any expectation of Peter's. The parable of the Fig-Tree (13:6-9) is told to *confirm* Jesus's demand for repentance in 13:1-5.

The introductions to parabolic discourse in chapters 14 and 15 are particularly interesting. Luke calls the lesson on hospitality given to Jesus's fellow guests a παραβολή (14:7), though it is neither veiled nor metaphorical. It serves to reprove the behavior Jesus had observed but does not directly attack any expectation of the guests. When Jesus does, in this setting, get down to parabolic discourse, (the parable of the Great Banquet, 14:16-24), he does so in response to a statement made by a guest regarding the kingdom: μακάριος ὅστις φάγεται ἄρτον ἐν τῇ βασιλείᾳ τοῦ θεοῦ (14:15). The parable shows something about the call to the kingdom, but it in no way functions to rebut the guest's exclamation, or his opinion. As in 19:11, the opinion is stimulated by an apparently eschatological statement by Jesus (14:4). The parable does not deny the blessedness of life in the kingdom, but it shifts the discussion to what is, in fact, happening in the ministry of Jesus: the rejection by those first called, and the invitation of the outcast. That this is the case is indicated by the thematic connection between the parable and Jesus's immediate call to the crowd in 14:25-33. In short, the parable of the Great Banquet responds to a statement about the Kingdom with an illustration of its emergence within the ministry of Jesus.

The most extended introduction to a parable is found in 15:1-3. The parables of the lost sheep (15:4-7), lost coin (15:8-10) and lost son (15:11-32) are told in response to the reactions of the Scribes and Pharisees to Jesus's ministry. They grumble because Jesus receives and eats with sinners. Each parable is clearly intended by

---

[36] Cf. J. D. Crossan, *The Dark Interval* (Niles, Ill.: Argus, 1975) 104-108.
[37] Mosely, "Audiences," 146; Jeremias, *Parables* 50, 46, 99.

Luke, not to refute this perception, but to confirm it. Each one shows that, in fact, Jesus's ministry precisely involves such a welcoming of those who are lost and sinful. These parables defend Jesus's ministry.

Luke's way of introducing parables is various. Only once does he explicitly refute the outlook of his listeners. Sometimes he uses the parable to confirm the viewpoint of the audience. Other times still he uses the introduction and parable as a way of illustrating something about the progress of his larger story. This is clearest in the parable of the Great Banquet and the parables of The Lost. It may well be the function of the Parable of the Pounds, as well. In any case, there is nothing in Luke's language or other usage to demand our seeing the parable as a refutation of the expectation expressed in 19:11.

C. The content of 19:11: what is being confirmed or confuted? There are at least three possibilities, here.

1. Usually the emphasis is placed on παραχρῆμα,[38] and its place in the sentence would justify this stress. What does it mean? Apart from Matt. 21:19, 20, it is a distinctively Lukan word, being used by him sixteen times and by the other NT writers not at all. Luke especially likes to use it for healings, to note the suddenness of physical change.[39] It always refers to palpable, physical event. This is the only place where its reference might be to an event of larger or more indeterminate proportions. The ταῦτα, referring back to 19:9-10, seems to place their expectation within an eschatological framework.[40] If the parable confirms the introduction, Jesus's entrance as βασιλεύς and the events of the passion are proximate enough to be called παραχρῆμα. But if this word is the target of disconfirmation, it is by no means necessary to conclude that the

---

[38] Cf., e.g., Plummer, 439.

[39] Cf. Luke 4:39; 5:25; 8:44; 47, 55; 13:13, 18:43; Acts 3:7. He also uses it for the sudden deaths of Sapphira (Acts 5:10) and Herod (Acts 12:23).

[40] The combination of "Son of Abraham," "Salvation," "Today," and "Son of Man," is evocative. There is a cluster of eschatological Son of Man sayings in the journey section (9:26; 12:8-10, 40; 17:22, 24, 26, 30; 18:8). Abraham appears in eschatological contexts in 13:28 and 16:22. Of greater interest, however, is the Lukan redaction of 3:6-8, in which σωτηρία and τέκνα 'Αβραάμ are closely joined. The statements of 19:9-10 are not, within the Lukan story, unusual. The coming of salvation is announced already in 1:69, 71 and 2:30. Jesus declares the Scripture fulfilled "today" in 4:21, and the bent woman is called a daughter of Abraham in 13:16. As in those places, the realization of salvation or healing is not future, but present, "for the Son of Man has come to save..." (19:10).

author is justifying a parousia delayed for generations. The con-
futation of παραχρῆμα could be taken care of within the temporal
range of Luke's narrative (any time past the σήμερον of 19:9), with
not an eye to a distant return of the Lord.

2. The verb ἀναφαίνω is in a position of greater emphasis even
than παραχρῆμα. It is usually taken to mean, simply, "appear." If
so, the question "in what sense," is still appropriate. Does it point
to a full-scale, visible realization of the kingdom, or specifically to
the return of the Son of Man for judgment? Or can an "appearance" be accomplished by some sort of symbolic manifestation
of the Kingdom, such as the proclamation of a king by his
followers? Again, the issue of confirmation or disconfirmation is
important.

It is necessary, in any case, to emphatically deny the assumption
that ἀναφαίνω is part of the technical language connected to the
parousia. This illegitimate transfer of meaning sometimes takes
place,[41] supported, of course, by the use of φαίνω and especially
ἐπιφαίνω in the New Testament. In II Thess. 2:8, ἐπιφάνεια and
παρουσία are used together. And in the Pastorals, ἐπιφάνεια has close
to a technical meaning in reference to the παρουσία (cf. I Tim. 6:14;
II Tim. 1:10; 4:1; Tit. 2:13). But Luke lacks this noun altogether,
as he does παρουσία. Luke uses the adjective ἐπιφανής once in the
citation of Joel 3:4 in Acts 2:20, with reference to the "Great and
Manifest Day of the Lord." As for the verb ἐπιφαίνω, it is used by
Tit. 2:11 and 3:4 in a sacral sense, but in both Lk. 1:79 and Acts
27:20, the use is non-technical. There is simply no basis for
transferring any technical sense from ἐπιφαίνω to ἀναφαίνω in Lk.
19:11.

Neither can we assume that ἀναφαίνω always means the same as
φαίνω,[42] although it sometimes does. Luke is the only NT author to
use it. In Acts 21:3, the aorist participle ἀναφάναντες means,
"catching sight of,"[43] and the only other use in the NT is here in
19:11. To conclude that it means simply "appear," however,
would be precipitous, for the uses of ἀναφαίνω in other writings of

---

[41] This seems to be implicit in the commentaries, and is made explicit in Ellis,
223.
[42] Luke uses φαίνω for a physical appearance in Lk 9:8 and for a mental impression in Lk 24:11. He uses ἐμφανής in Acts 10:40 for Jesus's resurrection appearance. Ἐμφανίζω is used in Acts 23:15, 22; 24:1; 25:2, 15 for "report."
[43] As in Philo, Ad Flaccum 27.

the time are more various. The verb in the passive voice frequently does mean, "to appear, to be manifested," as consistently in Josephus.⁴⁴ But this is not invariable. Philo uses it often in the sense of "to reveal," especially in contexts wherein something latent becomes visible.⁴⁵ By extension, he can speak of God "revealing" his own existence,⁴⁶ or the truth of a situation.⁴⁷ This meaning, in turn, shades easily into "manifest" in the sense of "demonstrate," or even "display."⁴⁸ The step is not far, then, to another use of ἀναφαίνω which is of special interest to the analysis of this passage. Philo speaks of God "revealing his judgment." As a verbal action, this sort of manifestation is tantamount to "announcing his judgment."⁴⁹ Finally, Philo speaks of actions which "reveal" or "declare" a royal figure to be divine.⁵⁰ This last usage is considerably older than Philo, and can be found in Pindar,⁵¹ Euripides,⁵² and, possibly, in Herodotus.⁵³

In the light of this, it is not at all impossible that Luke intended μέλλει ἡ βασιλεία τοῦ θεοῦ ἀναφαίνεσθαι to mean that "the Kingdom of God was going to be declared." This would find immediate confirmation in the proclamation of Jesus as King in 19:38. But this brings us to the final difficulty of 19:11, the meaning of βασιλεία τοῦ θεοῦ.

3. What point does Luke want to make about the Kingdom of God? If the function of the parable is to confirm the expectation of 19:11, then Luke illustrates something about this kingdom, and those who reject it. And by having Jesus proclaimed as king in

---

⁴⁴ Cf. Josephus, *JB* IV 377; VII 371˙and *Ant* XVII 120.

⁴⁵ Cf. *De Migr. Abr.* 183; *De Fuga* 28; *De Cong.* 124, 153; *De Spec. Leg.* II, 141, 152; IV, 51-52; *Ad Gaium* 120.

⁴⁶ *De Praem*, 44. Cf. also the two uses of ἀναφαίνω given in J. H. Moulton, G. Milligan, *The Vocabulary of the Greek Testament* (Grand Rapids: Eerdmans, 1930) 39.

⁴⁷ *De Jos*, 255.

⁴⁸ *Quod Omn. Prob.* 149; *De Praem*. 4. Plato uses ἀναφαίνω in this sense in *Critias* 108C.

⁴⁹ *De Vita Mosis* II, 228. The two uses of ἀναφαίνω in LXX Job 11:18 and 13:18 seem to me to bear the same meaning. In Job's forensic context "to appear righteous" implies, "to be declared righteous by the judge."

⁵⁰ In a recitation of Caligula's wrongdoing, Philo asks rhetorically, διὰ ταῦτα ὁ νέος Διόνυσος ἡμῖν ἀνεφάνης?

⁵¹ Pindar's 4th Pythian Ode 4:62 has the son of Polymnestus declared the (future) king of Cyrene: βασιλέ' ἄμφανεν Κυράνᾳ (Liddell and Scott).

⁵² In the *Bacchae* 528, there is a divine acclamation: ἀναφαίνω σε τόδ', ὦ Βάκχιε, Θήβαις ὀνομάζειν (Liddell and Scott).

⁵³ Herodotus III, 82.

19:38, he says something about the relation of Jesus to this Kingdom. This is straightforward. But if the point of the parable is to refute 19:11, several other possibilities present themselves. Already from Lk. 1:33, Luke told us that Jesus would rule over Israel forever. The question of the restoration of the kingdom to Israel is raised explicitly in Acts 1:6, and only obliquely answered. Three aspects of "Kingdom" must therefore be considered: the kingship of Jesus, rule over Israel, and the Kingdom of God. Do they mutually impinge? If the point of the parable is to clarify a misconception contained in 19:11, how does it do this? Does it assert that messianic rule over Israel is not the same thing as the Kingdom of God, although Jesus is proclaimed as king in the entry?[54] Does it assert that the rule of Jesus over God's people is not yet full realization of God's rule and Kingdom?[55] Much weight rests on a less than clear construction. This article cannot rehearse all the complexity of Luke's view of the Kingdom. But a simplistic view of 19:11 which, without qualification, identifies βασιλεία τοῦ θεοῦ with the return of Jesus at the parousia misses that complexity altogether and begs the question of the passage's meaning.

III. This is the final deficiency in the traditional understanding of the parable with its introduction: it makes Luke work against himself as an author. We are asked to believe that Luke, using traditional materials with considerable freedom and able to put this passage wherever he wished,[56] deliberately placed it here at the climax of Jesus's carefully plotted ascent to Jerusalem (with meticulous markings of the way and the exact point of entry). He put it at this point of crescendo, in order to show that, in fact, this entry of Jesus was not the "appearing at once" of the Kingdom of God. Why should Luke's readers need to be told that? Were they so confused?[57] If Luke wanted to clarify matters, he has done an extraordinarily poor job, for the placement of the parable here only heightens the kingly impression made by Jesus's entrance into Jerusalem. This is strengthened further by Luke's insertion of ὁ

---

[54] Dupont, "parabole," 381.

[55] Conzelmann, *Theology* 198; Hiers, "Delay," 148.

[56] A simple observation, but worth pondering. If Luke had control of his materials, and wanted to achieve the purpose suggested for this passage, why didn't he place the passage in a less ambiguous setting, for example *after* the entry of Jesus into Jerusalem, so that the reader could not miss the next "enthronement" as the ascension?

[57] Marshall, 702, sees the difficulty here, but passes over it.

βασιλεύς in 19:38, which makes the acclamation (ἀναφαίνεσθαι) explicit, and by his having the Pharisees respond immediately with a demand that this acclamation of Jesus as king be silenced. As to the connection between this royal entry and the kingdom of God, Luke has further muddied his own waters by making the phrasing of 19:38 (ἐν οὐρανῷ εἰρήνη καὶ δόξα ἐν ὑψίστοις) recall so emphatically the angelic praise of God in 2:14 (δόξα ἐν ὑψίστοις θεῷ καὶ ἐπὶ γῆς εἰρήνη ἐν ἀνθρώποις εὐδοκίας.

The entry is only part of the problem. The Lukan version of the Last Supper again speaks clearly of the kingly rule of Jesus, one to be given as well to the Twelve: κἀγὼ διατίθεμαι ὑμῖν καθὼς διέθετό μοι ὁ πατήρ μου βασιλείαν (22:29). The striking difference from the parallel Matthean logion has been elaborated before.[58] In Luke, the authority is a present one, and will be carried out by the Twelve in Luke's narrative of the Jerusalem community.[59] Again, if Luke wished to loosen the connection between the reign of God and the manifestations of it in Jesus's ministry, he only confused the issue by shaping this passage the way he did. He adds to the confusion further in 23:2 by the way he has phrased the charge against Jesus. Before Pilate, Jesus is accused of stirring up the nation and calling himself a Christ, a king (λέγοντα ἑαυτὸν χριστὸν βασιλέα εἶναι). Only Luke draws this close a connection between χριστός and βασιλεύς, and has reported it as Jesus's own identification. Finally, in a uniquely Lukan turn, the man crucified with Jesus asks to be remembered ὅταν ἔλθῃς εἰς τὴν βασιλείαν σου (23:42), and Jesus tells him that he will be with him that day in paradise (23:43).

Since all of these notes emphasizing the kingly identity of Jesus are uniquely Lukan, and all of them occur immediately after the parable with its introduction, we must take seriously the possibility that Luke intended his parable to *confirm* 19:11, for the progress of Luke's story after the parable shows us in fact a "manifestation" of God's Kingdom "immediately." The points I have made should at least cause the traditional interpretation of this passage as a teaching on the delay of the parousia to be put aside, and prepare

---

[58] J. Dupont, "Le logion des douze Trônes (Mat 19:28, Lc 22:28-30)," *Bib* 45 (1964) 355-392. One should especially note the solemn and legal resonances of διατίθημι, cf. *L-S*, s.v. and J. Behm, "διατίθημι," *TDNT* II, 104-106, who sees the ἵνα clause as the object of the verb.

[59] Dupont, "Logion," 381; Brown, Apostasy 64ff; Jervell, *Luke and the People of God* 94.

the way for a reading of the parable which takes seriously its function within Luke's larger narrative. The shape of the parable itself, the ambiguity of 19:11, and Luke's consistency as a writer call for such a reading.

The Lukan Context for the Parable

If it is so that Luke achieves his purpose not only by what he tells his readers but also by the order of his telling, it is important to see precisely where in his story Luke has placed this passage, and what that placement might signify. The parable comes at a critical turning point in three concurrent developments within Luke's story: the proclamation of God's Rule by the Prophet-Messiah, the division within the people Israel caused by this proclamation, and the formation of a new leadership for the restored portion of this people.

A. Jesus and the Kingdom of God. Luke does not *identify* the Kingdom of God with the Kingdom of Israel, or the kingship of Jesus. The Kingdom of God remains a transcendent reality, the effective rule of God, which is proclaimed throughout Luke-Acts,[60] but is never said to be realized fully.[61] As Jesus proclaimed the Kingdom of God (4:43) and sends out emissaries so to preach (9:2; 10:9), the missionaries of Acts continue to preach ἡ βασιλεία τοῦ θεοῦ: Philip (Acts 8:12), Barnabas with Paul (14:21-22), and Paul himself (19:8; 20:25) until the very end (28:23, 31). Jesus can speak of the "approach" (ἔγγυς) of the Kingdom as a future phenomenon (Lk. 21:31).

But there is another side to Luke's presentation of the Kingdom. Jesus promises not to eat or drink after the meal with his disciples before his death "until the Kingdom of God comes" (Lk 22:16, 18). Yet, Luke makes a point of Jesus eating and drinking with his witnesses after his resurrection (24:30, 43; Acts 1:4; 10:41), and these occasions are used by Jesus to teach them τὰ περὶ τῆς βασιλείας τοῦ θεοῦ (Acts 1:4). Here is the deep ambiguity in Luke's teaching on the Kingdom of God. The Kingdom is not the church, certainly, nor is it simply a spiritual reality. At the same time, it is not entirely future, or world-ending. People enter into it (Lk. 18:24) even if through suffering (Acts 14:22). Luke's eschatology is decidedly

---

[60] Cf. Prast, *Presbyter und Evangelium* 263-300.

[61] But Conzelmann goes too far when he asserts, "He knows nothing of an immanent development on the basis of the preaching of the kingdom," *Theology* 122.

more individualistic than some other NT writers (cf. Lk. 12:20; 16:22),[62] and his eschatology is not simply a temporal category.[63] At the heart of the ambiguity is the role played by Jesus as King over Israel. Luke may not have intended to resolve the ambiguity, but it is part of the puzzle into which this parable must be fitted.

From the beginning of the Gospel, Luke's reader knows that Jesus will reign (βασιλεύσει) over the House of Jacob, that his kingdom (βασιλεία) will have no end (1:33), because God will give him the throne of his father David (1:32). In Luke, prophecies have a way of getting fulfilled within his story, and so it is with this one. In the first eight chapters of the Gospel, the phrase ἡ βασιλεία τοῦ θεοῦ occurs five times, in each case with Jesus as its proclaimer (4:43; 6:20; 7:28; 8:1, 10). From the sending of the Twelve in 9:1, however, up to our parable in 19:11, the phrase occurs twenty-one times. Luke does more than intensify the number of references to the kingdom in this section. He associates the Kingdom explicitly with the words and work of Jesus, and he pictures the Kingdom as imminent, indeed immanent.[64] These two aspects are brought together in Jesus's response during the Beelzebul controversy, "If I cast out demons by the finger of God, ἄρα ἔφθασεν ἐφ' ὑμᾶς ἡ βασιλεία τοῦ θεοῦ" (11:20).

The prayer Jesus teaches his disciples during the journey, ἐλθάτω ἡ βασιλεία σου (11:2) is found in a context where that kingdom is appearing powerfully in the work and words of Jesus. It is because of this that he can tell the μαθηταί (12:22) to seek the Kingdom because, in fact, it has already pleased the Father to give it to them: μὴ φόβου ... ὅτι εὐδόκησεν ὁ πατὴρ ὑμῶν δοῦναι ὑμῖν τὴν βασιλείαν (12:32).[65] It is for this reason that the kingdom parables of the mustard seed and leaven, which stress immanent presence, are appropriate in this journey context (13:18-21),[66] and it is for this reason that Jesus's response to the Pharisees' interrogation about the coming of the Kingdom (ἰδοὺ γὰρ ἡ βασιλεία τοῦ θεοῦ ἐντὸς ὑμῶν

---

[62] Cf. J. Dupont, Les Béatitudes III Les Évangélistes (Paris: J. Gabalda, 1973) 136.

[63] This is developed in a small pamphlet of mine, Luke-Acts: A Story of Prophet and People. (Chicago: Franciscan Herald Press, 1981) 54-64.

[64] Cf. Luke 10:9, 11; 16:16; 17:20-21; 18:16-17; 18:24, 29.

[65] The use of the aorist should be noted here, as well as the complete absence of this element of realization in the parallel, Matt 6:33.

[66] Unless these small parables have this interpretative function within the Lukan journey narrative, their uprooting from the Markan setting (cf. Mk 4:30-32) which is taken over by Matt 13:31-33, is hard to understand.

ἐστιν, 17:20-21) must be seen as an interpretation precisely of this process: in the progress of Jesus toward Jerusalem, the authentic people of God and therefore the Kingdom of God, is coming into existence.

The kingdom has been connected to Jesus's work, and has been increasingly pictured as present. But Jesus himself has never yet been called a king. Only, just before the Zaccheus incident, he is twice called "Son of David" by the blind man of Jericho, which is a preparation. Right *after* the parable, however, we find Jesus himself proclaimed as βασιλεύς (19:38), accused of claiming to be Messiah-King (23:2ff), castigated as such on the cross (23:37, 38), begged there for a place in his kingdom (23:42), and, at the last supper, giving rule (βασιλεία) to his closest followers (22:29). Concerning this past point, we should note that Jesus gives to others what had already been granted to him (καθὼς διέθετό μοι ὁ πατήρ μου βασιλείαν). This should be kept in mind as we read the parable, for the nobleman gave rule to his servants after he had gotten the kingdom (λαβόντα τὴν βασιλείαν, 19:15). After the parable, in short, the Kingdom of God and the Kingship of Jesus are brought by Luke very close together.

This connection continues in Acts, though less obtrusively, for the point has been made for any careful reader. The question concerning the restoration of the kingdom to Israel "at this time" is not so much rebuffed as answered in terms of his followers' witnessing to *him* (Acts 1:6-8). Philip preaches about the Kingdom of God and the Name of Jesus Christ—the two are spoken in one breath (Acts 8:12). We find Paul accused of preaching another king, Jesus (Acts 17:7). And Paul's final testimony concerning the Kingdom of God is specified by his trying to persuade the Jews of Rome περὶ τοῦ Ἰησοῦ (28:23). At the very end, Paul preaches the Kingdom and teaches περὶ τοῦ Κυρίου Ἰησοῦ Χριστοῦ (Acts 28:31). Finally, we note that in Paul's sermon at Antioch of Pisidia, he strikes the Davidic (and therefore kingly) connection hard, by moving directly from David to Jesus τῷ Ἰσραὴλ σωτῆρα (13:23, cf. Lk. 2:11), a connection already established by Lk. 1:32, 69; 18:37-39; 20:41-44; Acts 2:34; 7:45, and picked up a last time by James in Acts 15:16.

As Luke sees God's people as consisting in more than the historical Israel, yet always rooted in the restored people (realized in the Jerusalem community),[67] so he sees the Kingdom of God as

---

[67] Cf. Jervell, *Luke and the People of God* 56-64, and N. A. Dahl, "'A People for His Name (Acts 15:14)'" *NTS* 4 (1957-8) 319-327.

transcending the rule of Jesus over the people Israel, yet always without denying the reality or legitimacy of that messianic rule. It is not contrary to God's Kingdom; in some sense, it is both sign and partial realization of that kingdom. And the place in the story where this connection is established is the Parable of the Pounds.

B. The rejection of Jesus by the leaders of Israel.[68] It is again in the journey narrative that Luke intensifies this part of his story. Zechariah had predicted a division in the people Israel caused by Jesus (Lk. 2:34). It was programmatically foreshadowed at Nazareth (4:16-30). And in 7:29-30, Luke identifies the nature of the split: the tax-collectors and sinners—the outcast—received God's prophets; but the leaders of the people—the Pharisees and Lawyers—rejected both John and Jesus. These are the "citizens" (19:14) who did not accept the prophetic messianic mission of Jesus. Because they rejected him, they rejected God's plan for themselves (7:30), and found themselves progressively excluded from the restored people forming about the Messiah.

In the journey narrative, Luke so organizes his materials that the reader gains the impression of a great crowd of disciples being formed about Jesus from among the crowd, as he makes his way to Jerusalem (the small band of 8:1-3 becomes, at the entrance to the city, a πλῆθος τῶν μαθητῶν, 19:37). At the same time, the leaders of the people, who constantly test and oppose the prophet, are being excluded.

Once more, the Parable of the Pounds proves to be a critical stage in this progress of the story. It is immediately preceded by the acceptance by Zaccheus of Jesus (Zaccheus, of course, being a chief tax-collector), and Jesus in turn proclaiming him a son of Abraham (19:9).[69] Typically, the opponents respond to the gesture of fellowship by grumbling (19:7, cf. 15:1-3). After the Parable of the Pounds, when Jesus is acclaimed as βασιλεύς, the Pharisees want the acclamation silenced (19:39). In response, Jesus speaks words of

---

[68] For these two sections of the argument, I rely on evidence developed more fully in *Literary Function* 46-121, and will therefore make my points without great elaboration.

[69] Notice how the talk of Abraham in 3:8; 13:15-16; 13:28 and 16:22 occurs within this theme of acceptance and rejection within the people. Luke makes the point repeatedly that the acceptance or rejection of Jesus determines inclusion within the people. Thus, in 19:9-10, salvation comes to Zaccheus, a son of Abraham because of his acceptance of Jesus.

judgment over their city (19:41-44), thus completing the pattern: the leaders who reject Jesus are themselves rejected.

That there will be a change in leadership over the people is indicated parabolically by the Parable of the Vineyard (20:9-18) which is recognized by the leaders as addressed to them (20:19). The representatives of the leadership shift at this point: the Pharisees and Lawyers are replaced by the members of the Sanhedrin as the opponents of Jesus. But it is still the leaders who oppose him, rather than the populace at large.[70]

In Acts, the Jerusalem narrative shows how the leaders of the people who rejected the voice of the Prophet whom God raised up (to continue his powerful presence in the words and deeds of his prophetic followers) were "cut off from the people" (Acts 3:23). Before the Spirit-filled words and deeds of the Apostles, the leaders were reduced to fear and impotence: authority over the people passed from their hands (5:26, 41-42).

They resisted the rule of the one who was the true heir of the throne of David his father (Acts 2:30, cf. Lk. 1:32), who was at God's right hand (2:35), and was seen as Son of Man standing at God's right hand (7:56). They resisted him by refusing the proclamation of him by those who proclaimed God's Kingdom in his name. They were never "slaughtered." But they were certainly, in Luke's story, "cut off" from the people of God.

C. The New Leadership over Israel. As the old leaders fall away from their place of authority, Luke shows us the preparation, installation, and ministry of a new group of leaders over Israel: the Twelve. From the sending out of the Twelve in 9:1ff, Luke joins two aspects of this leadership: 1) it is intimately connected with the work of Jesus—as he proclaims the kingdom and announces its presence by works of healing, so do they (9:2, 11): 2) it is symbolized by the disposition of possessions, especially by the distribution of food. The Twelve share with Jesus in the feeding of the five thousand (9:12-17). The Twelve (cf. 12:41) are like managers whom the master will place over the household servants (12:42).

After the Parable of the Pounds, as we have seen, the Twelve are, at the Last Supper, given βασιλεία over Israel (22:29-30), and this authority is symbolized in terms of service at tables (22:24-27).[71] In

---

[70] Cf. J. Kodell, "Luke's Use of Laos, 'People' especially in the Jerusalem Narrative," *CBQ* 31 (1969) 327-343; Johnson, *Literary Function* 117-119.

[71] Cf. Prast, *Presbyter und Evangelium* 233-262.

Acts, this authority is exercised by the leadership role the Twelve play within the restored Israel. They are established in power when faced with persecution (4:23-31). They exercise prophetic power within the people (5:1-11), and are the acknowledged leaders both within (4:32-37) and without (5:12-42). The authority they wield is again symbolized by their being in charge of the collection and distribution of goods. When the Twelve hand on the spiritual authority to the Seven, it is once more symbolized by table-service (Acts 6:1ff). In this progression as well, the Parable of the Pounds provides a point of pivot.

Reading the Parable in Context

The lines of interpretation should by now be abundantly clear. Who is the nobleman who would be king, and who in fact gets βασιλεία, so that he cannot only exercise it, but share it with his faithful followers? Jesus, who will immediately be hailed as king, dispose of βασιλεία, grant entrance to the thief, and, as risen Lord, continue to exercise authority through his emissaries' words and deeds. Who are the fellow citizens who do not wish to have this man as their ruler, who protest it, and then, defeated, are slaughtered before the king? The leaders of the people who decried the proclamation of Jesus as King, who mocked him as such on the cross, who rejected his mission as prophet, who persecuted his Apostles and who, at last, found themselves "cut off from the people." Who are the servants whose use of possessions is rewarded by ἐξουσία within the dominion of this king? The Twelve, who have been schooled in service (22:28), and whose βασιλεία over the restored Israel is exercised and expressed in the ministry of word and table-service.[72] When will all this occur? In the course of the story Luke is telling, beginning *immediately* with the messianic proclamation of Jesus in 19:38.

Not everything fits exactly. One cannot push the "slaughtering," for example, or suggest that the profitless servant who was rejected from leadership is Judas. Luke is not working with needle-point obsessiveness. But the parable works admirably to illustrate and interpret the next section of Luke's story. Indeed, it does nothing else so well. Reading the Parable of the Pounds in this

---

[72] Brown, *Apostasy* 64, connects the ἐξουσία of the parable to the βασιλεία of 22:29, but refers the first to the parousia.

fashion within the context of the Lukan story, we conclude that it does not deny but confirm the expectation of 19:11: Jesus *is* proclaimed as a King and does exercise rule through his apostles in the restored Israel. This is a "manifestation" of God's Kingdom. And those who refuse it, are cut off. The parable and its introduction together serve the literary function of alerting the reader as to just what will follow. It is, preeminently, the Lukan kingship parable.

LUKE'S PREFACE IN THE CONTEXT OF GREEK PREFACE-WRITING

by

LOVEDAY ALEXANDER

Manchester

In 1899 P. Corssen wrote in a review of Blass's *Philology of the Gospels*:

"Mit dem Evangelium des Lukas ist das Evangelium aus dem Dunkel der Conventikel auf den Büchermarkt hinausgetreten... Beweis das Prooemium... Mit solchem Raffinement schreibt Keiner, der im Verborgenen bleiben will, das ist berechnet auf ein großes Publikum".[1]

These words marked a turning-point in the scholarly treatment of the Lukan preface: a retreat from the primary exegesis of the plain meaning of the text (already declared a hopeless task by Aberle in 1863[2]), the beginnings of a quest for the meaning behind the words. And they suggest already one direction in which that quest would lead. For Corssen, a certain literary style ("solchem Raffinement") implies a certain audience ("ein großes Publikum") and points to a particular social setting for the work ("aus dem Dunkel der Conventikel auf den Büchermarkt hinaus"). The preface, he reasons, implies an intention on Luke's part to write 'Literature' in the more restricted sense of the word, 'Hochliteratur' or 'Belles-lettres' (the terms are inexact but for the moment useful).[3] Corssen's *obiter dicta* thus constitute what is virtually a programme for the subsequent study of the Lukan preface.

---

[1] P. Corssen, *Göttingische Gelehrte Anzeigen*, 1899, pp. 305ff.

[2] *Theologische Quartalschrift* 45 (1863), p. 99: The only sure result of recent research on the preface is "die Mehrdeutigkeit aller entscheidener Wörte und Wendungen in denselben". Aberle's own conclusion from this fact is that the ambiguity is deliberate, a sort of code necessary in days of persecution: a rather desperate expedient!

[3] For a pertinent and timely critique of the "Hochliteratur"/"Kleinliteratur" dichotomy, see P. L. Shuler, *A Genre for the Gospels* (Fortress Press, Philadelphia, 1982), pp. 11ff.

Once the decision had been made that the preface marked Luke's work as belonging, at least in aspiration, to the Greek literary world, the next step was to locate it more precisely within that world. Most critics argued that the conventional language and *topoi* of the preface set it squarely within one particular literary tradition, namely Greek historiography. This approach found its apogee in the work of H. J. Cadbury, especially in his detailed commentary on the preface appended to *The Beginnings of Christianity* vol. II (1922),[4] and in the series of articles in which he attempted to work out the implications of his reading of the preface for the understanding of Luke-Acts as a whole.[5] Cadbury's work has remained essentially unchallenged. Most subsequent scholarship has simply taken it for granted.[6] New readings of the preface have based themselves on theological argument rather than on a refutation of Cadbury's case.[7] Only in comparatively recent times has there been any serious attempt to tackle Cadbury on his own ground, by looking afresh at the literary background to Luke's composition.[8]

---

[4] H. J. Cadbury, *Commentary on the Preface of Luke*, Appendix C to *The Beginnings of Christianity*, ed. Foakes Jackson and Kirsopp Lake, vol. I, ii, *The Acts of the Apostles*, (London, 1922), pp. 489-510.

[5] See especially: "The Purpose expressed in Luke's Preface", *The Expositor* (June 1921), pp. 431-41; "The Knowledge claimed in Luke's Preface", *The Expositor* (Dec. 1922), pp. 401-420; "'We' and 'I' passages in Luke-Acts", *NTS* 3 (1956/7), pp. 128ff.

[6] Cf. e.g. E. Haenchen, *Die Apostelgeschichte* (Göttingen, 1965) on Acts 1:1, and similarly other standard commentaries. Cadbury provides the unexpressed foundation for such works as C. K. Barrett, *Luke the Historian in Recent Study* (London, 1961), and E. Plümacher, *Lukas als hellenistischer Schriftsteller* (Göttingen, 1972), and for the inclusion of Luke's work in A. J. Toynbee, *Greek Historical Thought* (London, 1924).

[7] E.g. G. Klein, "Lukas 1:1-4 als theologisches Programm", in *Zeit und Geschichte*, Bultmann Dankesgabe zum 80. Geburtstag (Tübingen, 1964), pp. 193-216. Against Klein, cf. H. Flender, *St. Luke: Theologian of Redemptive History*, tr. R. H. Fuller (London, 1967), p. 65 n. 3.

[8] This is not the place for a full bibliography, but note especially W. C. van Unnik, "Opmerkingen over het doel van Lucas' geschiedwerk (Luc. 1:4)", *Ned. Theol. Tijdschrift* 9 (1954-5), pp. 323-33; idem, "Once more St. Luke's Prologue", *Neotestamentica* 7 (1963), pp. 7-26; and Vernon Robbins, "Prefaces in Greco-Roman Biography and Luke-Acts", *SBL Seminar Papers* vol. II, ed. P. J. Achtemeier (Missoula: Scholars Press, 1978), pp. 193-207. Conzelmann, *Die Mitte der Zeit*[3] (Tübingen, 1960), p. 7 n. 1 argues that prefaces belong properly to epideictic literature, not historical, and thus mark a development from history to "monographs"; but he makes no real attempt to examine the uses and forms of prefaces in Greek historiography. See also now J. A. Fitzmyer, *The Gospel According to Luke I-XI* (Anchor Bible: Doubleday, N.Y., 1981), pp. 287-302.

There have always been difficulties, however, in this "received opinion". For the social historian of the early church there is a degree of implausibility in any view that would see Luke either as setting out consciously to write "Greek history" or as presenting an "Apology" for the new movement to Roman authority: either would seem to imply a high level of rhetorical culture for which there is little evidence even in Luke's own work, let alone in the rest of the New Testament.[9] And in literary terms Luke's preface, while it may look 'rhetorical' as against, say, the opening verses of Mark or Matthew, is not actually very successful rhetoric. It is obscure and ambiguous, overburdened with heavy compounds imprecisely used; the difficulty of interpreting it should in itself warn us against placing it on too high a level of literary competence.[10] Formally, too, there are many differences between Luke's preface and those of the Greek historians, differences perhaps ignored because they are so obvious. Thus Luke's preface is one sentence long where Thucydides' consists of 23 chapters, each at least four times the length of Luke 1:1-4; Luke does not contain any of the general moral reflections which are a mark of the Hellenistic historians; the Greek historians by convention speak of themselves in the third person rather than the first; and they never open with a second-person address.[11]

For all this there was nothing fundamentally wrong with the line of argument followed by Corssen and his successors. As Corssen

---

[9] For a perceptive analysis of the social problems, see Tessa Rajak, *Josephus* (London, 1983), p. 196 and n. 25: "It is unlikely that [Josephus'] origins permitted him to penetrate as an equal into any favoured literary coterie." Luke's preface has long been regarded as the literary high point of the New Testament: cf. besides the standard commentaries, Blass-Debrunner-Funk, *A Greek Grammar of the New Testament* (Cambridge, 1961) sect. 464; E. Norden, *Agnostos Theos* (Leipzig and Berlin, 1913), p. 316 n. 1: "diese Periode, die allgemein als die beststilisierte des ganzen NTs gilt...". The implication is that the rest of the NT fails to measure up to this standard—even Luke cannot keep it up for more than four verses! On the dangers of overestimating Luke's literary prowess, see A. Wifstrand, *L'Église ancienne et la culture grecque* (Paris, 1962), pp. 44ff; F. Blass, *Die Rhythmen der asianischen und römischen Kunstprosa* (Leipzig, 1905), p. 42.

[10] Cf. van Unnik, "Once More", p. 9: "Had he spared himself the trouble of writing such a master-sentence, he would have saved his later readers a nightmare of exegetical puzzles". E. Haenchen, *Der Weg Jesu* (Berlin, 1966), p. 1f: "Hätte [Lukas] den ersten Vers einfacher schreiben wollen, dann hätte es etwa geheißen: 'viele haben die Dinge erzählt, die bei uns geschehen sind'".

[11] Fuller discussion of these points may be found in my *Luke-Acts in its contemporary setting*, chap. II (see note 15 below). See also n. 24.

saw, literary analysis (of style, vocabulary and composition of the preface) must lead inevitably to certain conclusions about audience and social setting; and as Norden[12] and Cadbury perceived, this literary analysis must proceed by means of comparison with all the available contemporary literature. The fault lies not in the methodology but in its application: even Cadbury's *Appendix* (which at 21 pages is the longest as well as the most serious treatment of the subject)[13] fails to spread the net wide enough. What is needed is a new, thorough-going appraisal of the literary evidence, which takes in as wide a range of Greek prefaces as is possible, and makes use of the recent advances in the study of Hellenistic style.[14] From such a study new conclusions as to audience and social setting will emerge in due course; but the initial task is one for the literary historian.[15]

I. *The literary affinities of Luke's preface*[16]

Establishing the literary affinities of Luke's preface may be seen as a exercise in mapping. The outer limits of the field can be drawn without much difficulty. We need to look at Greek prose prefaces from the fourth century BC (by which time the classic literary forms were already established) down to the second century AD, the latest possible date for the composition of Luke-Acts. Within that period only extant prefaces will be considered: notices and *testimonia* ("x wrote a book and dedicated it to y") are interesting but only of use

---

[12] E. Norden, *Agnostos Theos* (Leipzig and Berlin, 1913), p. 316 n. 1.

[13] Norden's oft-quoted remarks on the preface (see preceding note) occur in a footnote to his treatment of Acts; Klostermann's discussion takes up only 3 pages of his commentary (*Das Lukasevangelium*: Handbuch zum NT, 2nd ed., Tübingen 1929). It is perhaps significant that Cadbury never actually steps aside from the work of exegesis to consider the methodological problems behind his use of "parallels".

[14] E.g. Jonas Palm, *Über Sprache und Stil des Diodoros von Sizilien* (Diss. Lund, 1955). There are also insights of a more general nature to be gained from an appreciation of the newer disciplines of stylistics and sociolinguistics.

[15] This article is a revised version of a paper read at Tyndale House, Cambridge in July 1983. I profited from the discussion of my views on that occasion, particularly from the comments of Professors F. F. Bruce, E. A. Judge and I. H. Marshall. My arguments presuppose the detailed work of my D.Phil. thesis, *Luke-Acts in its contemporary setting, with special reference to the prefaces* (*Luke 1:1-4 and Acts 1:1*), referred to hereafter as *LACS*. This will be published in revised form as an SNTS Monograph.

[16] "Luke's preface" should be taken to include Acts 1:1 here and wherever appropriate.

to us at a secondary level, since it is essential to our study to examine the actual *formalia* of dedication, the author's *ipsissima verba*.
It is not easy, however, to mark out a narrower area of relevance
within this large field. Faced with a bewildering amount of potential
comparative material, critics have tended to opt for one of three
ways of narrowing down the field. (1) They have found parallels in
a single author and posited him as the direct model for Luke. (2)
They have pointed to parallels in an area with which Luke's literary
links are already well established, e.g. Hellenistic Jewish literature.
(3) They have picked out a likely-looking area on the basis of *content*
(history, biography) and looked there for preface-topics (e.g.
discussion of sources, purpose of the work) similar to those found in
Luke. All three of these approaches are vitiated by a failure to
establish a wider frame of reference against which the significance
of such "parallels" can be assessed. Parallels in content or topic
can mask obvious or crucial differences in form, as I have already
observed in my remarks on the comparative length of Luke's and
Thucydides' prefaces. Parallels with individual authors[17] are mean-
ingless without the wider database which will enable us to say,
"Yes, Luke is like x, but he is *more like* y". This is so even in the
case of Hellenistic Jewish literature, where there is a positive *prima
facie* case for literary influence. None of the surviving prefaces in
that literature is close enough to Luke's to provide a clear model,
and thus we still have to ask whether Luke in his preface may not be
closer to other areas of Greek literature.

This does not mean that the only course left to us is to examine
every single Greek preface in turn within the allotted time span.
Such an examination would be virtually impossible to assimilate,
and would be in any case inherently problematic unless we have
some idea at the outset what we are looking for. We must begin
with a serviceable description of Luke's preface. We need to draw
up a list of its characteristics and to agree on the relative importance
of these characteristics for the purposes of establishing parallelism.
Since a preface is a formal literary convention, formal and syntactical characteristics should take precedence over topics. Style per-
force comes last, not because it is unimportant but because we still

---

[17] Except in the rare cases where the parallels are so overwhelming as to make
the case for direct literary dependence unassailable. There are no such parallels in
the case of Luke's preface.

lack an objective descriptive language for the nuances of Greek style in the sort of texts we will be dealing with. Terms like "literary" and "rhetorical" are not precise enough, and it is difficult to proceed securely beyond them, except by piecemeal comparisons with other authors. However, style provides an essential fourth component once we have located points of contact in form, syntax and content. Following this line of approach we can set out a hierarchical checklist of possible points of comparison, and thence proceed to draw up some kind of diachronic guide to the field under review, on the basis of which we can build up a picture of the generic and other relationships within the field, and so locate Luke's true position in a methodologically sound manner.

Luke's preface: A checklist of characteristics

An objective description of Luke's preface, based on the hierarchy suggested, might look something like this:

a) *Form*:
1. Short (one sentence)
2. First person
3. Second-person address: – name (inserted vocative)
   – pronoun (*soi*)
   – additional clause ("so that you may know")
4. Detachable: no connection with the following narrative
5. Second volume: name repeated in vocative with brief resumé of first volume

b) *Syntactical structure*:
6. Periodic
7. Main clause = author's decision to write
8. Causal clause preceding main verb = reason for writing
9. Adverbial clause dependent on first subordinate clause = nature of material
10. Participial clause dependent on main verb = information about author
11. Final clause after main verb = purpose in writing

c) *Topics*:
12. Other writers (= 8)
13. Nature of material (= 9)
14. Author's qualifications (= 10)
15. Benefit for dedicatee (= 11)

d) *Style*:
16. Traces of rhetorical style - periodic, feel for sonorous diction, impressive vocabulary; but rhetorical effectiveness limited
17. Contrast with following text in style, vocabulary and subject-matter (secular character)
18. Vocabulary cumbersome: multiple compound verbs, many *hapax legomena*, lack of clarity
19. Compression: large number of topics compressed into single sentence.

How may such a preface be summarily characterized? Looked at functionally, it has little to do with the precepts of the rhetorical tradition as stated in the dictum that the aim of a preface is "benevolos, attentos, dociles facere auditores".[18] Luke's preface is simply a short, detachable passage in which the author stands briefly aside from his own narrative to explain who he is, what he is doing, why and for whom. At its simplest, we might describe it as a *label* with an *address*:[19] and this is the kind of preface whose origins we must seek.

The development of explanatory prefaces in Greek literature

The fourth century BC was a period of transition in Greek culture in many respects: one is of particular significance for our quest. Writing, though widespread by the fifth century BC, was still essentially secondary to oral expression: its function was still seen as that of *hypomnēma* or *aide-mémoire*,[20] and the classic literary forms were still those of oral literature—epic and lyric verse, drama, rhetoric. By the fourth century writing had become a primary means of expression in its own right;[21] the classic forms had begun to take on a new life as written set-pieces (as for example with Isocrates' "written speeches"[22]), and new forms were emerging to meet the new situation. It was a transition that aroused theoretical interest among the thinkers of the day. Plato was particularly alert to the change and its potential hazards:

"Once a thing is put in writing, the composition, whatever it may be, drifts all over the place, getting into the hands not only of those who understand it, but equally of those who have no business with it; it does not know how to address the right

---

[18] Cicero, *De Inventione* I xvi, 22; *De Oratore* II 323. See further *LACS* chap. II. 1 n. 15 (p. 273).

[19] "Detachable" in literary terms, that is. These prefaces should not be confused with the projecting tags (σίλλυβοι) on which the titles of books could be inscribed: see F. G. Kenyon, *Books and Readers in Greece and Rome*[2] (Oxford, 1951), p. 62.

[20] Plato, *Phaedrus* 275d.

[21] Kenyon, *Books and Readers*, pp. 20-26, esp. pp. 24-5; P. Friedländer, *Plato: an Introduction*, translates and revised, Bollingen Foundation LIX (New York, 1958), vol. I, chap. V (pp. 109ff).

[22] Friedländer, *Plato* I, pp. 112ff; on "written speeches", pp. 110-111, and see n. 6 p. 357. Cf. C. Eucken, *Isokrates* (Berlin/New York, 1983), chap. III, "Das Problem von Schriftlichkeit und Mündlichkeit", and pp. 272f; R. L. Howland, "The Attack on Isocrates in the *Phaedrus*", Classical Quarterly 31 (1937), pp. 151-9, esp. p. 158.

people and not to address the wrong. And when it has been ill-treated and unfairly abused it always needs its parent to come to its help, being unable to defend or help itself.''[23]

Among the side-effects of the change from oral to written expression, in other words, are an increased need for *explanation* and a feeling that it may be desirable to name a specific *audience*.

There were several possible responses to the need for explanation. The use of a preface for personal explanation was already established as a possibility in the work of the fifth-century historians, but we can perceive here a marked reluctance to break the mould of impersonal narrative inherited from the epic tradition. There is no second-person address, and the classical historian tends to speak of himself in the third person, not the first.[24] Where there is a lapse into first-person explanation, as in Thucydides I 22 or Herodotus I 5, this is in no sense a detachable ''label''. It is often forgotten that Herodotus' first-person remarks on sources and methodology occur not in the preface but as *obiter dicta* attached to specific items of information.[25] Xenophon provides a much better example of an explanatory personal preface in the *De equitandi ra tione*, which begins with a discussion of the author's own experience of horsemanship, a description of his subject and readership, and an explanation of the relationship between his own work and that of his predecessors. This is an isolated literary phenomenon, however; the other *Scripta Minora* favour a more general kind of opening gambit, perhaps owing something to epideictic oratory. Isocrates exhibits a more artless response to the need for explanation in the *Antidosis*, which begins with a brief personal passage external to the normal *exordium* of the speech itself;[26] but this again is an isolated phenomenon.

---

[23] Plato, *Phaedrus* 275 d-e.

[24] On the third person ''sphragis'' see E. Herkommer, *Die Topoi in der Proömien der Römischen Geschichtswerk* (Diss. Tübingen, 1968), pp. 46ff. On the lack of second-person address, *ibid.* p. 48 n. 1: ''... daß im Geschichtswerk im Gegensatz zum Brief kein 'Du' angesprochen wird''; further, p. 25: ''Die Widmung von Geschichtswerken war bei den Griechen nicht üblich ... Auch zum Wesen der römischen Geschichtsschreibung gehört keine Widmung''.

[25] E.g. Herodotus II 29.1, III 115.2, IV 16.11.

[26] Isocrates, *Antidosis* (Or. XV), 1: ''If this discourse which is about to be read had been like the speeches which are produced either for the law-courts or for oratorical display, I should not, I suppose, have prefaced it by any explanation. Since, however, it is novel and different in character, it is necessary to begin by setting forth the reasons why I chose to write a discourse so unlike any other, for if I neglected to make this clear, my speech would, no doubt, impress many as curious and strange''.

Solutions to the problem of defining an audience were equally varied. Plato's own was a characteristically subtle one. The philosophical writings which he intended for the general public were presented as dramatic dialogues, in an attempt to provide an inbuilt dialectic and so simulate the living master-pupil interaction which Plato saw as essential to real philosophy.[27] The *Dialogues* inevitably still required some sort of 'scene-setting', but this was provided by an introductory or framework dialogue so that the dramatic mould of the whole was not broken.[28] Another (and simpler) solution was to adopt a literary form which allowed one to name a specific audience. The fourth century sees the beginning of a long tradition of protreptic and moral discourses and of substantial open "letters" addressed to named, real individuals. Both forms contain a personal address, but in both cases the address, to borrow a phrase of Werner Jaeger's, is "organic to the style as such".[29] Similarly poetic dedication could use the form of a lyric or didactic poem addressed to a named individual, but again in this case the address is integral to the form, not set in a detachable "label".[30]

It is perhaps significant that classical literature shows this reluctance to step outside the bounds of a given literary form to add the simple kind of explanatory label which we find in Luke 1:1-4. Certainly it is outside the normal canon of that literature that we first find evidence of this phenomenon, in the long and multiform tradition of *technical* or *professional prose* ('Fachprosa') which I have called

---

[27] *Friedländer*, Plato I, p. 113.

[28] On prefaces to dialogues, see M. Ruch, *Le Prooemium Philosophique chez Cicéron* (Strasbourg, 1958). Aristotle appears to have adopted an "explanatory" type of preface for his dialogues (Ruch, pp. 41-3, 325ff). Cicero, as Ruch argues, moves back more closely to the dramatic form (approached now with the eye of the historian, p. 332); however, in his addition of dedication Cicero breaks completely with dramatic convention (pp. 330ff).

[29] W. W. Jaeger, *Aristotle: Fundamentals of the History of his Development*, revised and tr. (Oxford, 1948), p. 56.

[30] Many of the classic poetic forms involve a personal address—e.g. didactic verse, lyric verse; but to call such poems "dedicated" would be to devalue the word to the point of emptiness. It seems reasonable to restrict "dedication" to describing what a poet might do with a *book* as such (Catullus provides a good example), and to exclude an address integral to a particular form. On this criterion Dionysius Chalcus (see O.C.D.[2] *art.* "Dedications") fails to qualify as the first "dedication"; Athenaeus, *Deipnos.* XV 669 d-e speaks of sending round a poem as a "toast" (in a sympotic contest), not of a book. Cf. T. Janson, *Latin Prose Prefaces*, Acta Univ. Stockholm, Studia Latina Stockh. 13 (1964), p. 18 n. 14.

"the scientific tradition".[31] It covers all subjects: medicine, philosophy, mathematics, engineering, rhetoric, right down to the magical sciences of the second century AD with treatises on astrology and the interpretation of dreams. Not unexpectedly, this is exactly where Plato had seen the problem arising in its most acute form. The Platonic dialogue was one solution, but Plato's example did not affect the vast output of technical literature in all these subjects which was *not* intended as "Literature", *not* initially for public consumption: in Aristotelian terms, the "esoteric" as opposed to the "exoteric" works. It is here that the preface as "label", with or without address, comes into its own.

Greek "scientific" prefaces

The earliest examples of this scholastic literature (up to the end of the fourth century BC) have no explanatory prefaces: they were not designed for circulation outside the school which produced them, and their *Sitz im Leben* is defined externally—i.e. the people who used them knew what they were. With the growth in complexity of the world of books in the third century we find more explanatory elements coming in: where the Aristotelian treatise typically begins with a bald general statement introducing the subject of the book, Theophrastus tends to spend an extra sentence defining the position of the subject within the total *corpus*.[32] Many scientific texts continue to be written in this way, either with no prefatory material, or with a purely bibliographical introductory sentence, right up to the fourth century AD.[33]

However the tradition also contains a group of texts which do have the kind of "label + address" preface we are looking for, that is, they have brief personal prefaces in which the author speaks of

---

[31] The term "scientific" is not ideal. I use it here not in its modern sense to exclude "Arts" subjects, but in a sense closer to the German "wissenschaftlich". "Academic", "technical", "specialist" and "professional" would all be appropriate in certain respects, but no one English word covers all the ground. It is important not to determine in advance whether these texts belong to the area we might call "trade" or "professional" manuals or to the more "academic" sphere: each case must be decided individually.

[32] E.g. *Hist. Plant.* III. 1 *init.* (Wimmer p. 32); *De Causis Plant.* I. 1 *init.* (Wimmer p. 165), II. 1 *init.* (Wimmer p. 192).

[33] E.g. Asclepiodotus, *Tactica*; Dionysius Thrax, *Ars Grammatica*; Cleonides, *Introductio Harmonica*; Demetrius, *De Elocutione*; Hephaestion, *Encheiridion*; Albinus, *Introductio* and *Epitome*.

himself in the first person and (frequently) addresses a second person by name. These prefaces are by no means uniform, but they do reveal a discernible pattern.[34] The critical factor in their development is the emergence of the second-person address, which here is *not* integral to the form of the treatise as such: the scientific tradition did not adopt the didactic convention of addressing a pupil directly, and the personal address never penetrates the treatise itself to any great extent.[35] Behind it lie two initially separate sets of circumstances, both characteristic of the Hellenistic age: the fact of patronage (generally royal), which produced dedication proper; and the fact of geographical distance between cultural centres, which produced written correspondence. I say "initially separate" because in the earlier texts there is a clear distinction between the two. Dedication to a patron uses the rhetorical form of address (vocative inserted after the first few words);[36] correspondence with a peer, a friend or colleague, uses letter-form.[37] Archimedes provides clear examples of both: on the one hand, the letters (and they are genuine letters) addressed to fellow-mathematicians in Alexandria to whom he was literally 'sending' his work; and on the other, the *Psammites* (*Arenarius*), dedicated in rhetorical fashion to the young prince Gelon of Syracuse.[38] However, the two forms merge remarkably quickly. The second-century BC astronomer Hipparchus vacillates between rhetorical and epistolary address to his

---

[34] For full analysis see *LACS*. The authors discussed in that study are: Diocles of Carystus (*Letter to Antigonus*); Archimedes; Apollonius of Perge; Hypsicles, *On the Dodecahedron and Eicosahedron* (= Euclid Bk. XIV); Hipparchus, *Commentary on the 'Phaenomena' of Aratus and Eudoxus*; Bito, *Kataskeuai*; Philo of Byzantium, *Belopoeica* and *Pneumatica*; Vitruvius; Hero of Alexandria; "Demetrius", *Typoi Epistolikoi*; Ps-Scymnus; Dionysius Calliphontis filius; Apollonius of Citium; Dioscorides; Erotian; Galen; Hermogenes of Tarsus; Ps. Thessalus; Artemidorus Daldianus; Vettius Valens; and Serenus.

[35] The extent to which the texts are affected by the personal address varies; sometimes the "you" is repeated spasmodically throughout, sometimes it never reappears after the preface.

[36] E.g. Bito, *Kataskeuai*, Preface 1 (E. W. Marsden, *Greek and Roman Artillery*, II (1971), p. 66.1 = Wescher p. 43); Apollonius of Citium, *In Hippocratis De Articulis Commentarius*, ed. F. Kudlien, *C.M.G.* XI 1.1 (1965), Prefaces to Bks I, II, III. Our earliest text, Diocles of Carystus' *Letter to Antigonus* (ed. W. Jaeger, *Diokles von Karystos* [1938] pp. 75ff) is in fact an exception to this rule.

[37] E.g. Apollonius of Perge, *Conica* (ed. Heiberg, Teubner 1891-3), Bks I, II, IV. There is no reason to suppose that this Attalus belonged to the royal house of that name.

[38] Archimedes, *Opera Omnia*, ed. Heiberg (Teubner 1910-15, repr. 1972). Letters: vol. I, pp. 2, 168, 246; vol. II, pp. 2, 262. *Psammites*: vol. II, pp. 216, 258.

"Aischrion", who could be equally friend or patron;[39] and at the same period one of the most "rhetorical" of all our prefaces is addressed by the mathematician Hypsicles to an equally unknown "Protarchus", not as we might expect to a monarch.[40]

Both forms of address can be seen to function also as explanatory prefaces from an early date. The letters of Archimedes, though clearly real letters, contain invaluable and detailed bibliographical and methodological information; it is presumably this doubling with the Theophrastean type of explanation which accounts for their preservation. By the first century AD we are finding short explanatory prefaces *without* address which yet follow exactly the formulaic pattern of addressed prefaces—as for example in Hero (1st or 2nd century A.D.) and Galen (end 2nd century A.D.), where the closing personal clause "so that you may learn" becomes a generalized "so that whoever wishes to may learn".[41]

Luke's preface in the context of Greek preface-writing

We have now in principle isolated a group of explanatory prefaces in scientific texts as meriting particular attention. The next step must be to institute a detailed comparison with Luke's preface. I have carried out such a comparison elsewhere[42] and need not repeat the exercise here. For the present argument it will be enough to point out the most striking similarities in terms of the checklist given above.

As to *form*: I have already indicated that these prefaces combine first-person explanation with second-person address in the detachable 'label + address' manner of Luke 1:1-4; the *formalia* Luke uses for introducing the second person and for the resumption in Acts 1:1 are well paralleled in the scientific prefaces. In *length* scientific prefaces vary: one of Archimedes' letters runs to eight pages, but there are many prefaces on the same scale as Luke's. In general there is a tendency for scientific prefaces to become shorter

---

[39] Hipparchus, *Comm. in Arati et Eudoxi Phaenomena*, ed. C. Manitius (Teubner, 1894), pp. 2, 120, 216.

[40] Hypsicles = (Euclid), *Elements* XIV, ed. Heiberg vol. V (Teubner, 1894), p. 2.

[41] Hero of Alexandria, *Pneumatica* I Pref. 7-9, (ed. Schmidt, vol. I (Teubner, 1899), p. 2, 7-9); Galen, *De typis*, Pref. = Kühn VII, p. 463 3ff.

[42] See *LACS* chaps II.3 and III.2.

and more compressed, while historical prefaces in the same period are getting longer. Scientific writers show a marked preference for a *periodic style* in their prefaces, contrasting with the normally paratactic style of the main text, and the *vocabulary* of their prefaces is very similar to Luke's; they share a fondness (among other things) for compound variations on the words for writing and composing. There is a contrast here with the prefaces found in Hellenistic Jewish literature, which display some similar formal characteristics but a more flowery, 'Alexandrian' vocabulary.

It is in fact possible to go through Luke's preface word by word and find parallels in the scientific tradition for virtually every feature (and I have argued that the few features which cannot be so paralleled are Lucan or Christian idiosyncrasies rather than links with any other Greek literary tradition). But the most striking parallels are surely those to be found in the *syntactical structure* which appears in these prefaces with surprising constancy, and in the arrangement of topics within that structure. It is the constancy of this pattern that encourages me to speak of "the scientific tradition" as a unity, despite the vast range of subjects covered by the different writers. I have chosen some of the clearest examples to set out in an appendix below, as the quickest way of demonstrating this point.

All these factors point to a conclusion that of all the Greek prefaces available for comparison, Luke's is closest to those of the scientific tradition; and that there is no single point in Luke 1:1-4 or Acts 1:1 where it is necessary to invoke any other Greek literary tradition. It remains to consider what this conclusion enables us to say about Luke-Acts as a whole and its author's place in the literary and social world of his time.

II. *Luke's preface and the literary and social setting of Luke-Acts*

What does it mean to say that Luke 1:1-4 is a "scientific preface"? Potentially this conclusion is one of great significance. If we can firmly say that Luke's work "belongs" to this category of "scientific literature" or "technical prose", then we have an immediate link in to a large and neglected area of "middlebrow" literature of the first century AD. The importance of this *Fachprosa* for New Testament linguistics has already been underlined by the work of Albert Wifstrand and more especially by his pupil Lars Rydbeck, whose study *Fachprosa, vermeintliche Volkssprache und Neues*

Testament appeared in 1967.[43] Rydbeck shows that the New Testament writers use a language identical neither with the vernacular *Koine* of the papyri (probably as near as we can get to the spoken *Koine* of the streets and market-places of the Eastern Empire), nor with the classicizing prose of the *literati*. It is a "Zwischenprosa", literate but not literary,[44] a *written* language designed primarily for conveying factual information; and it is chiefly preserved in the technical treatises of the scientific writers. As Abraham Malherbe has noted,[45] "almost half of Rydbeck's references (in the NT) are to Luke and Acts"; but Rydbeck does not discuss the preface itself, and he insists (p. 16) that his study is concerned with "linguistic-grammatical facts" and not with a "technical prose *style* as such". My analysis of the Lucan preface (which was completed in all essentials without a knowledge of Rydbeck's work) therefore provides a separate and independent link with this body of literature.

I would thus present my work as a contribution to the long-overdue task of "broadening our definition of literature",[46] that is, of widening the canon of contemporary literature with which the New Testament writings can properly be compared. It scarcely needs demonstrating that such a widening of the canon will shed light not only on literary and linguistic issues, but on the whole question of the social context of the New Testament as well. For the sociolinguist, "any use of language displays certain linguistic features which allow it to be identified with one or more extra-linguistic contexts".[47] In the case of the New Testament writings, this kind of evidence has a peculiar importance, for despite our best endeavours it remains true that there is a depressing lack of external evidence for the social history of the Church in the first century of its existence, and that the primary data for investigation must be the New Testament writings themselves. That is to say, these writings must be viewed not only as sources for nuggets of "social" information for the New Testament historian, but also as objects of

---

[43] Lars Rydbeck, *Fachprosa, vermeintliche Volkssprache und Neues Testament*, Acta Univ. Upsal. (Studia Graeca Upsal. 5), 1967.

[44] Cf. F. C. Grant, "not illiterate, but certainly nonliterary": *The Gospels: their origin and their growth* (New York, 1957), p. 28.

[45] A. J. Malherbe, *Social Aspects of Early Christianity* (Louisiana University Press, 1977), p. 41, n. 28.

[46] Malherbe, *Social Aspects*, p. 19.

[47] D. Crystal and D. Davy, *Investigating English Style* (London: Longman's Paperback, 1969), p. 11.

socio-historical investigation in their own right. We need to ask them concrete questions: What are the social dynamics implied in the relationship between the author and his readership? What are the social functions of the writings inside their own communities? How do these writings interact with the world at large? What kinds of people produced writings like these, and for whom?

The importance of this point has been rightly stressed by Malherbe,[48] but otherwise it has received comparatively little attention in the recent spate of work on the social history of the early Church.[49] The New Testament writings have been quarried for items of information for the social historian, with a remarkable degree of success; but they have not on the whole been studied as objects of social history themselves. It now seems clear that a significant element in many first-century congregations was composed of craftsmen or tradesmen, artisans, businessmen or businesswomen on a small or moderate scale. Lists of such crafts and trades figure both in Tertullian and in Celsus,[50] and on the evidence of the Epistles and Acts (such as it is) these kinds of people played a significant part, at least in the Pauline churches.[51] However the evidence as to the balance of social forces in the early churches may be added up,[52] there is surprising unanimity among scholars as to the major component in their composition, right from C. H. Roberts in 1954 ("the circle in which Mark moved in Rome— Jewish-Gentile traders, small businessmen, freedmen, or slaves..."), through Kreissig in 1967 ("den städtischen Kreisen wohlsituierter Handwerker, Händler und Angehörigen freier Berufe..."), and on up to Wayne Meeks in 1982 ("the 'typical' Christian... is a free artisan or small trader...").[53] The question

[48] Malherbe, *Social Aspects*, pp. 16-17.

[49] See the survey articles by Robin Scroggs (*NTS* 26 [1980], pp. 164-179) and J. Z. Smith (*Religious Studies Review* 1 [1975], pp. 19-25), and John Schütz's *Introduction* to the English translation of Gerd Theissen, *The Social Setting of Pauline Christianity* (Fortress Press/T. and T. Clark, 1982). Bibliography in Wayne A. Meeks, *The First Urban Christians* (Yale, 1983).

[50] Origen, *C. Cels.* III 55; Tertullian, *De Idol.* VIII 2-4. See for further references Wayne Meeks, *First Urban Christians*, chap. 2 notes 1-4 (p. 214); and cf. le Père Hamman, *La Vie Quotidienne des premiers Chrétiens* (Paris, 1971), pp. 54ff.

[51] E.g. Acts 16:4ff, 18:3; II Tim. 4:14; Col. 4:14.

[52] See Wayne Meeks, "The Social Context of Pauline Theology", *Interpretation* 36 (1982), pp. 267ff.

[53] C. H. Roberts, "The Codex", *Proceedings of the British Academy*, 1954, p. 187; H. Kreissig, "Zur sozialen Zusammensetzung der frühchristlichen Gemeinden im

that has not been asked (or not seriously pursued) is: How does this picture relate to our *literary* remains? What kinds and degrees of literacy would we expect to find among these classes? What sort of education did they receive? Did they produce—or even read—any literature of their own? If so, what was it like? Were their tastes the same as those of the dominant intellectual élite, or were they able to pursue their own interests and set their own standards?[54]

It is precisely here that I believe the New Testament critic has much to gain from taking a closer look at the "scientific tradition" of technical prose. This will of course be a long-term project; the study of *Fachprosa* has been neglected even on the classical side,[55] and in particular we still lack a thorough investigation of the social context of the scientific writers. In this essentially programmatic essay I can do little more than raise the questions, and try to tackle a preliminary problem which must strike any student of Luke-Acts presented with my rather paradoxical conclusions. I have argued that Luke's preface is evidence of a positive connection with the scientific tradition. But in what sense can Luke's two-volume *narrative* be described as "a scientific treatise"? I shall explore this problem with the aid of three models: (1) Luke as an imitator of scientific prefaces; (2) Luke as a reader of scientific texts; (3) Luke as a writer within the scientific tradition. What I am interested to discover through this series of models is just how far we can take the observation that Luke's preface is most like the prefaces of the scientific tradition.

Luke as an imitator of scientific prefaces

The simplest kind of literary dependence is that of copying a single model. This was put forward as an explanation of Luke's

---

ersten Jahrhundert u.s.w.", *Eirene* 6 (1967), p. 99; Meeks, "Social Context" (*Interpretation* 36 [1982]), p. 270. Meeks' conclusions are developed more fully in his *First Urban Christians*, chap. 2.

[54] The question of literary style in relation to social class is raised (in Deissmann's terms) but not pursued by Meeks, *First Urban Christians*, p. 52. Meeks does elsewhere mention briefly that Paul occasionally uses commercial language. John Schütz has recognized the urgent need for refinement of Deissmann's categories: see G. Theissen, *The Social Setting of Pauline Christianity*, Introduction p. 4.

[55] Cf. M. Fuhrmann in *Gnomon* 38 (1966), p. 467: "Die Untersuchung berücksichtigt sämtliche Gattungen der Prosaliteratur; inbesondere schenkt sie den sonst von der Forschung nicht selten vernachlässigten fachwissenschaftlichen Schriften hinlänglich Beachtung".

preface as long ago as 1874, in Lagarde's suggestion that Luke
1:1-4 is a rather incompetent imitation of the preface of
Dioscorides' *De Materia Medica*.[56] But my observations do not confirm this. I have located not stray resemblances to one preface or
another, but rather a *nexus* of parallels which add up to a family
resemblance. There are too many affinities with too wide a variety
of scientific prefaces to make the hypothesis of a single model (even
a lost one) convincing; and, after all, Luke's preface does make
sense in its own way. I would not see him, then, as an imitator; he
is composing freely, but in a certain style and within a certain pattern which is distributed widely throughout the scientific tradition.
The whole tradition may therefore be treated as a *matrix* in which to
pursue the investigation of Luke and his work.

More subtle, but equally unsatisfactory, is the suggestion that
Luke might deliberately have chosen ''a scientific preface-style'' as
some kind of signal to his readers about the kind of book his Gospel
was going to be. On the face of it the idea is not entirely ridiculous.
The scientific writers aimed at a sober, non-rhetorical presentation
of fact, unembellished by literary allusion or rhetorical decoration
(see further below). Such a style would be no more intrinsically inappropriate for Luke's Gospel than it is, say, for Vettius Valens'
horoscopes or Thessalus' astrological herbal, given the high level of
commitment of each author to his material.

What is inappropriate here is not the idea of presenting the
Gospel in ''scientific style'' as such; it is the whole notion of the
conscious adoption of this style that rings false. It is as if we were
imagining Luke running his eye along his (anachronistic) bookshelf
and picking out one style from among the many displayed—a procedure which would imply a very high level of literary self-
consciousness.[57] The linguists and sociolinguists have taught us (or
taught us to put into words what we had intuitively known all
along) that the choice of style can operate at a much deeper level of
a writer's consciousness. ''The type of language we are using,'' in
the words of Crystal and Davy's classic *Investigating English Style*,
''changes fairly instinctively with the situation''.[58] Or compare this
observation on present-day scientific language:

---

[56] P. de Lagarde, *Psalterium Hieronymi* (1874), p. 165.

[57] Cf. Morton Smith in *JBL* 90 (1971), p. 196: ''Nobody thinks of any
evangelist as a literary man sitting down to produce a composition of a recognized
form, in the way one might sit down to write a double ballade ...''.

[58] Crystal and Davy, *Investigating English Style*, p. 4.

"Whether or not a scientist has anything of importance to say about his subject, his way of saying it is to a very great extent laid down—sometimes in style-books, sometimes in his unconscious awareness of 'how scientific writers write'. A scientific journal will not accept an article unless it is written in what the editorial board believes an appropriate style; and this in the end comes down to following a large number of specific rules about grammar, vocabulary and general lay-out."[59]

It is along these lines—of the "unconscious", the "fairly instinctive"—that I suggest we approach the question of Luke's choice of style.

Luke as a reader of scientific texts

The "instinctive" or "automatic" choce I have suggested can, of course, still be made out of a wide range of options. An accomplished rhetor like Hermogenes would choose the "plain" style as suited to his teaching manuals, rather than the decorated style of full-blown rhetorical composition which he could command when he wished. Similarly, we might argue, perhaps Luke could have written in a more lofty style had he so desired; certainly it is not possible to prove otherwise. Nevertheless, it seems more economical to work 'from the ground up'. We know that Luke could command a *biblical* Greek style which is outside the range of Greek literary taste; but we have no evidence to suggest that he could command any more elevated *literary* Greek than he displays in the preface. Like so many of the non-rhetorical scientific writers, he seems to be constrained by inadequate control of literary resource, rather than by any need for deliberate obscurity or literary ambiguity. It seems most natural to suppose that the preface represents the upper limits of Luke's literary style, not a deliberate adoption of the "lowbrow".

Working from this 'minimal', economical view, I would suggest that Luke's choice of style should be seen in the first instance not as "scientific" but as *formal*. Faced with the daunting task of composing a formal opening to mark the presentation of his book to Theophilus, he draws on the only style he knows which is at all appropriate to the occasion. If we suppose that his experience of non-biblical literature (apart from the remote and impractical classics of

---

[59] D. Crystal, *Linguistics* (Penguin, 1971), p. 29. Cf. Morton Smith, *JBL* 90 (1971), p. 196: "... *automatically* cast in similar form ..." (my italics).

[60] Crystal and Davy, *Investigating English Style*, p. 5.

schooldays) was limited to the technical writings of a trade or profession, this preface-style would seem to him simply the "correct" style to use for a formal opening paragraph, the appropriate "linguistic manners" for the occasion.[60] Beginning a book is notoriously the most difficult point in its composition, especially for the inexperienced author; what more natural than to fall instinctively into the style used for such openings in the books he knows best?

The establishment of this point—that Luke is to be seen at the very least as a *reader* of some kind of technical manuals—is sufficient of itself to provide a secure jumping-off point for a better understanding of the man and his world. We need not trouble ourselves with the vexed and probably insoluble question of whether the author of Luke-Acts was or was not the physician of Col. 4:14. The mere fact of the preface immediately provides us with a firm link into the world of the crafts and professions of the Greek East *in general*, and makes all the more urgent a thorough investigation of the social dynamics of that world. Moreover, if the perception of the preface as the appropriate linguistic manners for the opening of Luke-Acts tells us something about the author, then presumably it will also tell us something about his readership—at least about his primary and named reader, Theophilus. It seems reasonable to look for an analogue for Luke's dedication among the patterns of dedication found in the scientific writers, most probably in the pattern which takes over in the Imperial period, and which is seen most clearly in Galen.[61] We must proceed with caution here. Little is known about the social standing of the scientific writers and their patrons and readers, not enough about the social realities of scientific dedication; reconstruction must be based on a careful and exhaustive reading of the texts. Nevertheless the literary link provided by Luke's preface warrants a thorough exploration of this area of ancient life as a background to Luke the author and his relationship with Theophilus.

Luke as a writer within the scientific tradition

It is one thing to establish that Luke has read some scientific literature and adopts the device of the preface as a suitable formal

---

[61] See further, *LACS* pp. 152ff.

opening for his own work. It is quite another to see him functioning as a writer, operating according to recognised procedures within a living tradition. Can we take this further step? Can the influence of scientific writing be traced any further on in Luke-Acts itself, or does it cease with the abrupt change of style at Luke 1:5?

That change of style may itself be regarded as a characteristic feature of scientific writing. At the end of the preface, the normal style of exposition is resumed—mathematical theorems, systematic divisions of the subject, or whatever—usually without apology. It is an aspect of the writers' habitual attitude to "literary style", an attitude of indifference, sometimes of active hostility to the canons of rhetorical composition. The same indifference is evidenced in the lack of literary allusion in these texts—again sometimes quite clearly deliberate, as when Apollonius of Citium *omits* a Homeric allusion which was in the Hippocratic text he was commenting on.[62] Both these negative aspects of scientific style can be paralleled in Luke-Acts. It has long been a puzzle how this apparently most 'literary' author of the New Testament could tolerate that stylistic break at 1:5, or why he seems unaffected by the habit of classical allusion which pervades most classical Greek literature.[63] For a scientific writer, both would be normal.

Yet such negative similarities are hardly sufficient to qualify Luke as a member of the class of "scientific writers". How can Luke's two-volume narrative, based on traditional material rather than on "eyewitness" research or the systematic sifting of new evidence, be compared with the treatises of Vitruvius or Hermogenes? What possible congruity can there be between Hero's *Mechanics* or Galen's *Anatomical Procedures* and Luke's story of the sayings and doings of a Galilean holy man and his followers? This is the nub of the problem with which the alignment of Luke's preface leaves us. As stated, it contains two issues: content and method. Both, I believe, can be resolved by a careful analysis of the actual practice of the scientific authors and of the functions of their writings.

---

[62] See further, *LACS* p. 140 and n. 30.

[63] G. Glockmann, *Homer in der frühchristlichen Literatur bis Justinus* (TU 105, 1968), pp. 17ff, 59ff. Glockmann finds it inconceivable that Luke should be completely ignorant of Homer (p. 65). See also N. Zeegers-Vanderhorst, *Les citations des Poètes Grecs chez les apologistes Chrétiens du IIe siècle* (Louvain, 1972), pp. 134-5; Malherbe, *Social Aspects*, pp. 41-5.

The problem of biographical content may be tackled in one of two ways. The first is to look at the uses of biography within the school traditions. Here most of the evidence comes from the philosophical schools. C. H. Talbert has made a number of important suggestions on this subject.[64] He sees Luke-Acts as falling into a pattern found in Diogenes Laertius, viz. *Life* of the founder of a school plus *Succession* or record of the transmission of authentic doctrine *via* the master's disciples. Talbert's picture is in need of refinement,[65] but he does present a useful collection of material demonstrating the interest of the philosophical schools both in biography and in the issue of "succession".

Evidence for biographical interest in the founders of other schools is less forthcoming. None of the surviving *Lives* of Hippocrates is early enough for our purpose, but these later *Lives* are based on earlier works with titles like *On the Medical Tradition* and *On the Sect of Hippocrates*.[66] Exactly how much biographical narrative these texts contained, and whether they would have looked at all like Luke-Acts, is unclear, but in principle they should provide a parallel worth pursuing. Other great figures of Greek science were remembered rather through biographical anecdote than through biography as such—as for example in the story about Archimedes told by Plutarch, *Marcellus* xivf. Here there is not the same ideological interest in the lifestyle of a founder as there is in the philosophical schools, but there were other reasons for preserving biographical details—bibliographical, chronographical, exemplary —as may be seen, for example, in the scattered notices (never part of a full 'biography') which make up the sum of our biographical in-

[64] C. H. Talbert, *Literary Patterns, Theological Themes and the Genre of Luke-Acts*, SBL Monographs 20 (Scholars Press, Missoula, Montana, 1974), chap. VIII; idem, *What is a Gospel?* (Fortress Press, 1977); idem, "Biographies of Philosophers and Rulers as Instruments of Religious Propaganda in Mediterranean Antiquity", *ANRW* II 16.2 (1978), pp 1619-1651.

[65] It is not clear how many (if any) full-scale biographies of philosophers were actually composed in this pattern from *within* the schools and before the second century AD. Ingemar Düring, for example, does not believe that Andronicus' edition of Aristotle contained a biography as such, merely a 'catalogue raisonnée' in which biographical information was ancillary to bibliographical interest: see I. Düring, *Aristotle in the Ancient Biographical Tradition*, Acta Universitatis Gothoburgensis/ Göteborgs Universitets Årsskrift LXIII (1957)/2, pp. 467, 413-425.

[66] See RE VIII.2 s.v. *Hippokrates* no. 16 (1802-3), and RE Suppl. VI, 1292-1305, in which Edelstein argues that the roots of the later "Lives" lie in a "Hippocratic legend" of Coan origin, in which Hippocrates is both "der ideale Mensch" and "Stadtheros", and which first arises in the second century BC.

formation on the mathematician Hippocrates of Chios.[67] There is then some evidence that biographical information played a definite role in the traditions of the schools, chiefly but not exclusively the philosophical schools. Whether there is sufficient evidence at the right date to provide a possible model for Luke-Acts, and whether this kind of biographical activity (which is for the most part ancillary to a pre-existent and independent body of oral or written teaching) provides a proper parallel to the role of Gospel traditions in the life of the early Church, must remain matters for more detailed investigation.

The alternative and, I believe, preferable approach to the problem of the biographical character of Luke's Gospel is to look to the scientific tradition in the first instance for parallels not in content but in function. The texts I have studied differ widely as to content, and insofar as form is determined by content there is no uniformity once we leave the prefaces behind. What they do have in common is (in large degree) a similarity of function. They derive more or less directly from a school context: they are "school texts", that is, not elementary, watered-down textbooks in the modern sense, but the written deposit of the *techne*, the distillation of the teaching of a school or a craft tradition as it was passed down from one generation to another.[68] Forms of presentation vary, some traditions preserving a style closer to that of the oral lecture, others reduced to different degrees of written systematisation;[69] but the variety of content is simply a reflection of the variety of teaching traditions embodied in the texts. On this analogy, Luke's biographical presentation of his material would equally be a reflection of the shape of the tradition he received: the Jesus tradition was already in biographical form—i.e. it was already shaped and focussed around the words and deeds of a single person—and that is how Luke records it.[70]

---

[67] RE VIII.2 s.v. *Hippokrates* no. 14 (1780-1801).

[68] This is, of course, a generalization of a complex situation. For fuller discussion see *LACS* pp. 39ff, 146.

[69] Oral: e.g. Aristoxenus of Tarentum, *El. Harm.*, III 59.6; P. Steinmetz, *Die Physik des Theophrastus*, Palingenesia I (1964), pp. 14ff. Systematic: see M. Fuhrmann, *Das systematische Lehrbuch: ein Beitrag zur Geschichte der Wissenschaften in der Antike* (Göttingen, 1960).

[70] "Already" — I mean not only in Luke's written predecessors (whatever they were) but in the living community tradition on which Luke ultimately depends. The relationship between the Gospel traditions and the preaching of the early Church is a matter of controversy: cf. Schuler, *A Genre for the Gospels*, pp. 13ff; H.

In sum, then, I would argue that the biographical content of the Gospel and Acts is by no means an insuperable obstacle to viewing Luke as a writer set firmly within the context of the scientific tradition. And on the positive side, the New Testament critic can only benefit from a more thoroughgoing investigation of that context. The scientific tradition provides the matrix within which we can explore both the social and the literary aspects of Luke's work, both the man himself and the nature of his writings.

I conclude by noting briefly some future lines of research. The following aspects of the scientific tradition (in part related to the social status and social attitudes of scientific writers, and in part to their literary methods) should prove fruitful areas of investigation for the student of Luke-Acts:

a) Many scientific authors probably exhibited the kind of "high status inconsistency" identified by Wayne Meeks as critical in forming the selfunderstanding of early Pauline Christianity.[71] Whatever the social standing of their subject-matter (rhetoric, for example, would rank high), its teachers and practitioners themselves would tend to be slaves or freedmen in great households, Greeks in Roman society, men obliged to support themselves by the exercise of their profession.

b) Greek culture had a deep-rooted scorn for any occupation (other than the traditional aristocratic pursuits of hunting, farming and soldiering) which involved working with the hands—cf. Plutarch, *Vita Periclis* ii and *Vita Marcelli* xivf. This attitude to manual labour was not shared by the scientific writers, who, though not craftsmen themselves, speak of the *technitai* with deep respect.[72] Thus the scientific tradition, here at odds with the dominant literary culture, may provide an alternative background to the New Testament references to manual labour, and especially to the vexed subject of Paul's tentmaking, which Luke mentions in a totally matter-of-fact fashion at Acts 18:1-3.[73]

Koester, "One Jesus and Four Primitive Gospels", *HTR* 2 (1968), pp. 206ff. Here I wish merely to draw attention to the logic of the ancient evidence, if my model of Luke as a "scientific writer" is accepted.

[71] Meeks, "Social Context" (*Interpretation* 36 [1982]), pp. 271ff; idem, *First Urban Christians*, pp. 22-23, 191.

[72] Galen, *De Comp. Med. Sec. Loc.* VI 1 = Kühn XII 894; Philo, *Belopoeica*, Th. 51.9ff.

[73] See Ronald Hock, "Paul's Tentmaking and the Problem of his Social Class", *JBL* 97 (1980), pp. 555-64; idem, *The Social Context of Paul's Ministry: Tentmaking and*

c) Respect for tradition is a prime value in scientific texts, and especially respect for the passing on of tradition by direct personal contact from master to disciple. The theme of 'the author's credentials' is not found in the earlier prefaces, but becomes commoner from the end of the Hellenistic period onwards, perhaps owing to the influence of the historical/geographical tradition. Even so, it is noticeable how many scientific writers tend to stress contact with tradition as a qualification, as well as (sometimes instead of) the personal experience or individual research which would be more typical of a historical writer.[74]

d) This respect for tradition does not exclude—in fact it often goes along with—extensive use of written sources. Especially interesting here are Philo of Byzantium, Vitruvius and Hero, all of whom, despite their professed reliance on "tradition", apparently present different recensions of written material from the school of Ctesibius.[75]

e) Respect for tradition does not exclude reworking of tradition; in fact it is characteristic of these texts (and a source of many headaches for their editors) that their material was constantly reworked and updated—hence the name 'Gebrauchsliteratur'.[76]

f) The ultimate derivation of their material from a school setting does not exclude a fair amount of individual variation, both in the amount of 'presentational' writing-up (especially where a text is dedicated) and in the imprint of the author on his material. In some cases, of course, the author is also the originator of his own teaching material (Galen). But the variation is limited. Even Vitruvius (for example), patronised by an aristocratic literary circle and dedicating his treatise on architecture to the young Octavian, produces what is essentially a systematic treatise of the type perfected in the schools, containing traditional material and using traditional formulae.[77]

Apostleship (Fortress Press: Philadelphia, 1980). Even if we accept Hock's argument that Paul's references to his own manual labour reflect a deliberate polemical stance (an argument which I do not find entirely convincing), the same cannot be true of Acts 18:1-3, which has no obvious polemical function.

[74] See *LACS*, pp. 64-70.
[75] See *LACS*, pp. 144-8.
[76] See *LACS*, pp. 146, 148.
[77] M. Fuhrmann, *Das systematische Lehrbuch*, chap. 7 and chap. 13, sect. 4.

APPENDIX

Syntactical analysis of Luke 1:1-4 and selected Greek scientific prefaces

A. *Luke*   *Date*: I/II A.D.

   Gospel   *Text*: Nestle. Lk. ch. 1 vv. 1-4.

1 Ἐπειδήπερ πολλοὶ ἐπεχείρησαν   Causal clause (*epei*): other writers
   ἀνατάξασθαι διήγησιν
   περὶ τῶν πεπληροφορημένων ἐν
   ἡμῖν πραγμάτων,

2   καθὼς παρέδοσαν ἡμῖν οἱ ἀπ'   Adverbial clause dependent on cl. 1:
       ἀρχῆς αὐτόπται καὶ ὑπηρέται   description of subject-matter.
       γενόμενοι τοῦ λόγου,

3 ἔδοξε κἀμοὶ   Main verb: author's decision.

4   παρηκολουθηκότι ἄνωθεν   Participial clause dependent on ind.
       πᾶσιν ἀκριβῶς   obj. of main vb.: author's qualifica-
                                          tions.

5   καθεξῆς σοι γράψαι, κράτιστε   Object clause: treatment of subject-
       Θεόφιλε,   matter. Address (rhetorical).

6 ἵνα ἐπιγνῷς περὶ ὧν κατηχήθης   Final clause: results for dedicatee.
   λόγων τὴν ἀσφάλειαν.

B. *Diocles of Carystus*   *Date*: end of IV B.C.

   Letter to Antigonus   *Text*: W. Jaeger, *Diokles von Karystos*
                                            (Berlin 1938) pp. 75ff.

1 ΔΙΟΚΛΗΣ 'ΑΝΤΙΓΟΝΩΙ ΒΑΣΙΛΕΙ   Address: epistolary

2 Ἐπειδή σοι συμβαίνει   Causal clause. Disposition of dedicatee
   μουσικωτάτῳ πάντων βασιλέων   (3-fold).
   γεγονέναι
   καὶ πλεῖστον χρόνον βεβιωκέναι
   φιλοσοφίας τε πάσης ἔμπειρον ὄντα
   τυγχάνειν καὶ τοῖς μαθηματι-
   κοῖς πρωταγωνιστήν,

6 ὑπολαμβάνων βασιλικήν τε καὶ   2nd causal clause (participial).
   οἰκείαν [τὴν] φιλοσοφίαν τὴν περὶ   Nature of subject-matter.
   τῶν ὑγιεινῶν ἀκοήν τε καὶ θεωρίαν

4 γέγραφά σοι   Main verb.
                                        Author's decision to write.

5 πόθεν αἱ νόσοι τοῖς ἀνθρώποις   Object of main verb: indirect question.
   συνίστανται   Contents of work.
   καὶ τίνων προγενομένων σημείων,
   καὶ πῶς ἄν τις αὐταῖς βοηθῶν
   ἐπιτυγχάνοι·

6 οὔτε γὰρ χειμὼν <ἂν> ἐν τῷ   Parenthesis: expansion of (5).
  οὐρανῷ συσταίη ποτὲ μὴ οὐχὶ
  σημείων τινῶν προγενομένων,
  οἷσπερ παρακολουθοῦσιν οἱ ναυτικοὶ
  καὶ οἱ πολύπειροι τῶν ἀνθρώπων,
  οὔτε πάθος ἐν ἀνθρώπου φύσει
  συσταίη ποτὲ μὴ οὐχὶ σημείου τινὸς
  προγενομένου.

7 σὺ δὲ πεισθεὶς τοῖς ὑφ' ἡμῶν λεγομένοις   Additional sentence at end: results for
  παρακολουθήσεις τῇ ἀκριβείᾳ τῇ   dedicatee.
  περὶ αὐτῶν.

C. *Demetrius*   *Date*: I BC, but progressively revised.

  Formae Epistolicae   *Text*: ed. V. Weichert, *Demetrii et Libanii*
                            qui feruntur **τύποι ἐπιστολικοὶ** *et*
                            ἐπιστολιμαῖοι χαρακτῆρες
                            (Teubner 1910) pp. 1-2.

1 **Τῶν ἐπιστολικῶν τύπων,** ὦ   Causal clause (genitive absolute).
  Ἡρακλείδη, **ἐχόντων** τὴν θεωρίαν   Nature of the subject-matter.
  τοῦ συνεστάναι μὲν ἀπὸ πλειόνων   Address: rhetorical, inserted after first
  εἰδῶν, ἀναβάλλεσθαι **δὲ** ἐκ τῶν ἀεὶ   few words.
  πρὸς τὸ παρὸν ἁρμοζόντων,
  καὶ καθηκόντων μὲν ὡς τεχνικώ-   Causal cl. contd.: faults of
  τατα γράφεσθαι, γραφομένων δ'   practitioners.
  ὡς ἔτυχεν ὑπὸ τῶν τὰς τοιαύτας τοῖς
  ἐπὶ πραγμάτων ταττομένοις
  ὑπουργίας ἀναδεχομένων,

2 **θεωρῶν** σε φιλοτίμως ἔχοντα πρός   2nd causal clause: part. agreeing with
  φιλομαθείαν   subj. of main vb.
                            Disposition of dedicatee.

3 **ἐπραγματευσάμην**   Main verb:author's decision.

4 **διά τινων συστήσειν ἰδεῶν**   Object of main vb.: indirect question.
  καὶ πόσας καὶ ἃς ἔχουσι διαφοράς,   Contents of work.

5 **καὶ καθάπερ** δεῖγμα τῆς ἑκάστου   2nd main vb · method of composition.
  γένους τάξεως **ὑποδέδειχα**

6   **προσεκθέμενος** μερικῶς τὸν περὶ   Part. agreeing with subj. of main vb ·
  ἑκάστου λόγον,   further details of composition.

7 ἅμα μὲν **ὑπολαμβάνων** καὶ σοὶ   2nd. participial cl. agreeing with subj.
  τοῦτο κεχαρισμένον ὑπάρχειν,   of main vb.
  εἴ τι τῶν ἄλλων περισσότερον   Results for dedicatee.
  εἰδήσεις τὸ λαμπρὸν τοῦ βίου
  τιθέμενος οὐκ ἐν τοῖς βρώμασιν,
  ἀλλ' ἐν ταῖς ἐπιστήμαις,

8 ἅμα δὲ κἀμὲ **νομίζων** τοῦ   3rd part. cl.: results for author.
  προσήκοντος ἐπαίνου μεθέξειν.

Second long sentence of preface contains reflections of a general moral nature.

D. *Hero of Alexandria*

Pneumatica I

Date: I/II A.D.

Text: edd. W. Schmidt et al.,
(Teubner 1899-1914) I p. 2

1	Τῆς πνευματικῆς πραγματείας σπουδῆς ἠξιωμένης πρὸς τῶν παλαιῶν φιλοσόφων τε καὶ μηχανικῶν,	Causal clause (genitive absol.): nature of subject-matter/other writers.
2	τῶν μὲν λογικῶς τὴν δύναμιν αὐτῆς ἀποδεδωκότων, τῶν δὲ καὶ δι' αὐτῆς τῆς τῶν αἰσθητῶν ἐνεργείας,	Participial cl. dependent on cl. 1: methodological classification of other writers.
3	ἀναγκαῖον ὑπάρχειν νομίζομεν καὶ αὐτοὶ	Main vb.: author's decision.
4	τὰ παραδοθέντα ὑπὸ τῶν ἀρχαίων εἰς τάξιν ἀγαγεῖν,	Object-clause: description of subject-matter.
5	καὶ ἃ ἡμεῖς δὲ προσευρήκαμεν εἰσθέσθαι·	2nd object-cl.: descr. contd.
	οὕτως γὰρ τοὺς μετὰ ταῦτα ἐν τοῖς μαθήμασιν ἀναστρέφεσθαι βουλομένους ὠφελεῖσθαι συμβήσεται.	Additional main clause: results for readers.

Second sentence of pref. (same length) gives bibliographical details.

E. *Galen of Pergamon*

De Typis

Date: end II A.D.

Text: ed. C. G. Kühn (Lips. 1821-33) VII 463

1	Πολλῶν πλατυτέρω ὑπὲρ τῆς περὶ τύπων θεωρίας πεπραγματευμένων,	Causal clause (genitive absol.): other writers.
2	ἀναγκαῖον ἡγησάμην αὐτὸς	Main vb.: author's decision.
3	ὁριστικώτερον καὶ κατὰ περιγραφὴν ἐπιδραμεῖν ταῦτα,	Object clause: specifies treatment of subject-matter.
4	οὕτως εὐκαταρίθμητον καὶ εὐκαταμάθητον οἰόμενος τοῖς νεωστὶ προσιοῦσι τῇ τέχνῃ τὸ πρᾶγμα,	Participial cl. dep. on subj. of main vb.: results for readers.
5	ὅν τε ἁπλοῦν καὶ μετὰ τὴν ἁπλουστέραν κατάληψιν εὐκολώτερον, καὶ καθάπερ ἐξ ἑτοίμου τοῖς πολλοῖς ἐντυγχάνον.	2 participial clauses dependent on object of previous clause: nature of subject-matter.
6	ἀρκτέον δ' ἐντεῦθεν.	Transitional formula.

'THE CHRIST MUST SUFFER': NEW LIGHT ON THE JESUS—PETER, STEPHEN, PAUL PARALLELS IN LUKE-ACTS

by

DAVID P. MOESSNER
Decatur, GA

The strikingly similar features of the central characters in Acts and Jesus in the Gospel of Luke have long been the subject of interest.[1] That Peter and especially Paul perform the same type of healings (Luke 5:17-26—Acts 3:1-10; 14:8-18), raise people from the dead (Luke 7:11-17; 8:40-56—Acts 9:36-43; 20:7-12), preach repentance to Jew and Gentile alike (Luke 24:44-48—Acts 10; 17:16-33), and suffer shame and rejection by their own folk (Luke 22:47-23:49—Acts 4:1-22; 21:27-22:29)[2] in imitation and in the "the name"[3] of their Master have raised fundamental questions concerning Luke's primary literary and theological aims in continuing the ὁ πρῶτος λόγος of Jesus' deeds and teaching in the "second word" of the Acts (Acts 1:1). Stephen, too, in the remarkable parallels between his death and Jesus' passion has generated fascination among critical scholars, though his position within the wider ranging Peter-Paul parallels has often escaped attention.[4] In Part I we shall present a brief overview of critical treatment of these parallels and suggest a historical perspective which comprehends Stephen along with Peter and Paul and provides an underlying pattern of coherence from which to focus the many similarities. In Parts II-IV we shall develop this pattern by applying it respectively

---

[1] One of the first critical comparisons of Jesus and Paul was by Bruno Bauer (*Die Apostelgeschichte eine Ausgleichung des Paulinismus und des Judenthums innerhalb der christlichen Kirche* [Berlin: 1850]); see the survey of research on the parallels in, W. Radl (*Paulus und Jesus im lukanischen Doppelwerk* [Bern: Lang, 1975] 44-59).

[2] Already in 1845 F. C. Baur listed these and other parallels *in detail* (*Paulus, Der Apostel Jesu Christi, Sein Leben und Wirken, seine Briefe und seine Lehre* [2d ed.; Leipzig: 1866-67; reprinted, Osnabrück: Zeller, 1968], 1. 104-5, 116-17, 179, 218-20, 245-47, etc.).

[3] Luke 24:47; Acts 4:7-10; 5:28; 23:13.

[4] Especially within the *Tendenz* critique; see Part I below.

to Stephen, Jesus and Peter, and Paul, before summarizing our conclusions.

I

In 1838 F. C. Baur noted the Peter-Paul parallels within the intention of Acts as part of his evidence of a thoroughgoing Paulinist apologetic to present "Paul as Petrine as possible and Peter as Pauline as possible" in bridging the Paulinist with the Petrine party into catholic Christianity.[5] Shortly thereafter in 1854 Baur's student, Eduard Zeller, in taking over Baur's problematic and corroborating M. Schneckenburger's Acts as a defense of Paul (1841),[6] introduced Stephen as a link between the Peter-Paul parallels and the Jesus of the Gospel, on the one hand, and between the primitive Petrine Christianity and the Pauline Gentile mission, on the other.[7] Zeller goes on to the curious observation that a common christological conception—viz., a mighty *prophet* who must suffer— underlies the Jesus-Peter/(Stephen)/Paul parallels. Particularly in the rage that Jesus, Stephen, and Paul experience from the rejection of "the Jews" it is clear that "Luke," the one and same author of both volumes, intends to bind together their common "person and ministry." And yet Zeller backs away from developing this christological cohesion.[8] Indeed, like his contemporaries, the Jesus-Peter/(Stephen)/Paul parallels are used *solely* in illuminating the apologetic character of Acts.

In the years following the demise of the Tübingen School's approach to Acts as a *Tendenzschrift*, scholars either neglected the Jesus-Peter/(Stephen)/Paul parallels altogether or mentioned them generally in conjunction with the principle of the master-disciple.[9]

---

[5] My translation of Baur ("Ueber den Ursprung des Episcopats in der christliche Kirche," *Ausgewählte Werke in Einzelausgaben* [ed. K. Scholder; Stuttgart-Bad Cannstatt: Frommann, 1963] 462); also cited in Radl (*Paulus*, 44).

[6] M. Schneckenburger, *Ueber den Zweck der Apostelgeschichte* (Bern: Fischer, 1841).

[7] "Stephen thus forms the proper link between Paul and the primitive church; in character and fate he is the type of the Gentile apostle" (*The Contents and Origin of the Acts of the Apostles, Critically Investigated* [2vols.; London: Williams & Norgate, 1875-76], 2. 176).

[8] Zeller, *Acts*, 2. 175-76, 200-01, 227-33; see F. Overbeck's criticism of Zeller on this point as discussed by Radl (*Paulus*, 48).

[9] R. B. Rackham's commentary on Acts is a notable exception (*The Acts of the Apostles* [Westminster Commentaries; 8th ed.; London: Methuen, 1919] xlvii-xlix); see A. J. Mattill, Jr.s' survey, "The Purpose of Acts: Schneckenburger

It was not until the flowering of *Redaktionsgeschichte* for Lukan studies in H. Conzelmann's, *Die Mitte der Zeit*, that the methodological way was clear to pose again the question of Luke's *own* literary-theological intentions in the Jesus-Peter/(Stephen)/ Paul parallels.[10] In his 1961 commentary on Luke, W. Grundmann modified Conzelmann's distinction between the *heilsgeschichtliche* epochs of Jesus and that of the church by asserting that Jesus' passion was intrinsically constitutive for the life of the church through the eschatological presence of the suffering Lord in the divinely ordained suffering of his witnesses. "Dabei wird eine deutliche Parallelität zwischen dem Herrn und seinen Zeugen sichtbar."[11] Grundmann's notion was echoed or reverberated with minor modulations in succeeding years[12] until in 1975 W. Radl drew out the fuller consequences for the *heilsgeschichtliche* approach by making the Jesus-Paul parallels a direct focus of investigation. His conclusions: in both individual detail and the overall structuring of his narrative the author of Luke-Acts purposely parallels Paul with Jesus to demonstrate to the Gentile, post-apostolic church under duress that its life is presented precisely through the presence of Jesus in the pattern of suffering that Paul and other apostles as well as their Lord himself underwent. Consequently, the period of Jesus and that of the church, though distinguishable, form one inseparable era of the fulfillment of the "good news of the Kingdom of God."[13]

At the same time that Conzelmann's history of salvation perspective had reached a zenith of influence, its redaction-critical foundation was beginning to crack under the weight of literary-critical

---

Reconsidered," *Apostolic History and the Gospel: Biblical and Historical Essays Presented to F. F. Bruce on His 60th Birthday* (ed. W. W. Gasque and R. P. Martin; Exeter: Paternoster, 1970) 113-15.

[10] *Die Mitte der Zeit: Studien zur Theologie des Lukas* (BHT 17; 3d ed.; Tübingen: Mohr [Siebeck], 1960).

[11] *Das Evangelium nach Lukas* (THKNT 3; 8th ed.; Berlin: Evangelische, 1978) 4; see esp. pp. 1-6.

[12] E.g., G. Stählin, *Die Apostelgeschichte* (NTD 5; 13th ed.; Göttingen: Vandenhoeck & Ruprecht, 1970) 4-5; cf. Radl, *Paulus*, 54-57; independently of Radl's work but in a similar direction, G. Muhlack (*Die Parallelen von Lukas-Evangelium und Apostelgeschichte*; [Theologie und Wirklichkeit 8; Bern: Lang, 1979]).

[13] *Paulus*; see esp. pp. 375-95. See also J. Roloff's analysis of the Lukan Paul and his discussion of Radl ("Die Paulus-Darstellung des Lukas," *EvT* 39 [1979] 510-31); though coming to the same basic conclusion, Roloff stresses more the individuality of Paul's historical mission in determining the particular character of the Gentile church.

studies which made the narrative world of Luke-Acts, rather than Mark, the *primary* context for discerning Luke's thematic intentions in one or the other of his two volumes.[14] An important consensus presently arising out of this methodological shift is the prominence given by Luke[15] to "prophetic" notions, whether in the structuring of his narrative around a promise (prophecy)-fulfillment scheme, or the central literary *figure* of the prophet who fulfills earlier prophecies and prophesies new fulfillments within the ongoing historical pattern. Foremost is P. S. Minear's, *To Heal and To Reveal*, in which he has developed extensively both the prophetic consciousness that pervades Luke-Acts and the special lineage of characters that mediates this world of the invisible but "compresent reality" of God.[16] Central to Minear's findings is the specific type of prophetic model in the "prophet like Moses." Using Peter's and Stephen's explicit identification of Jesus as the prophet of Deut 18:15-18 as strategic commentaries on the whole movement of Jesus and his followers in Luke-Acts, Minear points to the critical role that the suffering of *rejection* from Israel plays in integrating so many of the distinctive Lukan emphases: e.g., repentance and forgiveness; fulfillment of all the prophets; the universalism of the covenant to Abraham.[17] It thus becomes clear that, whatever particular purposes Luke has in mind for his audience(s), the *prophetic* parallels between Jesus and the *dramatis personae* of the Acts belong to the very warp and woof of his two-volume story.

More recent literary studies have confirmed independently Minear's picture and elucidated further the prophet like Moses prototype in Luke's narrative technique and overarching plot. For instance, in 1980 D. L. Tiede highlighted the deuteronomic prophetic-historical pattern of Israel's apostasy → punishment → vindication that undergirds Luke's re-interpretation of the prophetic promises of Scripture that are both fulfilled and promised in

---

[14] Already G. W. H. Lampe in 1955-56, though comparing with Mark and Matthew, emphasized the speeches in Acts as the best point of departure in determing the "peculiarly Lucan portrait of Christ" (p. 160 of "The Lucan Portrait of Christ," *NTS* 2 [1955-56] 160-75); see further, Radl (*Paulus*, 57-58).

[15] In these authors and in the rest of our study, "Luke" is the author of Luke-Acts, irrespective of the identity of the "we" in Acts.

[16] *To Heal and To Reveal. The Prophetic Vocation According to Luke* (New York: Seabury, 1976).

[17] *Heal and Reveal*, esp. 102-21.

the ministry of Jesus and the church in Acts. Although Tiede does not treat the Jesus-Peter/(Stephen)/Paul parallels directly, it is manifest that the pattern of rejection of the apostolic emissaries by the Jews in Acts resonates the rejection of Jesus in the Gospel as the prophet like Moses.[18] This "concept of the suffering prophet is . . . established as the framework for telling 'the good news of Jesus.'"[19]

The force of these prophetic features in both plot and characters is to provide an intrinsic rationale as well as an internal coherence for the Jesus-Peter/(Stephen)/Paul parallels. For it is decisive in this approach that the coherence be distinctively *christological* as over against the *heilsgeschichtliche* perspective. Whereas even in the earlier *Tendenz* critique, as in the salvation-historical, the parallel actions of the actors point away from themselves to a variety of possible mediums or agencies which *guarantee the continuity of salvation* (e.g., the Holy Spirit, the "word" of God, apostolic succession, fidelity to the law, etc.), in the christological it is the actions or events of the characters themselves, sc. a messianic pattern inhering in the fabric of the narrative itself, which bind the parallels into an organic whole. Peter, Stephen, Paul must suffer rejection like their Messiah, because that is the very manner in which the fulfillment of the messianic history takes place within the promised plan of God. Therefore it is also the case that this *christological-historical* perspective vouchsafes the continuity of salvation, however the various stages or phases of salvation may be conceived or divided.

Yet in some of the expositions of the prophetic patterns thus far, a lack of precision in clarifying concepts such as "the prophet like Moses" or "deuteronomic history" has tended to mitigate the significance of the parallels and even to make certain scholars wary of the whole prophetic "cast" of Luke-Acts. In what sense, for example, can the suffering of "the prophet like Moses" be tantamount to the motif of the "suffering prophet" of intertestamental Judaism?[20] Does a *deuteronomic*-prophetic dynamic refer to the course of Israel's history as a whole, as in the interaction of human freedom with divine providence, or to only certain salvific events,

---

[18] *Prophecy and History in Luke-Acts* (Philadelphia: Fortress, 1980) esp. 33-63. The Suffering Servant of Isaiah coalesces with the prophet like Moses and serves to justify the mission to the Gentiles as an apologetic for Paul (pp. 42-55). Cf. nn. 42 and 65.

[19] *Prophecy and History*, 43.

[20] E.g., Tiede, *Prophecy and History*, 40-44, esp. 140 n. 37.

etc.?[21] Moreover, are we not in danger of forfeiting the distinctive roles of the various characters in Acts by subsuming them to the status of prophet and then subordinating the various similarities with Jesus to prophetic parallels or "patterns"?[22] How can Peter, for instance, be linked with Paul as a prophet "like Jesus" or "like Moses" when his career never issues in formal charges such as blasphemy nor elicits the kind of rage from larger masses of Israel as we find with both Stephen and Paul?

The thesis of this study is that the inner dynamic of the christological-historical conception which binds the characters of both volumes as *prophets* is the specific Deuteronomistic view of Israel's history with respect to the reception of her prophets as messengers and mediators of Yahweh's salvation. In his monumental *Israel und das gewaltsame Geschick der Propheten*, O. H. Steck outlined this perspective for the Palestinian Judaism of ca. 200 BCE to 100 CE by amassing overwhelming evidence that *one* conceptual canopy of Israel's past and the role and fate of her prophets within that history covered all its literature.[23] He summarizes this basic orientation under four interlocking tenets:[24]

A.   The history of Israel is one long, unending story of a "stiff-necked" and disobedient people;

B.   God sent his messengers, the *prophets*, to mediate his will (i.e. the Law),

---

[21] Tiede, *Prophecy and History*, 30-33; Tiede, however, has done an excellent job in raising the literary issues surrounding Lukan historiography and in pointing to the rich and varied scriptural traditions that inform Luke's presentation of the "definite plan and prescience of God" (Acts 2:23).

[22] This is the tendency of L. T. Johnson's study (*The Literary Function of Possessions in Luke-Acts* [SBLDS 39; Missoula: Scholars, 1977]) of the prophets as "men of the Spirit" (pp. 38-121), though his pattern of the Prophet and the People is a penetrating illumination of the overall contour and dynamic of Luke's two-volume story.

[23] Subtitle of Steck's book: *Untersuchungen zur Ueberlieferung des deuteronomistischen Geschichtsbildes im Alten Testament, Spätjudentum und Urchristentum* (WMANT 23; Neukirchen-Vluyn: Neukirchener, 1967). We shall not concern ourselves with the *extent* of the Deuteronomistic view in Jewish literature of Palestinian provenance; that Steck has proved his contention for a vast amount of this literature is beyond question (see e.g., J. H. Elliot, *JBL* 87 [1968] 226-27).

[24] *Geschick*, esp. 60-80; it is particularly characteristic of Hasidic apocalyptic literature that the final judgment include the large portion of Israel that has not joined their repentance movement and to spare (in certain cases) Gentile nations/individuals that do repent. In any case, the final judgment is often depicted in terms of 587 BCE (Steck [p. 123] denotes this final judgment as *Tenet F2*; to avoid needless confusion we shall refer to an eschatological use of *Tenet D*). See Steck, *Geschick*, 153-89; cf. n. 31.

to instruct and admonish them in this will, and to exhort them to repentance lest they bring upon themselves judgment and destruction;

C.   Nevertheless, Israel *en masse* rejected all these prophets, even *persecuting* and *killing* them out of their stubborn "stiff-neckedness";

D.   Therefore, Israel's God had "rained" destruction upon them in 722 and 587 BCE and would destroy them in a similar way if they did not hearken to his word.

This understanding encompasses the wide divergences of the multi-hued Judaism of the intertestamental and early NT period and is an *inner* Jewish critique of its *own* history that can vary widely in tone and application. For instance, how faithfulness to the covenant law should be expressed or which group in fact in the past may have constituted a faithful remnant, etc. are all operative within this unifying view.[25]

The author of Luke-Acts shares this orientation to Israel's past but with a major modification: the cycle of stubborn disobedience has been definitively broken by the coming of the prophet like Moses, the Anointed One, Jesus of Nazareth, whose death for the sinful nation and raising up from the dead ushers in the *final* salvation, promised by the prophets, for the eschatological remnant of Israel. In this fulfillment, Jesus as the prophet like Moses stands unique. None of the apostolic suffering or martyrdom in Acts accomplishes the decisive saving act as the suffering and death and resurrection of the Lord's Messiah.[26] Once the Acts begins, Israel is offered, a second time, through the prophet-apostles, the final redemption sealed through the prophet like Moses and appropriated through repentance for the final forgiveness/removal of sin. At the same time, refusal of this offer by Israel *as a whole* evokes the pronouncement of eschatological judgment, again promised by the prophets, that is to say, the pronouncement of *Tenet D* which is conceived as the final judgment of God upon Israel for rejecting its prophet *par excellence*, the one whom Moses himself prophesied. Therefore Peter and the other apostles, Stephen, and Paul are bound to the fate of the Prophet-Messiah like Moses. Rejection of their message of repentance is a rejection of their prophetic calling and thus of the prophet like Moses himself whose authoritative

---

[25] *Geschick*, 196-222.

[26] For the view that the cross has atoning significance as Jesus dies as the prophet like Moses, see the author's, "Jesus and the 'Wilderness Generation': The Death of the Prophet Like Moses According to Luke," *Society of Biblical Literature 1982 Seminar Papers* (Chico: Scholars, 1982) 319-40.

presence has sent them and propels them onward. Peter, Stephen, and Paul, then, are Deuteronomistic rejected prophets whose sending to Israel (*Tenet B*) ends in persecution and even death (*Tenet C*). It is this fundamental view of Israel's continued disobedience that is the linchpin of cohesion of the Jesus-Peter/Stephen/Paul parallels.

In Part II we shall see how Stephen's speech and tragic fate point both back to the culmination of Israel's rejection of the prophet like Moses, at the end of the Gospel and early Acts comunity, and forward to the career and fate of Paul. Before tracing this climax in the last section of Acts, however, we shall demonstrate in Part III that Jesus' own sending to Jerusalem as a Deuteronomistic rejected prophet in the Gospel serves as the bedrock for the landscape to follow in the Acts. At no point shall we raise the separate, though closely related and important, question of which particular situation(s) or problem(s) Luke is attempting to address with his vivid portrayal of Israel's reception of her prophets. Such issues lie beyond the scope of the present study.

II

Recent literary criticism has demonstrated the pivotal juncture of Stephen's speech (Acts 7) in illuminating the overarching plot of Luke's two volumes.[27] Stephen first enters the story of Acts in the conflict arising between "Hellenists" and "Hebraists" in the young Christian community (Acts 6). But no sooner is this threat apparently relieved (6:7) when the reader is thrust into the tragic end of his ministry. Why does Luke give such "short shrift" to Stephen's career which he then concludes, oddly, with a lenghty speech, in fact, the longest speech of the Acts? The reason becomes evident when the content of his speech is read as a commentary on the state of Israel's reception of its messianic salvation. Stephen is a transition figure. His own death marks the beginning of concentrated persecution of the church by the leaders of Israel (8:1-4; 9:1-2; 11:19), even as it foreshadows the growing opposition of the *people* of Israel as a whole that will meet Paul at nearly every turn.[28]

---

[27] See e.g., E. Richard, *Acts 6:1-8:4. The Author's Method of Composition* (SBLDS 41; Missoula: Scholars, 1978) 311-59; Johnson, *Possessions*, 70-76.

[28] See below, Part IV, (iv).

Already before this speech is recounted Luke drops a hint of what is to come. Stephen ignites the fury of Diaspora Jews resident in Jerusalem from the synagogue that includes Cyrenians and those from Asia. Luke will tell his readers before long that it was Christian converts from Cyrene dispersed from Jerusalem because of Stephen's persecution who along with men from Cyprus first preached the "Lord Jesus" to non Israelites at Antioch (11:19-20; cf. 13:1). And then somewhat later Paul himself will be sent out from Antioch on a mission to Israel and the Gentiles in which Jews from Asia will emerge as his chief opponents (13:1-3; 14:27-28; 19:23-20:1, 16; 21:27; 24:18). Thus, opposition to Stephen results in journey missions which carry to the "end of the earth" the messianic salvation prophesied by "Moses" and "all the prophets" (3:18, 21-25; 7:37, 52; 8:28; 10:43; 13:27, 40-41; 15:15-18; 24:14; 26:22-23, 27; 28:23, 25). The plan of Acts 1:8 takes a decisive step forward.

It is in Stephen's defense before the Sanhedrin in 7:2-8:3, however, where Luke fuses the fate of Stephen's reception by Israel to the fate of Jesus in the Gospel. Wearing the mantle of the prophet,[29] Stephen sets out to defend the Jerusalem community's relationship to the God of "our fathers" by recounting Israel's past. The journey motif that pulsates throughout this rehearsal not only serves as a convenient scaffolding for the leading ideas; it is itself integral to the view of Israel's history that informs the entire presentation:

(i) Upon a revelation of God in Mesopotamia (7:2), Abraham moves to Haran after being commanded to "go out" and "come" to the "land" which God will show him (v 3). But Haran is not the promised "land" since God "leads him to migrate" to "the land" "in which you are now living" (v 4). From the outset, then, movement to the "land" of revealed promise is the dynamic pivot of the plot. It appears that by the end of verse 4, Stephen already anticipates the climax by pointing out to his hearers in Jerusalem that they are standing in the very land of the fulfilled promise;

(ii) But the fulfillment did not come so quickly in their journeying history, simply because Abraham himself received no inheritance in the land. Instead, God promised "possession" (v 5) only after "his

---

[29] See esp. Minear, *Heal and Reveal*, 102-11, 116-21, 133-42; Johnson, *Possessions*, 38-78.

descendants'' were to become "enslaved" as "strangers" in a "foreign land." Only then after some four hundred years would they "journey out" and come "to worship" "in this place" (τόπος) (v 7b). That is to say, first another journey is necessary—and indeed a journey to the place in the promised land—before the promised inheritence could be realized;

(iii) But even before this journey Stephen recounts the journey into slavery (vv 9-16). First, out of scorn from his brothers, Joseph is sold into bondage in Egypt. But delivered from his afflictions, raised up within the house of Pharaoh, and elevated above all the people of Egypt by God himself, Joseph becomes an anticipation of the Exodus deliverer[30] by feeding the "twelve patriarchs," Jacob and his relatives, who are "sent" or later "journey down" to escape a devastating famine. Though unrecognized by his brothers on their first visit, this Joseph who was *cast aside* by his own becomes exalted among them as their "deliverer";

(iv) Since "the time of *promise* was drawing near" (v 17), this glorious period was not to last for long. Moses, himself one of the brethren of Israel (v 20) but raised in the house of Pharaoh (v 21), also goes unrecognized by his own when he visits and "delivers" (v 25) one of them from the oppression of the Egyptians. On his return to reconcile a feud among his brethren he is spurned and "*cast aside*" (v 27). Thus he must flee to Midian, an alien in his own "house," as well as a sojourner in a foreign land; (vv 29-34). It is only then that Moses, in the desert of Mt. Sinai, trembles in fear at the *voice* of the Lord (φωνή κυρίου) in the midst of burning fire and receives a calling to be *sent* (ἀποστέλλω) on a *journey* to his people to deliver them from Egypt. So it is as the days of the long-awaited promise to Abraham and the patriarchs are beginning to be completely full that the Exodus journey begins (vv 35-45). But although already repudiated by his people, Moses becomes their "ruler" and "*deliverer*" to "*lead* them out" with "wonders and signs in Egypt, the Red Sea, and in the desert for forty years" (vv 35-36). It is there on the journey that he prophesies of one whom "God will raise up from your brethren *like me*" (v 37—Deut 18:15), and receives "living words" "in the desert" "upon the mountain." Yet—despite all

---

[30] Like Moses, Jesus, and Stephen Joseph is *sofia*, v 10 (Luke 2:40, 52; Acts 6:3, 10; 7:22. cf. Luke 21:15); like Jesus and Stephen he has *charis*, v 10, before God and the people (Luke 2:40, 52; Acts 6:8; 7:46; cf. 2:47).

of this—he is scorned and *"cast aside"* a second time by his brethren, "our fathers," who "turned in their hearts back to Egypt" (v 39). This epoch-making rejection is epitomized by the calf to which they sacrificed and "were rejoicing" in the "works of their hands" (v 41). Thus a perverted rejoicing in the wilderness *at the mountain* forms the quintessence of a froward people whom God not only gave over to idolatrous worship, but also to the foreign land of *Babylon* (i.e. *Tenet D*) "just as it it written in the book of the *prophets*" (vv 42-43). Consequently, before the promise is fully realized, the pronouncement of the judgment of *Tenet D*[31] falls over the Exodus journey "to the *place*" in the land;

---

[31] *Tenet D* often refers to the actual punishment in the past of the Northern kingdom (722 BCE) and/or Babylonian exile and destruction of Jerusalem in 587 BCE (see Steck, *Geschick*, 63 n. 8). However, in certain strands of later Deuteronomistic thinking the pronouncement of impending judgment became an integral part of the prophetic calling (*Geschick*, 123 n. 5, 140, 193-95, 218-22). *Tenet D* is found *inter alia* in: *Hebrew OT*—Deut 28:45a, 46, 48-57, 59-62a, 63b-68 (cf. vv 45b, 47, 62b); 2 Kgs 17:18, 20 (cf. vv 7-17, 19); 2 Chr 24:23-24 (cf. vv 18-22); 36:16b-21 (cf. vv 12-16a); Ezra 9:7b, 9a, 13, 14b (cf. vv 7a, 10b-11, 15b); Neh 1:8b (cf. vv 7-8a); 9:27a, 30b, 32, 36-37 (cf. vv 13-14, 16-17a, 18, 26, 28a, 29-30a, 33b-35); Jer 7:32-34 (cf. vv 25-28); 25:8-14 (cf. vv 3-7); 26:6 (cf. vv 2-5); 29:17-18, 30b (cf. vv 19-20a); 35:17 (cf. vv 13-15); 44:2, 6, 11-15 (cf. vv 3-5, 7-10); Zech 1:2 (cf. vv 3-4, 6); 7:12c-14 (cf. vv 11-12b); Dan 9:7b, 11b-14a, 16, 17b-18a (cf. vv 5-6, 8, 9b-11a, 14b, 15b); Ps 79:1-5, 7 (cf. v 8a); 106:40-42 (cf. vv 6-7, 13-14, 16, 19-21a, 24-25, 28-29a, 32-39); *Deutero-canonical* and *Pseudepigrapha*—(see immediate contexts for *Tenets A-C*)—Tob 3:4b; Bar 1:20; 2:1-5a, 6-7, 9, 13-14, 20-26, 29-30; 3:4b, 7a, 8; Pr Azar 4, 5, 8-10, 14, 15; *T. Levi* 10:4; 15:1-3; 16:4-5a; *T. Jud.* 23:3-4; *T. Iss.* 6:2, *T. Zeb.* 9:6; *T. Dan* 5:8; *T. Naph.* 4:2, 5; *T. Ash.* 7:2, 6; 1 *Enoch* 89:56, 66, 90:25-26; 91:12, 14-15; *Jub.* 1:13; *Pss. Sol.* 8:28; 9:1a, c, 2a; 17:20; *As. Mos.* 3:1-6; chap. 8; *Bib. Ant.* 12:4; 13:10; 19:7; 4 Ezra 3:27; 14:32-33; 2 *Apoc. Bar.* 1:4-5; 4:1; 31:5; 44:5-6, 12b, 15b; 46-6b; 77:4b; *Qumran*—4QDibHam 2:11; 3:6-14a; 5:3b-6a, 16b-18a; 6:7-8, 11-13; 1QS 1:26; CD 1:3b-4a, 12-13a; *NT* and early *Patristic*—Matt 22:7; 23:29-31; Mark 12:9 par.; 1 Thess 2:16; *Barn.* 5:11; Justin *Dial.* 16:4; *Joseph*—*Ant.* 9.13. 2 §266; 9.14.1 §281; *Rabbis*—*Pesiq. R.* 138a; 146a.

As is clear from these examples, the language of *Tenet D* is as varied as the literary contexts and backgrounds in which it is expressed. Although many images are stereotyped (e.g., "desolate/deserted land," Jer 7:34b; 25:11; 44:2, 6; Zech 7:14; 2 Chr 36:21b; *T. Jud.* 23:3; *T. Ash.* 7:2; etc. or "scattered/dispersed," Zech 7:14a; Tob 3:4b; Bar 2:4b, 13, 29; 3:8; *T. Levi* 10:4; 16:5; *T. Jud.* 23:3; *Jub.* 1:13; etc.), *Tenet D* defies strict form-critical delimitations—to be sure, incorporating various judgment oracles as the prophetic "woe" (*Wehespruch*) (Steck, *Geschick*, 51-53, 63 n. 8) etc.—and thus exhibits less stereotypical formulation as a *whole*. What is crucial in identifying *Tenet D* is its logical sequence within the dynamic *complex* of the Deuteronomistic view, i.e. within *Tenets A-C*, which must clearly pervade the literary context. This methodological procedure will be followed for our entire study. See also n. 24.

(v) The journey, however, continues, led by "the tent of witness" which was with "our fathers in the desert" as it was built by Moses (v 44). This tabernacle formed the focal point for "our fathers" when God thrust out the nations during the time of Joshua and up to the days of David who "found favor before God." Though David wanted to "find" a "dwelling place" for the God of the house of Jacob, it was his son Solomon who built him a "house" (vv 45-47). But there is not doubt that this building of the Temple did *not fulfill* the promise to Abraham that his posterity (i.e. "house") would "journey" "to this place" to "worship" God (v 7 → v 17). For Stephen immediately qualifies the importance of the Temple by reminding his hearers that God does not dwell in such "hand" or "man-made" structures "just as the prophet (Isa 66:1) declares: 'Heaven is my throne . . . . What is the *place* (τόπος) of my dwelling? Did not *my* hand make all these things?'" (vv 48-50);[32]

(vi) The journeying history for the "house of Jacob" was not over; the *coming* of the Righteous One was still to come. But now instead of relating the events of this period, Stephen abruptly changes his tack altogether by lashing into his audience with a most "scandalous" accusation: "You stiff-necked folk (σκληροτράχηλοι), uncircumcised in your hearts and ears! As your fathers did so you yourselves continue to do—you always resist the Holy Spirit.'" (v 51). Here the classic indictment of *Tenet A* could not be more forcefully expressed.[33] Stephen's hearers are no different than their stubborn ancestors who continually resisted the redemptive gestures of God.[34] Though mention of the "Holy Spirit" contemporizes the Christian community's understanding of the messianic fulfillment, it is clear that the crowd's resistance continues the *same* unceasing obstinacy that Israel has always shown to the messengers of God's redemptive pleading:[35] "Which of the *prophets* did not your

---

[32] Cf. N. Dahl, "The Story of Abraham in Luke-Acts," *Studies in Luke-Acts: Essays Presented in Honor of Paul Schubert* (ed. L. E. Keck and J. L. Martyn; Nashville: Abingdon, 1966) 142-48. Dahl comes to a similar interpretation of the Temple polemic within the speech.

[33] See e.g., Neh 9:16-17a, 29; 2Kgs 18:14; Jer 7:24, 26; Bar 2:30, 33; *Jub.* 1:7, 20; etc.

[34] E.g., Bar 1:19: "From the day when the Lord brought our fathers out of the land of Egypt until today, we have been disobedient to the Lord our God, and we have been negligent in not heeding his voice."

[35] For this obstinate resistance against the *Spirit* of God who spoke the law and warned Israel *through the prophets*, see Neh 9:30, cf. v 20; Zech 7:12b; 1QS 8:15-16.

fathers persecute? Indeed, they killed these who proclaimed beforehand the coming of the Righteous One, the one whom you yourselves have now betrayed and murdered'' (v 52). Hence with *Tenet B* implicit, Stephen moves directly from *Tenet A* to *Tenet C*, sc. to Israel's persecuting and killing of all the prophets that has now climaxed in the killing of the Righteous One, the *prophet like Moses!*[36]

But right at the point when the audience might expect the solemn tones of *Tenet D* to fall once again[37]—but now upon them—the narrative takes yet another surprising turn. Suddenly Stephen is gazing ''into heaven'' at the ''glory (δόξα) of God,'' seeing ''Jesus standing at the right hand of God'' and declaring to his audience the majesty of his beatific vision. As these ''blasphemous'' words enter into ears that are still smoldering from the outrageous assertions of his speech, the crowd's hostility can no longer be contained as they drag Stephen outside the city and stone him.

Before we enumerate the parallels between Stephen's dying moments and Jesus' passion that Luke takes pains to draw, we must take stock of the orientation to Israel's history and sketch the characters that now color Luke's presentation:

Moses. Stephen's speech is dominated by Moses and the *Exodus*, i.e. vv 17-45 of vv 2-50 or ca. 60% of the speech: *1.* Moses' calling to lead the people on a journey of redemption issues from the voice of God in brilliant light; *2.* This journey sending is to be the fulfillment of the ''God of glory's'' promise to Abraham that this posterity would worship God in the *place* (v 7 → 17), i.e. in Jerusalem where the tent of witness had been laid to rest and the Temple built (vv 44-47);[38] *3.* Yet the Exodus did *not* fulfill the promise simply because the entire journey was fraught with the perverted repudiation of God's chosen deliverer and mediator of living words and ended with an idolatrous use of the ''house'' or Temple. What is more, Israel's history from that time forward continued the calloused rejection (*Tenet A*) of the voice of God through his messengers (*Tenet B*) by killing the prophets (*Tenet C*). Thus, God ''delivered''

---

[36] For the move from *Tenet A* to *C* with *B* as the historical background, see the immediate contexts of the passages cited in n. 33, esp. Neh 9:26-30 and *Jub.* 1:7-12; cf. Zech 7:8-14.

[37] See n. 31 *fin.*

[38] For the importance of the ''central place'' in deuteronomic thinking, see e.g., E. W. Nicholson (*Deuteronomy and Tradition* [Oxford: Blackwell, 1967] 53-57); for the Deuteronomistic history, e.g., F. M. Cross (*Canaanite Myth and Hebrew Epic* [Cambridge: Harvard, 1973] 278-85).

them over to Babylon (*Tenet D*). Especially illuminating is the role of the calf in this reconstruction of the past: its idolatry sets the precedent for Israel's entire history of stiff-necked resistance.[39] Therefore, *Tenet D* follows immediately after this seminal perversion of the true worship of God (cf. v 7) though the Babylonian exile be hundreds of years removed.[40] (vv 39-43). Another journey of redemption by the Righteous One must come;

Jesus. Even though there is no direct depiction of Jesus' coming, the whole of Israel's journeying history culminates with him: *1*. No description of a divine authorization of his calling is presented; *2*. Jesus' coming is the consummation of the calling of Moses to lead Israel on the Exodus journey to the place in the land of promise for the true worship of God. Already on the Exodus Moses himself prophesied his "raising up" to be a "prophet . . . like me"; *3*. With the spurning of Moses coupled to the tragic fate of the prophets, it is certain that the reception of Moses' "living oracles" of the law which in Deut 18:15 promises a "prophet like me," is anticipated in the persecution and killing of the prophets before it is fulfilled in Jesus' coming as the Righteous One who is "murdered" by a stiff-necked folk who continually failed "*to keep the law!*" (v 53). That is to say, Jesus is like the prophets quintessentially as the *prophet like Moses*. He brings Israel's journeying history of unrelenting disobedience to God's messengers to its fulfillment;

Stephen. Stephen's speech and vision link him inseparably to Moses and the prophet like Moses: *1*. His recital of Israel's history of disobedience is confirmed by the vision of the "God of glory" whose glory first appeared to Abraham with the promise and now encompasses Stephen's ministry and leads it into the journeying salvation to the "end of the earth"; *2*. Stephen's charge denies the fulfillment of the Exodus salvation to *worship God* in Jerusalem *for his audience*. They always resist the Holy Spirit and did so by rejecting the coming of Jesus, the Righteous One. By implication it is the

---

[39] As for instance in Deuteronomy; see D. P. Moessner, "Luke 9:1-50: Luke's Preview of the Journey of the Prophet Like Moses of Deuteronomy," *JBL* 102 (1983) 582-87. See also n. 40.

[40] A similar telescoping of Israel's history is found in *Jubilees* 1 in which the Deuteronomistic view of Israel's disobedience is programmatic: *A* 1:7-11; *B* 1:12a; *C* 1:12b; *D* 1:13. *Tenet D* follows immediately upon a summary description of the monarchy as one *unending period of idolatry* (vv 10-12) that continues the idolatry *from Mt. Sinai!* (vv 3-9, cf. vv 21-22). Emphasis on the defilement of the central place in Jerusalem is also pronounced (vv 10, 27-29).

Christian community that participates in this fulfillment; 3. His accusation of a monolithic repudiation and even killing of the prophets and the prophet like Moses is matched by the rage of his audience that kills him as well. Accordingly, his vision of Jesus the Son of Man[41] with the glory of God draws him directly into Jesus' fate of rejection as the prophet like Moses.

As Luke concludes his description of Stephen, his legacy in the line of Jesus as the prophet like Moses and of all the rejected prophets is sealed. In his dying breath Stephen utters the words of Jesus on the cross (Acts 7:59—Luke 23:46) but now directly to the "Lord Jesus" himself. Moreover, his echo of Jesus' prayer on the cross for forgiveness (Acts 7:60—Luke 23:34) now takes on the added dimension that the same leaders (Sanhedrin) of Israel are continuing their rejection of Jesus by stoning Stephen. When we join to this continuity the oft-cited parallels between the charges against Jesus and Stephen, the portrait of Stephen as a type of the Deuteronomistic rejected prophets and antitype of the prophet like Jesus (Moses) is poignant indeed: "We have heard him [Stephen] speak blasphemous words against Moses and God" . . . . for "this man never ceases to speak words against this holy *place* and the law, for we have heard him say that this Jesus the Nazorean will destroy this *place* and will change the customs which *Moses* delivered to us" (6:11, 13-14). The Temple, the central place of all Israel, has become the center of the contested claims to the true vision of Moses and the worship of the God of glory. For it was Jesus' blasphemous words before the Sanhedrin that "from now on the Son of Man shall be seated at the right hand of the power of God" (Luke 23:9) which sparked the final surge of hostility that ended on the cross . . . . Meanwhile, "Saul was consenting to his death" (Acts 8:1a).

III

Do the accents of Stephen's stance towards Israel's past resonate with Luke's account of Jesus in the Gospel or does Stephen stand out as a "singular saint"? Our scope does not permit a rehearsal of the correspondences between the callings of Jesus and of Moses in

---

[41] Of the 25 previous uses of this phrase in Luke's first volume, 14 instances are linked *directly* to the "shame," rejection, or suffering/death of this figure.

Deuteronomy that the author has discussed elsewhere.[42] But we can summarize several of the characteristic contours of the Gospel landscape.

The Transfiguration

1. Only Luke speaks of Moses, Elijah, and Jesus appearing together "in glory" and the three disciples beholding "his glory" (τὴν δόξαν αὐτοῦ, 9:32). As "all Israel" previously had witnessed this divine "glory" on the mountain (Deut 5:24), so Peter, John and James, representing the twelve disciples and thus the twelve tribes of all Israel are privy to the divine glory now concentrated in Jesus. But before Peter can begin to accomodate the divine glory engulfing Jesus and Moses and Elijah, the latter two disappear and a cloud descends into the brilliant light (vv 33-34). Again only Luke by following the word order of the LXX emphasizes that the voice from the fiery cloud reverberates the divine command concerning the *prophet like Moses* spoken by the Lord himself to Moses *at Mount Horeb* and repeated by Moses at the borders of the land of promise on the Exodus journey (Deut 18:15-20): "hearken to him" (αὐτοῦ ἀκούετε, 18:15b—Luke 9:33b).[43] The glory of the mountain calling of Moses to mediate the life-giving voice to the people on the Exodus[44] has been transferred to Jesus as the prophet like Moses. For he it is who utters "living oracles" (cf. Acts 7:38b) to Israel and now with "the voice" is "found *alone*" (9:36a).

2. Jesus' calling to be the prophet like Moses is grounded and clarified only in Luke as an "exodus" *journey to Jerusalem* predicted already by Moses and Elijah (9:31). When verse 31 is linked back with Jesus' own prediction nearly a week earlier that he as the Son of Man must be rejected and killed by the "elders, chief priests, and scribes" (9:22, 28) and connected forward to verse 51 where "the days of his *taking* up," a euphemism for his death (and exaltation),[45]

---

[42] "Prophet Like Moses," 583-600; a comprehensive study of the entire Lukan journey by the author will be appearing as, *Lord of the Banquet: The Prophet Like Moses of the Lukan Travel Narrative* (9:1-19:44), in the AThANT ser., Theologischer Verlag, Zürich.

[43] In both the MT and LXX of Deut 18:15-22 it is clear that vv 16b-20 are a retrospect on the events at Horeb in 5:23-31.

[44] See D. P. Moessner, "Prophet Like Moses," 583, 587, 589.

[45] See J. A. Fitzmyer (*The Gospel According to Luke I-IX* [AB 28; Garden City: Doubleday, 1981] 828) for linguistic discussion.

are already beginning to be *fulfilled*, then it is evident that the "exodus" that Jesus fulfills *in* Jerusalem is one that he fulfills also on his way *to* Jerusalem, that is, on a journey to the center of the nation.[46] Moses and Elijah, the two great prophets of the Exodus,[47] are thus pointing ahead to a journey that culminates with the prophet like Moses reaching Israel's leaders in the central place of the whole people, viz. the Temple precincts. But as the heavenly voice also declares, Jesus the prophet like Moses accomplishes this uniquely as God's "Chosen Son" (9:35b).[48]

3. Again it is distinctive to Luke's narrative that precisely at the point in which the exodus fulfillment is being discussed, the representatives of the twelve tribes of Israel are "asleep!" (v 32a). This detail may appear inconsequential at best until it is also noticed that: (i) Luke is interested, too, in the fact that they "wake up" (v 32); (ii) Upon waking up the disciples' observance of the divine glory leads to a response totally inappropriate to that disclosure—"not knowing what he [Peter] was saying" (v 33b), leading to (iii) the fear the disciples bear when the cloud overshadows them and the voice commands them to hearken to Jesus (vv 34b-35). The disciples have missed the divine voice in Moses, Elijah, and Jesus. "Hearken to him" consequently becomes the mandate of the coming journey. Like Moses and Elijah, Jesus is sent to Israel with the voice of God (*Tenet B*). But thus far, reluctance and incomprehension and fear mark Israel's reception.

Luke grafts the behavior of the disciples among the crowds below

---

[46] For the connection between 9:31 and verse 51, see J. H. Davies ("The Purpose of the Central Section of Luke's Gospel," *SE* II [= TU 87; Berlin: Akademie, 1964] 164-69) and P. Schubert ("The Structure and significance of Luke 24," *Neutestamentliche Studien für Rudolf Bultmann* [BZNW 21: Berlin: Töpelmann, 1954] 184-85).

[47] See e.g., 1 Kgs 19:4-18; Sir 48:7-8; cf. 1 *Enoch* 89:51-52. The Jewish Torah reading of Exod 32:11-33 (golden calf and Moses pleading for the people) is followed by the *haphtorah* reading of Elijah's challenge on Mt. Carmel to the worshipers of Baal! (1 Kgs 18:1-39). For "Elijah's cup" at Jewish Passover celebrations and the use of Mal 4:5-6 (MT 3:23-24) at the Great Sabbath before the Passover feast, see A. Wiener, *The Prophet Elijah in the Development of Judaism: A Depth-Psychological Study* (London: Routlege and Kegan Paul, 1978) 133-35.

[48] Resonance with the "voice from heaven" in Jesus" baptism (Luke 3:22 "my beloved/chosen Son") is clear and confirms Jesus' calling on that occasion, esp. for the *disciples*. See e.g., I. H. Marshall, *The Gospel of Luke* (New International Greek Testament Commentary; Exeter: Paternoster, 1978) 388 ("elect one" connects both 9:35 and 3:22 through the Servant's calling to suffer, Isa 42:1); Fitzmyer, *Luke*, 793, 802-03. See also n. 65.

on the plain to the texture of the disciples' behavior on the mountain in a way that confirms and elucidates further the peculiar
features of the transfiguration narrative. After descending and
learning that his disciples were incapable of casting out a demon,
Jesus immediately denounces the *whole* generation as "faithless and
crooked" (v 41) and decries a prophetic calling which must continue to bear up and bear with such an obstinate folk. Indeed Jesus
echoes Moses' cry of lament at the base of Mt. Horeb: "How long
am I to be with you and bear you" (Luke 9:41—Deut 1:12). And
unlike Matthew and Mark it is the disciples themselves who pro-
voke Jesus' reaction and become patent examples of a froward
generation. For in uninterrupted sequence and "crowded" setting
Jesus tells the disciples that the "Son of Man will be delivered into
the hands of men" (v 44b).[49] Not only is the Sanhedrin going to
"kill" Jesus (v 22), so is "this generation" that is deaf to the voice
of God in their midst: "for they [the disciples] were not comprehen-
ding this word and it was concealed from them that they should not
perceive it, and they were afraid to ask him about this word"
(9:45). Reluctance, incomprehension, and fear again emerge as the
salient signs of "this generation." But Luke does not end here. The
disciples now begin to argue which of them is the "greatest" (vv
46-48; cf. Deut 1:12 at Mt. Horeb!). Jesus sets a child at his side to
illustrate the *proper* response to the *authority* of his *sending* (ἀποστέλλω,
v 48). The disciples betray their imperviousness to the voice of God
in Jesus yet again as they pride themselves in their "privileged"
position which had prevented one who did successfully exorcise
demons "in Jesus' name" (ἐν τῷ ὀνόματί σου, v 49; contrast vv 48,
40b). Like their Horeb counterparts in their perverted twisting of
the voice of God in the molten calf, so the disciples' glimpse of the
divine glory on the mountain reveals their own self-glory on the
plain.[50] They are *one* with the "men" of "this generation" as a
faithless and stiff-necked lot![51]

---

[49] Vv 23-25 along with probable paronomasia on ὁ υἱὸς τοῦ ἀνθρώπου with χεῖρας
ἀνθρώπων (see J. Jeremias, *TDNT* 5 [1967] 715) indicate a generic sense of
"man," or the generation of Jesus' day. In 17:25 it is expressly stated that "this
generation" rejects "the Son of Man" and thus is responsible for Jesus' suffering.

[50] That *John* (v 49) leads the disciples' response ties the disciples' behavior here
even more tightly to the three disciples on the mountain.

[51] For the incomprehension, fear, strife, and imperviousness to discipline as
characterizing "all Israel's" response to Moses in Deuteronomy, see Moessner,
"Prophet Like Moses," 583-87, cf. 588-95.

Before moving to Luke's "journey section," we can capsulize what has already become strikingly apparent: Stephen's portrayal in the Deuteronomistic tones of the stubborn rejection of the prophets Moses and Jesus has already been anticipated in the Transfiguration: *1.* Like Moses Jesus receives a calling to a journey sending from the *voice* of the Lord in brilliant *light.* But now Jesus is to *fulfill* Moses' sending with "living oracles" as the "prophet like me"; *2.* Jesus' journey is an Exodus to the Temple in Jerusalem to consummate Moses' Exodus to the central place of all Israel for the true worship of God; *3.* From the very outset the entire journey is characterized as one of suffering the stubborn rejection of the people *as a whole.*

—*Tenet B* stands behind the prophetic conception of a sending as mediators of the redemptive voice of God, no. *1,* while it is equally clear that *Tenets A* and *C* inform the reception of the prophet, no. *3.* Only no. *2* stands alone as the callings of Moses and Jesus, the prophet like Moses, on the Exodus to the nation's center.

The Journey (9:51-19:44)

i) Not only does Luke launch his journey narrative with a resounding rejection of Jesus that recalls the repudiation of Elijah by a Samaritan,[52] but he also ties his sonorous announcement in 9:51 to a string of journey notices which will remind the reader that Jesus' Exodus *as* the voice of God from the mountain to Jerusalem is indeed moving forward.[53] More than this, Luke will tell his readers that as Jesus progresses through the "towns and villages of Israel, teaching in their streets" (13:22) the crowds continue to swell around him until these "myriads" become a "multitude of crowds" (11:29 → 12:1 → 14:25). As the prophet like Moses Jesus gathers all Israel on their Exodus to Jerusalem.[54]

ii) Within this dynamic framework at the midpoint, two quarter-points, and at the end of the journey Luke marks in the chilling cadences of the Deuteronomistic prophetic fate the reception accorded Jesus the prophet like Moses:

---

[52] 2 Kgs 1:2-16; cf. Luke 9:54 (James and John!); cf. also 1 Kgs 19:19-21 and Luke 9:61-62.

[53] 9:53; 10:38; 13:22, 33; 14:25; 17:11; 18:31; 19:11, 28, 41.

[54] See e.g., 9:23, 59-62; 10:1-16; 11:23; 12:32-34; 13:31-35; 14:15-15:32; 18:18-19:40.

a) *11:47-51* At the end of a large crowd tableau (11:14-36) in which Jesus levels the four different responses of "marveling" amazement (v 14b), charge of alignment with Beelzebul (v 15), "testy" skepticism (v 16), and naive admiration (vv. 27-28) *to one mass* of an "evil generation" (v 29), he turns to the Pharisees at table who emerge from the crowd (v 37) as its leaders (vv. 43-44, 46, 52; 12:1b). Their scholars in the *law* "are witnesses and consent *to the deeds of your fathers*" (*Tenet A*) by "building the tombs of the prophets whom your fathers killed" (*Tenet C*) (vv 47-48). Indeed, the Wisdom of God had *sent* prophets and apostle-messengers (προφήτας καὶ ἀποστόλους, v 49) to Israel (*Tenet B*) who had been killed and persecuted in order that "this generation" would now be spattered with "the blood of *all* the prophets shed from the foundation of the world. . . from the blood of Abel to the blood of Zechariah who perished between the altar and the sanctuary" (*Tenets C & D*). "Yes, I tell you, it shall be required of this generation" (*Tenet D*)[55] (vv 50-51). The history of Israel has been one unending stiff-necked rejection of her prophets, reaching from its patriarchal roots all the way to the very heart of the nation in the sanctuary of its Temple! And now as 11:52-12:1 divulge, Jesus the prophet greater than Jonah and wiser than Solomon (11:29-32) has *entered* into this destiny to bring Israel's history for *this generation* to its climax;

b) *13:33-35* Strange as it may seem on the surface, Luke has Jesus pronounce a judgment oracle[56] upon Jerusalem and its Temple long before Jesus ever reaches the nation's center (13:34-35; cf. 17:11). But now in light of the prophetic penetration of Israel's stubborn stance already voiced by Jesus in the journey sending, the position of this prophecy of doom is understandable. For Luke has just presented Jesus in the burgeoning crowds (12:1-13:9), in their synagogues (13:10-21), and in their streets (13:22-30) teaching, admonishing, and warning the people of Israel about the "leaven of

---

[55] For blood vengeance "required," cf. Gen 9:5; 42:22; 2 Sam 4:11; Ps 9:12(13); for avenging the "blood" of the prophet(s), see 2 Kgs 9:7; 2 Chr 24:20-22, 25; cf. Ezek 33:6, 8. On the formulation of *Tenet D*, see nn. 24, 31; cf. Deut 18:19. For Luke 11:50-51 as a prophetic *Drohwort*, see Steck (*Geschick*), 52.

[56] With 13:35a cf. Dan 9:17b; Bar 2:26; esp. *T. Levi* 15:1; *Pesiq. R.* 138a; 146a; for a similar judgment oracle on the "house" as the palace and "lineage" of the king, cf. Jer 12:7; 22:5. In 1 *Enoch* 89:56 and 2 *Apoc. Bar.* 8:2; 64:6 "God" is described as actively leaving the Temple; see also nn. 24, 31.

the Pharisees'' which ''eats and drinks in the presence''[57] of Jesus
and entertains the *signs* of the present time[58] but refuses to repent
before the voice of God in their midst. ''I tell you, unless you repent
you will *all* likewise perish'' (13:3, 5). By the time Luke has reached
the midpoint of the journey narrative, the crowds of ''this generation'' have already been fully identified with their leaders as
''hypocrites'' (11:37-12:1 → 12:56). It is no wonder, then, when
Pharisees again emerge from ''the crowds'' in 13:31 to ''engage''
Jesus, he responds with the classic Deuteronomistic castigation of a
disobedient people and yet simultaneously with the pathos of the
prophet like Moses whose efforts to gather the people have gone
unrequited: ''Jerusalem, Jerusalem, You killer of prophets and
stoner of those (*Tenet C*) who are sent (τοὺς ἀπεσταλμένους) to you
(*Tenet B*). How often I have wished to gather your children as a hen
gathers her brood under her wings but you have not so wished!
Look, your house is forsaken'' (*Tenet D*). As in 11:47-12:1 it is clear
that Jesus' special prophetic sending to Jerusalem fully
recapitulates the tragic fate of all of Israel's prophets, ''for it cannot
be that a prophet should perish away from Jerusalem'' (13:33b).
But now it is even clearer that as Jesus goes toward Jerusalem, the
whole nation's destiny goes with him;

c) *17:25-30* Farther along the journey (cf. 14:25) Pharisees and
their scribes once again (15:1-2) demonstrate that ''this
generation'' remains deaf to the special mouthpiece of God in their
midst. When a heated exchange ensues (16:14-18), Jesus counters
with a parable (vv 19-31) mirroring Israel's monolithic callousness
and the categorical warning, ''If they do not hearken to *Moses and
the prophets*, neither will they be convinced if some one should rise up
from the dead'' (*Tenet C*) (v 31). *Tenets A* and *B* lie behind this ar-
ticulation of Israel's past here, while it is also the case that Jesus'
prophetic commission is tied to that refusal of all the prophets and
yet stands unique as an eschatological sending. Subsequently,
Jesus' encounter with the solid front of unresponsive lepers of the
Jewish nation (17:11-19) sets the stage for Jesus meeting yet once
more with Pharisees whose blindness to the ''sign'' of God's effective rule standing in their midst (17:20-21) has become patent for
the whole nation. For Jesus immediately warns the disciples against

---

[57] 13:26.
[58] 12:54-56.

falling prey to "this generation's" demand for proofs of God's redemption to Israel (ἰδοὺ ὧδε, 17:23 → 21 → 11:30, 32). "This generation" will, in fact, inflict suffering and rejection (17:25) (*Tenet C*) upon Jesus, the Son of Man, and then continue on unchanged *like the generations of Noah and Lot* (*Tenet A*) to "eat and drink," "buy and sell," totally hardened by the redemptive pleadings of the past (*Tenet B*), and oblivious to the future day of the Son of Man;

d) *19:41-44* As Jesus' entourage nears Jerusalem (cf. 18:31-34; 19:11) the large band of disciples fulfill Jesus' prophecy in 13:35b by heralding him as the "king, the one who comes in the name of the Lord" (19:38). Aglow with the "mighty works" they had "*seen*" (v 37b), they are joined by the many of the crowds who are electric with expectation that Jesus' approach to Jerusalem signals the immediate "*appearance*" of the Kingdom of God (19:11). But given the dynamic of the reception of the prophet on the journey, that Jesus—precisely in the midst of this messianic fervor—both weeps over Jerusalem and prophesies her destruction in the dirge[59] of *Tenet D* seems only fitting: "not one stone upon another will they leave in you" (19:44a); for Jesus knows full well that the time is coming quickly when the disciples will no longer cry out praise but link hands with the multitudes and leaders of Israel who cry out for his death. His final interaction on the journey with the leaders of "this generation," the Pharisees, provides a poignant conclusion: 'When the disciples become silent, then (as in Hab. 2:11) the toppling stones of ruin will shreak out against the perpetrated evil' (19:40 → 44).[60] Thus Luke ends his journey as it began: Jesus laments a wilderness generation closed to the "living words" that would have made for peace with God (v 42a → v 38b). Because it is a "faithless and twisted generation" that "has not known the time of your *visitation*," the *Exodus visitation* (LXX Gen 50:24-25; Exod 3:16) of God must now become his visitation for destruction (e.g., Jer 6:15; Isa 29:6).

To sum up ii), Luke's special journey section reveals in both contour and content, dynamics and depiction, a view of Israel's reception of Jesus from the mountain of revelation to the central place

---

[59] Cf. Jer 6:6-21; Isa 29:1-4.

[60] See A. Schlatter, *Das Evangelium des Lukas: Aus seinen Quellen Erklärt* (Stuttgart: Calwer, 1931) 409-10; for the grammatical construction, see BDF §§363, 373.

that is thoroughly and distinctly Deuteronomistic. For as Jesus, the Anointed and Chosen Son, is received like all the prophets before him, he brings this persistent history of disobedience to its consummation uniquely as the *prophet like Moses*.

iii) The Temple in Jerusalem is both the focus and the vortex of Jesus' journeying from the mountain in Galilee. Jesus himself determines resolutely (9:51) to consummate (τελειοῦμαι, 13:32b) his prophetic calling to gather Israel and crown their Exodus deliverance by journeying to the center of their worship of God. Only at the central place can Israel's destiny be won. But he is also drawn there, irresistibly, as if by a mighty whirlwind of intractable disobedience that also must fulminate in Israel's fate at the central place (13:33). In each of the *three* programmatic pronouncements of *Tenet D* on the journey (11:47-51; 13:31-35; 19:41-44), the Temple (οἶκος) becomes the epitome of opposition. In 11:50-51 the long history of the blood of all the prophets has flowed to its penultimate climax "between the altar and the sanctuary!" In 13:35a Israel's "house" is described as "forsaken" in the imagery of the departure of the presence of God from the Temple that will take place in the destruction of Jerusalem![61] And finally in 19:41-44, with the journey coming to a close, Jesus pronounces a final judgment that sums up the whole course of the journey. Although the Temple is not singled out in vv 41-44, Jesus immediately enters the Temple in verse 45, declaring that *"my house* will be a house of prayer, but you have made it a lair of robbers." That is to say, Jesus' journey to Jerusalem culminates in the Temple to lay claim to the *true worship of God*. But it is precisely here, in the atmosphere of the "plundering" of the worship, that the opposition which leads irreversibly to Jesus' death sets in without delay. At once Luke, in an overview (19:47-48) and several episodes (20:1-21:4), describes the authority of the teacher of Israel which provokes a coalition of the people's leaders to seek his death. And Luke will conclude this Jerusalem section with Jesus in the Temple prophesying the destruction and exile of the nation—in strokes reminiscent of 587 BCE[62]—while

---

[61] See nn. 56, 31.

[62] See C. H. Dodd, "The Fall of Jerusalem and the 'Abomination of Desolation,'" *JRS* 37 (1947) 47-54; independently, B. Reicke, "Synoptic Prophecies of the Destruction of Jerusalem," *Studies in New Testament and Early Christian Literature. Essays in Honor of Allen P. Wikgren* (ed. D. E. Aune; Leiden: Brill, 1972) 121-34.

pointing to the Temple as the omega point of this destruction: "Not one stone upon another shall be left" (21:6 → 19:44 → 19:40). Both the fate of the prophet like Moses and the nation are sealed in Jesus' journey to the Temple.

Peter and the Death of Jesus in the Early Acts Community

What again must seem singularly strange is the sudden twist Luke's story takes in chap. 22. It is Judas, one of "the twelve" (22:3), who makes the decisive move to "deliver" Jesus over to the scribes and chief priests—those just portrayed as the plotters of Jesus' demise. But what Jesus at the base of the mountain had proleptically perceived about a "crooked generation" and prophetically predicted about "the hands of men" (9:44) has come to pass. Even more ironic is the role Peter plays in the final consolidation of "this generation" to put Jesus to death:

i) At the Passover meal (22:14-38) when Jesus announces that "the hand" of the one who will "deliver him over" is with him *at table*, the disciples once again begin to argue which of them is the greatest (22:24-27 → 9:46-48). They thus not only repeat their behavior at the mountain but also mimic the leaders of this generation by *striving for rank at table* (22:24-27 → 20:46 → 14:7-11 → 11:43). In the midst of this quarreling Peter is designated the crucible for Satan's sifting that *the twelve* (ὑμᾶς 22:31) must uniquely undergo before ultimately they "eat and drink" and "judge" in the Kingdom of God. Peter's reply of readiness to go to prison and death indicates again that "he was not knowing what he was saying" (22:33—9: 33b);

ii) Peter's denial (22:54-62), following upon the *sleeping* of the disciples at the crucial moment of testing in the garden (vv 40-46), welds the incorporation of the twelve into "this generation" and preludes the monolith that will form around Pilate, "king of the Gentiles" (22:25a). After Jesus is condemned for assenting to be the "Son of God"—as the mountain voice had already proclaimed—and shuttled back to Pilate from Israel's king (23:8 → 9:9) who mocks Jesus' royal-messianic status (23:11 → 2b-3), the crowd now termed "the people" (ὁ λαός), join together with the chief priests and their "rulers"[63] to demand the death of this false

---

[63] It is not the case that the Pharisees-scribes disappear altogether once the Jerusalem ministry and passion narrative are treated. To be sure, "Pharisees"

prophet and messianic pretender (23:13-25; 24:19-21). The whole people of this generation is assembled, and it is into their hands that Pilate delivers Jesus over (παραδίδοναι, 23:25 → 48 → 21-22 → 20:20 → 18:32 → 9:44; cf. 24:7, 20). Not only has Peter's confession of Jesus' Messiahship (9:20) been twisted into its exact oposite by the whole nation, but his calling to *suffer* with Jesus on the journey to Jerusalem, which was *confirmed by the heavenly light* while he and the other disciples were *sleeping* (9:20-27 → 30-32), has also become the very antithesis for him, the disciples, and the whole people (cf. 14:25-27);

iii) As Peter was the leader of the disciples in death, so is he also in the new life of the prophet like Moses (24:19, 27). The first to see the risen *glorified* Christ, to whom *Moses* and *all* the prophets had pointed (24:26-27 → 34), it is he who leads the disciples in reconstituting the *twelve* as the authoritative witnesses to Israel of the resurrection (Acts 1:15-26). Moreover, on the day of "First Fruits" it is Peter who represents the twelve and the larger group of disciples by declaring to the gathered people of Israel from all over the world that the eschatological Spirit has been "poured out" by the exalted Jesus (Acts 2:5-36). When ca. 3000 of his audience repent and are baptized "in the name of Jesus Messiah" (vv 38, 41), they along with the disciples constitute the "first fruits" of the renewed, eschatological Israel who *worship at the Temple* and gather at the central place to witness to the unrepentant Israel (2:46; 3:1, 11; 5:20, 42; cf. Luke 24:53). Accordingly, it is once again Peter who *at the Temple* proclaims that Israel can now become heirs of the *promise to Abraham* by repenting of their killing of Jesus, the prophet like Moses (3:18-26; cf. 2:39), and who, before the Sanhedrin exclaims that "you" are the "builders" of Ps 118:22 who reject the "stone" "that has become the head of the corner" (4:11, 5-12).

---

does not occur after 19:39; but the plot to put an end to Jesus' public influence as it is conceived already in 6:7 (climax of 5:17-6:6) and developed through the Pharisees-scribes' (lawyers') resistance in the journey section (11:37-54; 12:1; 13:31-33; 14:1-24; 15:1-32; 16:14-31; 19:39-40) is continued by the "scribes" (now functionaries instead of religious party) of the Sanhedrin. The closest links are through the scribes' public reputation which in 20:45-47 is directly connected back to Jesus' accusations against the scribes at table (11:43, 46; 14-7-11; cf. 18.9-14 and 20:47b). As in 20:47 it is the Pharisees' scribes of 11:47-52 who will receive the "greater condemnation" for their detrimental influence upon the people.

Within this general orientation to what has transpired *with Israel* in the death and resurrection of Jesus, it is intriguing to see that the Deuteronomistic view, through *Peter*, informs the more specific explanation of *how* the fate of Jesus fulfills the final salvation in the overall plan of God for Israel's history:

Tenet A. Israel has remained a "crooked generation" (Acts 2:40—Luke 9:41; cf. Deut 32:5) that has out of "ignorance" (3:17) and "wickedness" (3:26b) "denied" and "killed" the "Righteous One" (3:13-14). "Ignorance" and "wickedness" are classic descriptions of culpable disobedience in deuteronomic language.[64] And that "ignorance" for Peter does not relieve Israel of its responsibility for the killing of Messiah is clear by the juxtaposition of the *demand* for repentance (3:17-19—οὖν!). One must be "rescued" from this "evil" lot (2:40b);

Tenet B. God "sent" (ἀποστέλλω) his servant[65] Jesus to Israel first, after having raised him up (ἀναστήσας, 3:26a). This "raising up" most likely refers to Jesus' earthly mission or sending, that is, to the "raising up" of the prophet in his calling, as in verse 22.[66] In any case, qua the Deuteronomistic conception, a prophet is *sent* to *proclaim* the will of God "in order to bless you in turning every one of you from your wickedness" (v 26b). To procure the blessing of the law or will of the Lord in the midst of perverse disobedience is the very raison d'être of the prophets' calling.[67] But even more significantly, Jesus has already been sent to do this to fulfill Moses' *prophecy* of the "prophet . . . like me (v 22). You shall hearken to him in whatever he tells you" (v 22b). Furthermore, this sending brings to fruition the prophecies of *all the prophets*. Thus we find again what we have discovered in Stephen's speech, the Transfiguration, and the journey. As a prophet, Jesus is sent to Israel with the living oracles of the prophet like Moses whose coming consummates all the prophets;

---

[64] E.g., Deut 4:25; 9:18; 27; 13:5, 11; 15:9; 17:13; 18:20, 22; 19:16; 25:2; 32:28; cf. 4:6; 9:4-5; 11:2; see also Moessner, "Prophet Like Moses," 584.

[65] Analysis of the use of *pais* and Servant of Isaiah christological notions, which function in Luke-Acts to express the *positive* conception of the mission to Gentiles (e.g., Luke 2:32; Acts 13:47; 26:23), lies outside the present scope, and their relationship to the Deuteronomistic rejected prophets must be the subject of a future study.

[66] See Moessner, "Wilderness Generation," 338-39.

[67] E.g., Neh 9:26, 29-30.

Tenet C. "To be rescued" from the "froward generation" of Israel for Peter's hearers means disentanglement through *repentance/turning* from the objective guilt or "wickedness" of killing Israel's Christ (vv 19, 26b; 2:38a). We do not find the charge that they have killed all the prophets, as in Stephen's speech and Jesus' journey; the tone is considerably less invective here. Nevertheless, we do find the assertion that the stubbornness (*Tenet A*) which led to Jesus' death is the fulfillment of what *all* the prophets (3:18) had forecast, viz that "God's *Christ* must suffer" (3:18—Luke 18:31-33; 9:20-22; cf. 24:26-27; Acts 7:37, 52). From verse 24 it is certain that this fulfillment includes the suffering that the Messiah must undergo precisely as the prophet like Moses (v 22). Consequently, what in fact has taken place in Jerusalem (v 14) fulfills what Moses and Elijah in glory on the mountain had prophesied (Luke 9:31) and what Stephen will later recount (Acts 7:37, 52);

Tenet D. The pronouncement of judgment upon Israel as a whole is lacking in the early speeches of Peter in the Acts as well as in Stephen's speech. With thousands responding to the cry for repentance, clearly the eschatological Israel is being formed out of the unrepenting Israel. Peter thus quotes Deut 18:19 (enriched by Lev 23:29) to declare that those individuals who fail to hearken to the voice of the prophet like Moses will be destroyed *from the people.* Gone is Jesus' blanket condemnation and prophecy of doom for the nation as a whole. "Removal of sin" (3:19) and "turning away from wickedness" (v 26), rather, are the signs of these eschatological times (v 24).

We can draw together our results for the *Jesus—Peter parallels* that we have discovered are grounded in the Deuteronomistic view: *1.* Peter, representing the twelve tribes of the eschatological Israel, is the authoritative witness of the *glory of God* in Jesus, the prophet like Moses, on the Exodus journey from the mountain in Galilee to his raising up in glory in the ascension in Jerusalm (Acts 3:13; Luke 24:26, 34). He not only witnesses the calling in great light of Jesus as the prophet like Moses and the disciples' calling to obey him, he also thunders again the heavenly voice in Jerusalem: "hearken to him"; *2.* Peter journeys with Jesus on the Exodus to the Temple and becomes the leader of the renewed eschatological Israel that makes the central place of all Israel the center of their worship. And it is there that he declares that the promise to Abraham has been fulfilled in the prophet like Moses whom God sent to "his

brethren'' and raised up and glorified from the dead; 3. Peter participates fully in the *crooked* generation that, like their fathers,
denied the Righteous One. Yet at the Temple he proclaims that
their killing of the prophet like Moses fulfills all the prophets in
finally breaking up Israel's monolith of disobedience to God's
voice. Thousands of Israel respond to his plea for repentance.

Although Peter becomes one with the prophet like Moses in the
suffering and rejection inflicted by the *leaders* of the unrepentant
Israel (Acts 4:5-31; 5:17-41, esp. v 26; 12:1-17), his later career of
suffering remains outside of Luke's greater interest to trace the prophetic career of Paul, to which we now turn.

IV

We have already met the character who occupies roughly one-
quarter of Luke's overall story material at Acts 8:1 where he was
''consenting'' to Stephen's death along with the other ''witnesses''
(7:58). After the journeys to Samaria and Gaza (8:4-40) spawned
by Stephen's stoning, we meet ''Saul'' again in 9:1 where Luke
picks up the thread of his persecution of the church from 8:3 and
weaves together Paul's ''conversion'' on the Damascus road
(9:1-19). Before analyzing Paul's last journey to Jerusalem we shall
see how his calling, expanded by the parallel accounts in 22:6-21;
26:12-23, develops out of the larger christological-historical pattern
that undergirds Luke's narrative.

The Calling

The immediate contexts of all three accounts stress the paramount position of Saul in opposing *to the death* the disciples of ''the
Way,'' those bound to the ''name of Jesus of Nazareth.'' Not only
that, but Jerusalem had continually been the center for this
persecution, even though Saul journeyed to foreign cities under the
commission of the guardians of the *Temple* worship, the chief priests
(9:2, 14; 26:12), and the leaders of the people, the ''whole council
of elders'' (22:5):

1. Like the mountain transfiguration, a great light from heaven
''flashes'' and a voice from heaven sends the overwhelmed Paul on
a journey mission (9:3-6; cf. 22:13-15). Parallel to the curious
detail, that on the mountain the ''trembling trio'' actually *see* Jesus
in flashing light before *hearing* the heavenly voice, is the twofold insistence that Paul was both to *see* and *hear* ''Jesus,'' the ''Righteous
One'' (22:7, 14-15; 26:13-14, 16; cf. 9:7, 27—Luke 9:32,

35-36)—now with the difference that the voice is that of the "Lord" Jesus himself. In short, whereas Peter's (the twelve's) and Stephen's callings are directly confirmed by the heavenly light of the glorified Jesus, Paul's calling is *initiated* from the glory of that light (22:11);

2. Like the mountain revelation, so Paul is sent on a journey mission which eventually will take a decisive turn in the Temple as Paul journeys to Jerusalem for the purpose of worshiping God (20:16; 24:11, 17-18). Now, however, his calling to all peoples—Israel and the nations alike—becomes a sending *away* from Jerusalem, and more particularly, *from the Temple*, which is confirmed by a vision of the "Lord" Jesus in that very sanctuary (22:17-21). Once again the fate of Paul like Jesus and Stephen will be settled at the central place!;

3. Like the mountain theophany and as in Stephen's vision, Paul's calling is one to suffering rejection by his own people (9:16 δεῖ. . .παθεῖν; 22:18, 21; 26:17). What distinguishes this opposition as the dynamic pivot of his calling in Paul's case is the threefold insistence that his persecution of the Christian Way was in truth the persecution of Jesus—the Righteous One—himself (9:1-2, 4-5, 13-14; 22:4-5, 7-8; 26:9-11, 14-15). This solidarity in suffering is further enhanced by the way Luke has tied Stephen's death to Paul's *calling*: i) Paul is not merely an active witness in Stephen's "murder" (cf. 9:1), he himself becomes the representative *par excellence* of the 'stiff-necked" generation of Stephen's audience by inflaming the ensuing efforts to extinguish the Christian movement (22:4-5; 26:9-11). After his "about face" Paul becomes a victim of his own ravages, first in Damascus (9:23-25), and then in Jerusalem where the non-believing *Hellenists* try to kill him (9:29; cf. 6:1, 8-14); ii) In what Luke undoubtedly intends as a recounting of this Jerusalem visit, Paul, before the lynching crowds at his last Jerusalem visit, relates his calling in the Temple when he had once again seen the "Righteous One"[68] and had confessed that the fury of the Jews against him was directly related to his own shedding of Stephen's "blood" (22:17-21). Through the heavenly vision of all that 'he had seen and heard" of the suffering Righteous One, Paul becomes one with Jesus and Stephen in his mission of suffering (22:14-15, 18, 21; 26:16; cf. 9:27).

---

[68] The *auton* in 22:18 has *ton dikaion* in verse 14 as its antecedent.

The Final Journey to Jerusalem

After relating Herod's threat on Peter's life during the *Passover* (12:1-19) and then Herod's own death (vv 20-24), Luke presents in 12:25-15:35 and 15:36-19:20 two major journey missions of Paul and his cohorts: first from Antioch (cf. 11:25-26, 30) to Cyprus and south-central Asia Minor back to Antioch and on to *Jerusalem* for the apostolic assembly; and then from Antioch through Asia Minor, Macedonia, Achaia, and return via *Jerusalem* to Antioch followed by a return to Asia Minor and a long stay in Ephesus. In 19:21-28:31 we encounter the longest journey section[69] and the one in which a number of extraordinary parallels to Jesus' passion journey have long been noted.[70] We shall discuss only those constitutive of the christological-historical pattern:

(i) Only Paul's third and final journey, as in Jesus' third[71] and final journey to Jerusalem, is prefaced by "a resolve in the Spirit" (19:21)/"resolute determination" (Luke 9:51), to reach Jerusalem, before passing on to Rome. Again Luke is signalling that the divine order (δεῖ, 19:21b) of salvation[72] is building to a new climax;

(ii) This divinely-directed journey follows a period which initiates a fulfillment of time. As in Luke 9:51, when the days of Jesus' itinerant ministry within Galilee come to a close the days of his "taking up" in Jerusalem are *already* being "filled to completion" (συμπληρόω), so in Acts 19:21 as Paul's mission in the eastern Mediterranean has become "fulfilled" (πληρόω) he must press forward to Jerusalem and Rome;

(iii) As in Jesus' journey, so in Paul's a foreboding rejection serves as the frontispiece (Acts 19:23-41—Luke 9:52-56). This scene is followed by intermittent predictions along the journey of suffering and death awaiting Jesus/Paul in Jerusalem (Acts

---

[69] For this division of the journey sections, see e.g., F. V. Filson ("The Journey Motif in Luke-Acts," *Apostolic History and the Gospel* [see n. 9] 68-77).

[70] See e.g., Rackham, *Acts*, xlvii and *passim*; M. D. Goulder, *Type and History in Acts* (London: SPCK, 1964) 34-51, 60-61; cf. Radl's (*Paulus*, 44-59) survey; Mattill, "Schneckenburger," 114-22; *idem*, "The Jesus-Paul Parallels and the Purpose of Luke-Acts: H. H. Evans Reconsidered," *NovT* 17 (1975) 15-46; D. P. Moessner, "Paul and the Pattern of the Prophet like Moses in Acts," *Society of Biblical Literature 1983 Seminar Papers* (Chico: Scholars, 1983) 203-12.

[71] Luke 2:22-28 and 2:41-51; 4:9-12 is not presented as a *journey* account.

[72] See E. Fascher, "Theologische Beobachtungen zu δεῖ," *Neutestamentliche Studien für Rudolf Bultmann* (see n. 46) 228-54.

20:22-25; 21:4, 10-14; cf. 20:38; 23:11; 27:10—Luke 12:49-50; 13:31-35; 17:25; 18:31-34);

(iv) As in Jesus' journey, so in Paul's the sense of impending doom in Jerusalem stems from a gathering storm as the journey advances. Already the riot in Ephesus is no isolated incident but a programmatic development within a skein of rejection scenes uncoiling to an explosion in Jerusalem. As the second journey begins (15:36), John Mark—who had dropped out "of the work" (15:38) at Pamphylia (13:13) before the first series of persecutions mostly from "Jews" were inflicted (13:45, 50-51; 14:2, 5-6, 19-20) and had thus not learned firsthand that "we *must* (δεῖ) enter the Kingdom of God *through many tribulations*" (14:22b)—is excluded by Paul for further participation in his calling (9:16; 22:18; 21, 26:17). Paul then circumcises Timothy for the mission "because of the Jews in those places!" who knew "his father *was a Greek*" (16:1-4). Strangely forbidden to preach in *Asia* (16:6), Paul and companions then confront a new series of persecutions largely again by unrepenting countrymen in Macedonia and Achaia (17:5-9, 13-15; 18:6, 9-10, 12-17) who as a whole[73] violently object to Paul's contention that Jesus is the Messiah and precisely so as one who "had to suffer" (τὸν χριστὸν ἔδει παθεῖν, 17:2-3 → 10b-11 → 18:4-5). Now on his return to Jerusalem Paul does stop at Asia where he argues with Jews in Ephesus who, however, encourage him to stay. But again Paul mysteriously leaves Ephesus, promising to return only "if God wills" (18:21 → 16:6). After returning through Galatia and Phrygia from Antioch,[74] Paul eventually arrives again at Ephsus but only after Apollos goes from Ephesus to *Corinth* and there "powerfully confutes the Jews" in demonstrating that "Jesus is the Christ" (18:28). As Paul resumes his arguing in the synagogue he does meet some "hardening" and "reviling" (19:9);[75] but by the end of his stay the opposition of the craftsmen associated with the Artemis temple has been so overwhelming against the "Way" and

---

[73] Beroea (17:10-12) is the only exception; otherwise only "some" Jews repent in the other cities to add to the core or remnant of the repenting eschatological Israel (17:4; 18:4).

[74] This retracing of the cities already visited is the consistent practice of Paul in Acts (14:21; 15:36, 41; 16:1, 4; 18:23); therefore 18:21 stands out all the more in creating narrative *dissonance*.

[75] Notice how Paul is *identified* with Jesus in the *opposition* by the seven sons of a Jewish high priest (19:13-17); the coming opposition to Paul in the Temple by the high priest (22:30-23:5) is adumbrated.

even against Jews that to all appearances Jewish opposition has paled to insignificance (vv 23-41). All the stranger, then, that Luke immediately follows with "a plot by the Jews" in Greece (20:3) which forces Paul to return by land to Asia Minor and then has Paul "sail past" Ephesus "so that he might not have to spend time in Asia" while at the same time "he was hastening . . . to be in Jerusalem on the day of Pentecost" (20:16).

The shroud of mystery covering Ephesus and Asia is finally pierced in the final legs toward Jerusalem:

a. *Ephesian Elders at Miletus*: 20:17-38, *Vv 18-20*: The *whole period in Asia* has been a patient endurance of *persecution* by "plots of the Jews"; *Vv 22-25*: Paul remains resolutely determined to "complete" (τελειόω) the course given to him by the Lord Jesus by *going to Jerusalem* where "imprisonment," "afflictions," and probable death have been divinely impressed upon him; *Vv 26-31*: Paul links his fate in *Jerusalem* to the fierce opposition that he has encountered in *Asia* and even to "men" from "the flock" who "will arise" and propound "twisted"/"perverted" things (διεστραμμένα, 20:30; cf. Luke 9:41!) after his departure (vv 29-30). But Paul stands apart from the "blood of all" that will be required from a faithless stance to "the whole will of God" that he has dared to preach and that God has secured "through the blood of his own,"[76] viz. through the suffering and death of the Christ (cf. v 21b).[77] As Jesus earlier had linked his arrival in Jerusalem to the *blood* required of the generation that continues to reject God's prophets, and as Paul at his calling had linked his own journey missions to the shedding of Stephen's *blood*, so now Paul joins his own persecution and death to his arrival in Jerusalem on account of the "twisted folk" of "the Jews" in rejecting his mission. He has just summarized his calling

---

[76] The language of "own" (*idios*, v 28b) reflects the filial character of the heavenly message at the baptism (Luke 3:22b "*my* beloved Son) and Transfiguration (9:35b "*my* Chosen Son"). See e.g., F. F. Bruce, *Commentary on the Book of the Acts* (NICNT; Grand Rapids: Eerdmans, 1954) 416 n. 59 (*idios* equivalent to *yachid*, "only," as translated by *agapetos*, *eklektos*, or *monogenes*).

[77] Whether or not "Christ" is the more original reading in verse 21b, the larger context of the argument with the Jews in Macedonia and Achaia supports the conclusion that the fierce opposition in Ephesus from the "plots of the Jews" (20:19-20a, 23-25, 26-31) stems from the burning contention that the "Christ" had to suffer and that Jesus is the Christ (see above); furthermore, verse 21b is speaking about "faith" and not the suffering or death of Jesus as the content of preaching.

to them, i.e. to Jews and Greeks, as a messenger of *repentance* (*Tenet B*), including the "typical" tasks of "teaching" and "exhortation" of the prophet. Moreover, his pronouncement of judgment on the "blood guilt" of the Asian audience reverberates this same pronouncement against the Jews in Corinth who had reviled him for "bearing witness. . . that the Christ was Jesus" (18:4-6 → 17:2-5). Before the Ephesian elders, then, *Tenets B* and *D*[78] are explicit, while *Tenets A* and *C* set the tone of the whole farewell address. A monolith of rejection is moving into place! (20:38);

b. *Tyre and Caesarea*: 21:4, 8-14. In "every city" (20:23) the Holy Spirit is "bearing witness that imprisonment and afflictions await" Paul. But though the "brethren," who prophesy "through the Spirit," try to dissuade him, he remains "bound by" or "in the Spirit" (20:22; cf. 19:21) to do the "will of the Lord" (21:14b) and thus remains ready "to be imprisoned and to die in Jerusalem" (21:13; cf. Luke 22:33!). Like Jesus "the Jews will bind the man ... and deliver him over into the hands of the Gentiles" (21:11—Luke 18:32);

c. *Paul's Arrival in Jerusalem*: 21:15-36. Paul soon learns that he is known among the "myriads" of believing Jews in Jerusalem as one who teaches *all the Jews* in the *Diaspora* to "forsake Moses" (v 21). With his journey missions once again linked directly to his fate in Jerusalem, it hardly comes as a surprise when we read that Jews *from Asia* are the ones who lay their hands on Paul and place him at the mercy of "the crowd" of "Israel" and of "the whole city and the people" (λαός) who demand his death (vv 27-28; cf. 24:19b-20; 25:24). Nor is it coincidental that they accuse Paul of defiling the worship of the Temple by having taken Trophimus, the *Ephesian* and a "*Greek*," into its environs. The riot over the temple of Artemis has now culminated in the uproar over "this holy place" (v 28b).

To sum up, as was true for Jesus, so also for Paul "that it cannot be that a prophet should perish away from Jerusalem" (Luke 13:33b; cf. Acts 21:31a);

(v) Accordingly, it is also the case that as with Jesus and Stephen the Temple forms the fulcrum of hostility against those "prophets and apostles sent to" her (Luke 13:34a). For it is Paul's appearance in the Temple which foments the convulsion leading to the charge

---

[78] See nn. 31, 55.

of blasphemy and despoiling the worship of that place (24:6). Later in his defense before Felix Paul will declare that he journeyed to Jerusalem in order to worship (24:11), and as a loyal Israelite he went to the central place during the Feast of First Fruits to bring alms and offerings for his nation (24:17; cf. 20:16, Deut 16:9-12). And more significantly, before Festus and Herod Agrippa Paul will aver that he is on trial "for hope in the *promise* . . . to the fathers" which has given meaning and purpose to the whole Temple cultus and is fulfilled in the raising up of one from the dead (26:6-8). But instead of recounting the events of Jesus' death and resurrection, Paul launches into an account of his own calling to suffer in which he sums up his whole career as one of *proclaiming repentance* to both Jews and Gentiles. Indeed it is because of this message of repentance that "the Jews seized me in the Temple and tried to kill me" (26:21). But, finishes Paul, he is only doing what *"Moses* and *all the prophets* said would come to pass," viz. "that the *Christ must suffer* and, being the first to rise from the dead, he [Christ] would proclaim light both to the people and to the Gentiles" (26:22b-23).[79] As with Stephen, Paul's solidarity with the one who journeyed to Jerusalem to die to fulfill Moses and all the prophets is complete (cf. Acts 23:11);

(vi) Thus it is also true that as in Jesus' arrest and trial, so in Paul's, representatives of the *whole* nation—the Sanhedrin, the people (λαός), and Herod, "king" of the Jews—along with their Roman governor and his authorities collaborate to decide his fate (Acts 21:30-32, 36, 39-40; 22:30; 23:1-5, 12-22; 24:1-9; 25:1-12—Luke 22:66-23:25; cf. Acts 4:27). And as with Jesus, so with Paul the people and their chief priests and elders demand his death, while the Roman governor three times pronounces his innocence (Acts 21:27-31, 34-36, 40-22:1, 22, 30-23:5, 12-15, 29; 25:2, 15, 18-20, 24-25, 30-31; 28:17-19—Luke 23:1-25);

(vii) But again it is the charges against Paul which encapsulate the christological-historical pattern of the rejection of the prophet like Moses and of all the prophets. He is accused of: (a) Teaching all the Jews of the Diaspora against "Moses," sc. against circumcision and the "customs" (Acts 21:21; cf. 6:14; 26:3; 28:17), and summarized as not "observing the law" in 21:24; (b) Teaching against "the people and the law and this place" and of defiling the

---

[79] See n. 65.

Temple with Greeks (21:28; cf. 24:6); (c) Creating agitation
"among all the Jews in the world" and of being a leader of the
"sect of the Nazoreans" (24:5; cf. 6:14; Paul and the "Nazorean,"
22:8; 26:9); (d) "Offending against" "the law of the Jews, the
Temple, and Caesar" (25:8); (e) "Actions against the people and
the customs of our fathers" (28:17). These charges can be grouped
together as against the law (Moses), the people (nation), and the
Temple, as a member of the "Nazoreans"—the very same accusations against Stephen—and in addition, against Caesar. Now in
Jesus' arrest and trial he also is charged with "agitating the
people" (Luke 23:5), "perverting" them with false teaching (23:2,
5, 14), and resisting allegiance to Caesar (23:2). "Law,"
"people," "Caesar" are precisely the charges against Jesus,
especially as they reached a fever pitch in Jesus' teaching in the
Temple (19:47-20:47);

(viii) Finally, though Paul unlike Stephen is not killed by the end
of Acts, Paul's journey to Rome does fulfill the journeys to "the
end of the earth" begun by the stiff-necked rejection of the prophet
like Moses and of Stephen in Jerusalem and commanded by the
"raised up" prophet like Moses as a fulfillment "that the Christ
must suffer and on the third day rise from the dead and that repentance and forgiveness of sins should be preached in his name to all
nations, beginning from Jerusalem" (Luke 24:46-47; cf. Acts 1:8).
This is the reason Paul utters Isa 6:9-10 exactly when and where he
does. For his preaching of repentance in the name of the risen
Christ who had to suffer at the hands of his own people has pro-
gressed to all nations *through* the unrelenting history of rejection of
God's messengers to Israel (*Tenets A & C*): "Go *to this people* and
say, 'You shall indeed hear but never understand . . . . For this
people's heart has grown fat, they have become hard of hearing . . .
lest they should *hearken* . . . and *turn* for me to heal them" (Acts
28:26-27). Paul, the great prophetic pleader of repentance to Israel
(*Tenet B*), in nearly every city of his journeying had to turn to the
Gentiles, "for they will hearken" (28:29b). Now in Rome and thus
from there to the "end of the earth" (Isa 49:6; Acts 1:8; Luke 2:32)
Paul sounds again the "your fathers" (28:25b) of Stephen (7:51-52)
and Jesus (Luke 11:47-48). As the monolith had begun to con-
solidate against Jesus on the Exodus journey to Jerusalem, provok-
ing the pronouncements of *Tenet D*, so along Paul's journeys which
culminated in the monolith of rejection in Jerusalem Paul has also

uttered *Tenet D* (Acts 13:40-41, cf. vv 46-47; 18:6, cf. 20:26).[80] But it is precisely through this christological-historical pattern of the Deuteronomistic rejection of the prophet like Moses and his prophet-apostles that the Exodus salvation, the "glory of Israel," is extended as "light to the Gentiles" in "the presence of all peoples" (Luke 2:31-32).[81]

We can now draw together our conclusions with a schematic profile of the three constitutive elements of the pattern of the prophet like Moses and his rejected prophets:

1. The calling to a journey sending to Israel is revealed by the voice of the Lord in "glorious" light.

Jesus	(Peter)/Moses/Stephen	Paul
(Luke 9:29-35)	(Acts 7:30-32)	(Acts 9:3-15; 22:6-15; 26:13-18)

> *Peter's* (Israel's) calling to journey with Jesus is confirmed in the Transfiguration and echoed to the gathered Israel in Jerusalem (Acts 3:22, 26).
> The journey missions from *Stephen's* witness are confirmed by the heavenly light (Acts 7:55-56).

2. The journey is the consummation of Moses' sending on the Exodus deliverance to the central place, the Temple, in Jerusalem for the true worship of God.

Jesus	(Peter)/Moses/Stephen	Paul
(Luke 9:31, 51-19:46)	(Acts 7:7, 17, 35-47, 52b)	(Acts 11:19-30; 13:2-19:20, 21-28:31)

> *Peter* (the twelve) is the authoritative witness of this journey from the mountain in Galilee to the fulfillment of the eschatological Israel at the central place in Jerusalem (Luke 9:32, 35; Acts 3:22-26).
> *Stephen's* witness leads (Acts 8:1-4; 11:19-20) to *Paul's* journeys which extend the Exodus salvation to the Gentiles from the Temple (Acts 9:15; 22:15-21; 26:17b-18) and which eventually culminate decisively at the central place of all Israel (19:21-28: 31).

3. The journey sending to the central place is a calling to suffering and rejection from the whole people of Israel. But through the persecution and even death of the prophets, Israel's unrelenting history of stubborn resistance is fulfilled precisely as it is broken in the Israel that repents and extends its salvation to the Gentiles, as foretold by Moses and all the prophets.

---

[80] See nn. 31, 55.
[81] See n. 65.

Jesus	→	(Peter)/Moses/Stephen	→	Paul
Luke 9:31-50,		(Acts 7:23-43,		(Acts 9:15-30;
51-19:46)		51-53)		22:14-21; 26:16-23)

Jesus is the "Christ" as the suffering prophet like Moses who is "raised up" from his violent death to bring the new life ("glory") of the Exodus salvation to Israel and the nations (Luke 24:26, 45-47; Acts 26:22-23).

Peter (repenting Israel) suffers rejection by the leaders of the nation before the monolithic rejection of the salvation of the prophet like Moses forms once again (Acts 4:5-31; 5:17-41; 12:1-17).

Stephen suffers rejection and violent death as a transition figure between the opposition of the leaders and the consolidating monolith of the people as a whole (Acts 7:54-8:4).

Paul suffers rejection of the people as a whole as the "glory of Israel" is extended to "all peoples" (Acts 19:21-28:31; Luke 2:31-32).

PREPARATION FOR PASSOVER (LUKE 22:7-13): A QUESTION OF REDACTIONAL TECHNIQUE

by

JOEL B. GREEN

Berkeley, California

1. *Introduction*

Gerhard Schneider's work on Luke 22:54-71, published in 1969, did much to identify a method suitable for coming to terms with the complex source- and redaction-critical issues related to the study of the Lukan passion narrative.[1] This was due primarily to Schneider's refusal to be drawn into quick decisions on critical questions; instead, he adopted a remarkable broad approach, combining minute literary-critical analysis with the larger questions of style, form, and theology. If Schneider did not at that time fully see the potential of treating Luke-Acts as a literary and theological unity and if he perhaps too readily equated redactional activity with literary creativity, his work nonetheless stands as an important landmark for methodological integration in studies of the Lukan passion story.

Unfortunately, subsequent study of the Lukan passion account has fallen short of the standard set by Schneider. For example, Vincent Taylor's work on *The Passion Narrative of St. Luke* (1972) focused too heavily on simple word statistics (i.e. on the mere counting of words, without regard for source-critical questions) and failed to reach the level of methodological comprehensiveness demonstrated by Schneider.[2] Joachim Jeremias's *Die Sprache des Lukasevangeliums* (1980) was more advanced linguistically, but, like Taylor, Jeremias

---

[1] Gerhard Schneider, *Verleugnung, Verspottung und Verhör Jesu nach Lukas 22, 54-71: Studien zur lukanischen Darstellung der Passion* (München: Kösel, 1969). See also his more recent essay on "The Political Charge against Jesus (Luke 23:2)," in *Jesus and the Politics of His Day*, ed. Ernst Bammel and C. F. D. Moule (Cambridge: Cambridge University, 1984) 403-414.

[2] Vincent Taylor, *The Passion Narrative of St. Luke: A Critical and Historical Investigation* (Cambridge: Cambridge University, 1972).

too quickly assumed that if Luke made use of a *Sonderquelle* in constructing his passion story its characteristic vocabulary would have been identical to that of L, as reconstructed from Luke's earlier chapters.[3] In other words, he did not allow for the possibility of an independent, narrative, passion source. On the other hand, Jeremias was sensitive to linguistic evidence from the Acts of the Apostles—the lack of which had a negative impact on aspects of David Catchpole's otherwise significant investigation of Luke 22:54-71 in *The Trial of Jesus* (1971).[4] To Catchpole's credit we should add that his study is in some ways to be preferred over that of Schneider because of Catchpole's greater ability to see the larger, structural picture of the denial and trial scenes. In his study of Luke 23 in *Der Tod Jesu im Lukasevangelium* (1978), Anton Büchele demonstrated a keen eye for structure; however, in his heavy reliance on simple word statistics for his source-critical decisions, Büchele—like Taylor and the much earlier John C. Hawkins (who was followed by Joseph A. Fitzmyer)—made no allowance for influence on Luke from his sources.[5] The lack of sensitivity to Luke's total theological *programme* and linguistic preferences detracted from the effectiveness of the recent essay by Frank J. Matera on Luke's crucifixion narrative (1985). Moreover, like Schneider, Matera too easily equated Lukan "redaction" and Lukan "creation."[6]

Other studies might be noted, but perhaps mention of one further, recent, full-scale investigation of the Lukan passion account will suffice to demonstrate the unenviable state of affairs we are in with respect to redactional work on Luke 22-23. In 1985 Jerome Neyrey authored *The Passion according to Luke: A Redaction Study of Luke's Soteriology*.[7] In this investigation Neyrey hoped to move the

[3] Joachim Jeremias, *Die Sprache des Lukasevangeliums: Redaktion und Tradition im Nicht-Markusstoff des dritten Evangeliums* (Göttingen: Vandenhoeck & Ruprecht, 1980).

[4] David R. Catchpole, *The Trial of Jesus: A Study in the Gospels and Jewish Historiography from 1770 to the Present Day* (Leiden: E. J. Brill, 1971) 153-220.

[5] Anton Büchelle, *Der Tod Jesu im Lukasevangelium: Eine redaktions-geschichtliche Untersuchung zu Lk 23* (Frankfurt am Main, 1978); John C. Hawkins, *Horae Synopticae: Contributions to the Study of the Synoptic Problem* (Oxford: Clarendon, 1899); Joseph A. Fitzmyer, *The Gospel according to Luke*, 2 vols. (Garden City, New York: Doubleday, 1981/85) 1:109-113.

[6] Frank J. Matera, "The Death of Jesus according to Luke: A Question of Sources," *CBQ* 47 (1985) 469-485.

[7] Jerome Neyrey, *The Passion according to Luke: A Redaction Study of Luke's Soteriology* (New York/Mahwah: Paulist, 1985)—on which see review in *JBL* (forthcoming). See his earlier articles: "The Absence of Jesus' Emotions—the Lukan

inquiry beyond the traditional questions of source criticism and historicity, focusing instead on redaction-critical issues. Despite some very helpful insights, particularly with respect to the promise of taking seriously the unity of the Third Gospel and the Book of Acts, it cannot be said that Neyrey succeeded in his purpose. The main problem, however, is that the state of the discussion is such that we are not yet ready to be moved beyond "traditional questions", for we have yet to achieve anything even approaching a consensus on the source-critical issue. This is demonstrated by Neyrey himself, for he constantly bases his interpretation of Luke on source-critical assumptions, with hardly an attempt at an adequate defense, and this severely undermines the redaction-critical case he wants to make.

Perhaps the most significant issue in the study of the Lukan passion narrative, and more broadly in the study of the Lukan redactional technique, has received surprisingly little explicit attention in the studies we have noted: How free a redactor is Luke?[8] Since the publication of Hans Conzelmann's groundbreaking study of the theology of Luke[9] it has largely been accepted that Luke is a self-conscious theologian.[10] To merely take this as a sweeping, guiding principle when studying the passion story, however, is to beg many questions—the most important being, To what extent is "Luke's theology" the theology of his sources? How freely did he redact his sources? To what degree did he feel bound to the themes and emphases of his sources? Apart from an essay treating this question within the context of the Lukan form of the parable of the sower by I. Howard Marshall (1969),[11] questions of this nature have largely

---

Redaction of Lk. 22, 39-46," *Bib* 61 (1980) 153-171; "Jesus' Address to the Women of Jerusalem (Lk. 23.27-31)—A Prophetic Judgement Oracle," *NTS* 29 (1983) 74-86.

[8] The identity of the author of Luke-Acts is disputed. The use of "Luke" in this essay is a matter of expediency, for our argument does not depend on the question of authorship.

[9] Hans Conzelmann, *The Theology of St. Luke* (London: Faber & Faber, 1960; reprint ed., London: SCM, 1982).

[10] Even those who take issue with Conzelmann's interpretation and approach would grant Luke this status—e.g. the earlier responses to Conzelmann by Helmut Flender, *St. Luke: Theologian of Redemptive History* (London: S.P.C.K., 1967); and I. Howard Marshall, *Luke: Historian and Theologian* (Grand Rapids, Michigan: Zondervan, 1971).

[11] I. Howard Marshall, "Tradition and Theology in Luke (Luke 8:5-15)," *TynB* 20 (1969) 56-75.

gone unasked. In this context it is noteworthy that Marshall concluded that Luke exercised a "fair degree" of freedom in reproducing his source—but that the theological contours of the Lukan redaction were to be found already in Luke's Markan source. Even Luke's theology of salvation, which is at center stage in this parable in the Third Gospel, fits into this framework:

... Luke's theology is one that is based on his sources, and he certainly cannot be accused of altering the basic content of the tradition which he received. Lucan interpretation is there but it is less in extent than it is often thought to be.[12]

What of the Lukan redaction of the passion narrative? Must we dismiss from the outset the possiblity that Luke was guided by a concern for fidelity to his sources and not always by some ulterior theological motive? Must we attribute every change from Mark's account to Luke's to some theological agenda rather than to the use of additional sources?[13] Within the context of the larger discussion regarding the possiblity of a pre-canonical passion source, we propose to set forth a test case for determining the extent to which Luke is willing to redact his sources. This we will do by focusing on one pericope—namely, Luke 22:7-13, the story of the preparation of the Passover. The rationale for this choice is the general unanimity regarding the source question: most agree that Luke's version of this narrative was based solely on its counterpart in the Second Gospel.[14] That is, almost no one holding to Markan priority would suggest that in these verses we have interference from a non-Markan narrative source on the Lukan redaction.[15] It is legitimate, then, to focus on this text, inquiring into the extent of Luke's redactional activity in the context of the passion account.

---

[12] Marshall, "Tradition and Theology," 74; cf. pp. 73-75.

[13] Reginald H. Fuller raises this very issue in a more general way in "Luke and Theologia Crucis," in Sin, Salvation, and the Spirit: Commemorating the Fiftieth Year of The Liturgical Press, ed. Daniel Durken (Collegeville, Minnesota: Liturgical, 1979) 215-216.

[14] So Rudolf Bultmann, The History of the Synoptic Tradition, rev. ed. (New York: Harper & Row, 1963) 279; Taylor, Passion, 44-46; Heinz Schürmann, Der Paschamahlbericht (Münster: Aschendorff, 1953) 75-104; I. Howard Marshall, The Gospel of Luke: A Commentary on the Greek Text (Grand Rapids, Michigan: Wm. B. Eerdmans, 1978) 789-792; Gerhard Schneider, Das Evangelium nach Lukas, 2 vols. (Gütersloh: Gerd Mohn, 1977) 2:441-443; Jeremias, Sprache 285; Fitzmyer, Luke, 2:1376-1384.

[15] Among those who hold to the two-document hypothesis, the sole exception to this uniform opinion appears to be Étienne Trocmé (The Passion as Liturgy: A Study in the Origin of the Passion Narratives in the Four Gospels [London: SCM, 1983]

To be sure, as Marshall himself noted,[16] this approach is not without its risks. (1) Among these the most significant (which Marshall did not list) is the current ambivalence in some quarters regarding the long-accepted solution to the Synoptic Problem. If Luke were making use of the First Gospel rather than the Second this would naturally alter the argument of this essay. Without delving into a much longer investigation here we can do little more than assert our own hypothesis—namely, the two-source theory— and refer to our own brief survey of the problem and, more significantly, to the recent and important work of C. M. Tuckett, which goes a long way toward undermining the two-Gospel hypothesis and undergirding the two-document theory.[17]

(2) A second uncertainty inherent to our task originates in the possibility that Luke has not redacted his passion source or sources in a relatively consistent way. In this regard one thinks immediately of the earlier work of Cadbury and others,[18] which suggests Luke

---

29-30), who argues that here, too, Luke is using a non-Markan source. Most fundamentally, Trocmé's viewpoint is based on his assumption that the Gospel of Mark first circulated without a passion narrative, and that Luke made use of a copy of Mark in this form—an argument we do not find convincing (see my review in *EvQ* 56 [1984] 185-188). More particularly, he argues: (A) Matthew follows the Markan narrative more faithfully than does Luke; (B) the chronological remarks of 22:7, 14 could come from an alternative source; and (C) Luke attributes the initiative to Jesus—a feature unknown in the Matthean and Markan parallels but closely linked to the words of Jesus in 22:15. To this we may reply: (A) Our own computations have shown that on the basis of word statistics alone Luke and Matthew are comparable in their use of Mark. Even if that were not the case, however, questioning Luke's redaction on the basis of the Matthean is a highly dubious exercise. (B) There is virtually no difference in meaning in the chronological reference in 22:7 when compared with that in Mark 14:12 and, as we shall indicate below, Luke's wording is consistent with his own style. (C) Accentuating Jesus' initiative here dovetails with the more general tendency in Luke to demonstrate how Jesus was in control of the events of his passion, as we shall see.

[16] Marshall, "Tradition and Theology," 60.

[17] Joel B. Green, "The Death of Jesus: Tradition and Interpretation in the Passion Narrative," (Ph.D. dissertation, University of Aberdeen, 1985) 43-59 (forthcoming from J. C. B. Mohr [Paul Siebeck]); C. M. Tuckett, *The Revival of the Griesbach Hypothesis: An Analysis and Appraisal* (Cambridge: Cambridge University, 1983).

[18] Henry J. Cadbury, *The Style and Literary Method of Luke* (Cambridge, Massachusetts: Harvard, 1920); idem, *The Making of Luke-Acts* (London: Macmillan, 1927) esp. 213-238; F. C. Burkitt, "The Use of Mark in the Gospel according to Luke," in *The Beginnings of Christianity*, part one: *The Acts of the Apostles*, vol. two: *Prolegomena—II: Criticism*, ed. F. J. Foakes Jackson and Kirsopp Lake (London: Macmillan, 1922) 106-120; James Hope Moulton, *A Grammar of New Testament Greek*, vol. four: *Style*, by Nigel Turner (Edinburgh: T. & T. Clark, 1976) 45-63; et al.

has imposed on his composition a notable unity of style. We might anticipate from this that Luke has exercised a consistent redactional technique throughout the passion account. Nevertheless, with respect to this study, in the end we can only hope to take an initial, if programmatic, sounding of the evidence for Luke's redactional activity in the passion narrative. We cannot rule out from an analysis of this one pericope the possibility that Luke has departed significantly in his redaction of the larger passion story from the standard he sets for himself here; however, we can adduce an *a priori* lens through which to investigate other parts of Luke 22-23.

(3) A final caveat which must be registered at the prolegomenous stage concerns the possibility that Luke has been influenced in his redaction not by additional written, narrative materials, but by oral sources. As we shall see, in this short pericope there is room for oral influence, and this should caution us against viewing every shift from the Markan rendition as necessarily a Lukanism.

With these considerations in view we are ready to proceed to an examination of the Lukan text of the preparation of the Passover.

2. Analysis

Luke 22:7a: ἦλθεν δὲ ἡ ἡμέρα τῶν ἀζύμων, ...
Mark 14:12a: καὶ τῇ πρώτῃ ἡμέρᾳ τῶν ἀζύμων, ...

In contrast to both Mark and Matthew, Luke gives the chronology of the preparation-event in an independent clause, and in doing so enhances the flow of the narrative by speaking first of the approach (ἤγγιζεν—22:1), then of the arrival (ἦλθεν) of the Passover.[19] While the combination ἐγγίζω ... ἔρχομαι is not otherwise found in Luke-Acts, Luke uses ἔρχομαι *de tempore* 8 of the 12 times it appears at the hand of the Synopticists. All three evangelists employ it in the parable of the bridegroom (Matt 9:15; Mark 2:20; Luke 5:35), and Luke 18:30 parallels Mark 10:30 in a reference to "the age which is to come." The final usage of the term in Mark (14:41: "the hour has come") has no strict parallel in Luke. In other Lukan references the context is eschatological (17:22; 21:6; 23:29; Acts 3:19[20]), except in Acts 13:44, where we are told that

---

[19] Cf. already F. Godet, *A Commentary on the Gospel of St. Luke*, 2 vols. (Edinburgh: T. & T. Clark, n.d.) 2:282; Alfred Plummer, *A Critical and Exegetical Commentary on the Gospel according to S. Luke*, 5th ed. (Edinburgh: T. & T. Clark, 1901) 492.

the Sabbath had come. It is in this last text that we find the closest semantic parallel to 22:7.

The introduction of the aorist of ἔρχομαι helps stylistically, but inasmuch as Luke drops the Markan reference to the "first" day, he opens the door to further difficulties. Does he think the Feast of Unleavened Bread lasted only one day? A minority of textual witnesses (d it sy^{s.c.}) attempt to smooth over this obstacle by substituting τοῦ πάσχα for τῶν ἀζύμων. However, elsewhere Luke follows current practice by apparently indentifying the Feast of Unleavened Bread and the Passover, and it is likely that he is only continuing to follow popular usage here.[20]

Luke's use of δέ, substituting for Mark's καί, corresponds to normal Lukan redaction.[21]

Luke 22:7b: ἐν ᾗ ἔδει θύεσθαι τὸ πάσχα.
Mark 14:12b: ὅτε τὸ πάσχα ἔθυον, ...

'Εν (supported by 01 A W Θ 063 0135 f^{1.13} Majority text) + the temporal dative is consistent with Lukan preferences,[22] and probably should be adopted as the best reading. Luke is not especially fond of ὅτε, so it is not surprising that he has edited it out here. Of the 12 times it appears in Mark, Luke has: substituted a participial construction 3 times (Mark 1:32/Luke 4:40;[23] 4:10/8:9; 11:1/19:28); otherwise rewritten Mark to exclude the adverb 2 times (Mark 4:6/Luke 8:6; 15:41/23:49 [?]); offered no parallel 5 times (Mark 6:21; 7:17; 8:19, 20; 15:20); and borrowed the term only once, in a Jesus-logion (Mark 2:25/Luke 6:3). Otherwise Luke employs ὅτε in non-Markan texts in 2:21, 22, 42; 4:25; 6:13;[24] 15:30; 17:22[?]; 22:35). These instances of ὅτε cannot simply be regarded as due to Lukan redaction since they could have

---

[20] See Luke 22:1; Acts 20:6(?); Josephus, *Ant.* 2.15.1; 14.2.1; *Bel.* 5.99; *J.W.* 5.3.1; SB 2:813-815; Samuel Sandmel, *Judaism and Christian Beginnings* (New York: Oxford, 1961) 213; Marshall, *Luke*, 791; Fitzmyer, *Luke*, 2:1382.

[21] Cf. Turner, *Style*, 57; Schürmann, *Paschamahlbericht*, 76; Cadbury, *Style*, 142-147.

[22] The temporal dative + ἐν is used by Matt—37 × ; Mark—17 × ; Luke-Acts— 147 × (Luke—120 ×). Schürmann (*Paschamahlbericht*, 79) regards this as Lukan.

[23] Luke's genitive absolute represents characteristic Lukan style—cf. Turner, *Style*, 59; Fitzmyer, *Luke*, 1:108.

[24] The source behind this text is debated. For the possibility of a non-Markan tradition here see Heinz Schürmann, *Das Lukasevangelium*, vol. 1, 3d ed. (Freiburg: Herder, 1984) 318-319, 323; Tim Schramm, *Der Markus-Stoff bei Lukas: Eine literarkritische und redaktionsgeschichtliche Untersuchung* (Cambridge: Cambridge University, 1971) 113-114.

originated in other sources (i.e. from L, Q, and/or a special passion source). Luke may have added the term in 22:14 (Mark 14:17) and 23:33 (Mark 15:22). Ὅτε is also found in 22:35, for which there is no parallel in the Second Gospel, and 10 times in Acts. The deletion of the adverb here is consistent, then, with Luke's overall stylistic preferences, and should be seen within the framework of his larger editorial decisions (1) to move away from Mark's Semitic ἔθυον—for which Luke substitutes the articular infinitive and (2) to add the imperfect of δεῖ—which denotes "the compulsion of law or custom."[25] It is unlikely that we should read this statement of necessity apart from the oft-noted Lukan emphasis on the δεῖ of Jesus' passion.[26] Luke's portrayal of circumstances surrounding the suffering and death of Jesus is dominated by the conviction that his passion was a matter of divine necessity. This motif is evident in the passion account itself but also in numerous anticipatory and retrospective references to Jesus' death throughout Luke-Acts (e.g. Luke 9:22; 13:33; 22:22, 37; 24:7, 26, 44; Acts 1:16; 17:2-3; et al.). Against this background we should understand that, in Luke's view, the necessity of the passover sacrifice parallels and anticipates the necessity of Jesus' (= Messiah's) death, suggesting that all is happening according to a pre-determined purpose.

Luke's redaction of the Markan text in 22:7 has thus been shown to be minimal but not without purpose. In addition to introducing his own stylistic and terminological preferences Luke has accented the historical feel of the narrative, more closely connecting this pericope with the introduction to his passion narrative. Moreover, he has provided a dramatic hint that the events of the account, now beginning to unfold, are taking place "of necessity". Already at this early point in the account of Jesus' suffering and death, then, the *heilsgeschichtliche* import of this fateful cycle of events comes to expression.

Luke 22:8: καὶ ἀπέστειλεν Πέτρον καὶ Ἰωάννην εἰπών· πορευθέντες ἑτοιμάσατε ἡμῶν τὸ πάσχα ἵνα φάγωμεν.

---

[25] BAG², 172; cf., for this requirement, Exod 12:6; otherwise: Luke 11:42; 13:14; Acts 15:5; 18:21.

[26] For this emphasis in Luke see, e.g., Eduard Lohse, "Lukas als Theologe der Heilsgeschichte," in *Die Einheit des Neuen Testaments* (Göttingen: Vandenhoeck & Ruprecht, 1973) 150-153; David L. Tiede, *Prophecy and History in Luke-Acts* (Philadelphia: Fortress, 1980) 97-125; Marshall, *Luke: Historian and Theologian*, 104-107; Büchele, *Der Tod Jesu*, e.g. 175-176; et al.

Mark 14:12c-13a: λέγουσιν αὐτῷ οἱ μαθηταὶ αὐτοῦ· ποῦ θέλεις
ἀπελθόντες ἑτοιμάσωμεν ἵνα φάγῃς τὸ πάσχα; καὶ ἀποστέλλει δύο
τῶν μαθητῶν αὐτοῦ καὶ λέγει αὐτοῖς· ὑπάγετε...

The two most noticeable peculiarities of the Lukan narrative vis-
à-vis the Markan appear here—where Luke (1) emphasizes Jesus'
initiative in having preparations made for the meal and (2) names
Mark's "two disciples" as Peter and John. As for the first point of
divergence, Luke's structure thus more closely parallels the similar
narrative in 19:29-40, where Jesus sends two disciples to bring a
colt for Jesus' entry into Jerusalem. Within the passion story a
similar emphasis on Jesus' active role is found in 22:47-48, where
Judas's attempt to greet Jesus is cut short by Jesus. While this
emphasis is not nearly so prominent in the Lukan as in the Johannine passion story, it is clear nevertheless that Luke wants the
reader to recognize that Jesus is not a mere pawn but is himself an
active agent in these passion events.

Among the evangelists Luke is alone in naming the two disciples
sent to prepare the meal. It may be that Luke borrowed this information from oral tradition, but it should not be overlooked that
Peter and John are important to Luke's account. In the early sections of the Acts narrative (see 3:1, 3, 11; 4:13, 19; 8:14) they
appear as representative leaders of the infantile Christian movement. Otherwise these two are mentioned along with James but
apart from the other disciples in Luke 8:52; 9:28; Acts 1:13. As
some exegetes have recognized, in naming these two disciples as
those who prepare the meal, Luke presents the "leaders" as
"servants" of the others, illustrating in an ironic way the point of
one segment of Jesus' farewell adress: the one who rules should be
as the one who serves (22:24-27).[27] Indeed, it is not inconceivable
that, for Luke, this event should be seen in the background of the
dispute over relative greatness among the disciples in 22:24.

As he often does, Luke edits out Mark's historic present,[28]
substituting in its place the aorist of ἀποστέλλω. Mark's αὐτοῖς has
been dropped, an editorial move which is in line with Luke's
tendency to eliminate superfluous personal pronouns serving as

---

[27] See Heinz Schürmann, "Der Dienst des Petrus und Johannes (Lk 22,8),"
in *Ursprung und Gestalt: Erörterungen und Besinnungen zum Neuen Testament*
(Düsseldorf: Patmos, 1970) 274-276; Schneider, *Luke*, 2:442-443; Fitzmyer, *Luke*,
1:1382.
[28] See Cadbury, *Style*, 158-159; Fitzmyer, *Luke*, 1:107.

indirect objects.[29] However, this is not a consistent redactional procedure for Luke, as we shall see shortly.

Πορεύομαι appears some 88 times in Luke-Acts. Luke substitutes it for Mark's ὑπάγω at 5:24; 8:48; 22:22; and for ἀπέρχομαι at 4:42; 9:12. He apparently borrows it from Q at 7:6, 22; 11:26; 15:24. Of the 49 occurrences of the term in the Third Gospel, however, most are in contexts wherein the evangelist is following neither Mark nor Q. Lloyd Gaston omits πορεύομαι from his list of characteristic Lukan vocabulary, but notes that Luke does use the term editorially from time to time.[30] Marshall suggests that the verb may have been used already in Luke's source(s) to denote the "way of Jesus" (cf. 9:51; 13:22; 22:33).[31] Given the fact that the text of Luke 22:8b appears to represent only a rewriting of the Markan parallel (14:12c) within the framework necessitated by Luke's decision to emphasize Jesus' initiative, it seems an inescapable conclusion that the change from ὑπάγω to πορεύομαι in this verse is a Lukanism as well. In this context its significance seems more stylistically than theologically motivated.

Contrary to Fitzmyer's judgement that 22:8 "is wholly of Lukan composition"[32] then, we must insist that Luke has only edited the Markan text (which, perhaps, Fitzmyer had intended to assert). In doing so the Third Evangelist has underscored Jesus' role as an active agent in the passion story and allowed Peter and John to illustrate in an acted parable (and thus anticipate) Jesus' teaching on servanthood in the table-talk of 22:25-27.

Luke 22:9: οἱ δὲ εἶπαν αὐτῷ· ποῦ θέλεις ἑτοιμάσωμεν;
Mark 14:12c: λέγουσιν αὐτῷ οἱ μαθηταὶ αὐτοῦ· ποῦ θέλεις ἀπελθόντες ἑτοιμάσωμεν ἵνα φάγῃς τὸ πάσχα;

Luke prefers the phrase εἶπον πρός + accusative over εἶπον + dative, as Jeremias has observed.[33] In fact, when εἶπον + dative appears in the Third Gospel it almost always derives from Luke's sources (e.g. 3:14; 4:3; 5:27; 6:39; 7:13, 22; 8:25, 48; et al.).

---

[29] See Turner, *Style*, 58; Fitzmyer, *Luke*, 1:108.

[30] Lloyd Gaston, *Horae Synopticae Electronicae: Word Statistics of the Synoptic Gospels* (Missoula, Montana: Society of Biblical Literature, 1973) 66; cf. Schürmann, *Paschamahlbericht*, 90.

[31] Marshall, *Luke*, 809; cf. Friedrich Rehkopf, *Die lukanische Sonderquelle* (Tübingen: J. C. B. Mohr [Paul Siebeck], 1959) 15-17.

[32] Fitzmyer, *Luke*, 2:1376.

[33] Jeremias, *Sprache*, 290.

Nevertheless, *contra* Jeremias, even when amending his sources
Luke is capable of employing the phrase εἶπον + dative (e.g. 6:10;
9:20). In his opening phrase (22:9), Luke is only following Mark,
substituting εἶπον for λέγω. Indeed, this whole verse merely
represents a Lukan abbreviation of the Markan parallel in light of
his redactional interests as noted above on 22:8. No substantive
changes require further explanation in 22:9.

Luke 22:10a: ὁ δὲ εἶπεν αὐτοῖς· ἰδοὺ εἰσελθόντων ὑμῶν εἰς τὴν πόλιν
συναντήσει ὑμῖν ἄνθρωπος κεράμιον ὕδατος βαστάζων·
Mark 14:13b: ὑπάγετε εἰς τὴν πόλιν, καὶ ἀπαντήσει ὑμῖν ἄνθρωπος
κεράμιον ὕδατος βαστάζων·

Again, the changes here are not substantive theologically. Luke's
opening ὁ δὲ εἶπεν αὐτοῖς is needed because of the earlier Lukan
redaction of the narrative flow, in which he has Jesus initiate the
dialogue. On εἶπον + dative, see above on 22:9. Mark's parataxis
has been avoided by Luke, who substitutes in its place his own
ἰδού + genitive. Luke favors the genitive absolute over Mark's καί
parataxis.[34] Luke is fond of ἰδού (Mark—8 times; Luke-Acts—79
times),[35] but has an aversion to ὑπάγω (see above on 22:8). His
preference for συν- compounds is widely-known[36] and this explains
his substitution of συναντήσει for ἀπαντήσει. The last segment of the
sentence (ὑμῖν...βαστάζων) is identical in Mark and Luke.

Luke 22:10b: ἀκολουθήσατε αὐτῷ εἰς τὴν οἰκίαν εἰς εἰσπορεύεται, ...
Mark 14:13c-14a: ἀκολουθήσατε αὐτῷ καὶ ὅπου ἐὰν εἰσέλθῃ...

In this phrase Luke has restructured his Markan source for
stylistic reasons. The Third Evangelist normally avoids ὅπου
ἄν/ἐάν; it appears only once in his two-volume narrative, in an
apparent reproduction of Q in 9:57 (cf. Matt 8:19). His redaction
of Mark 6:10 (Luke 9:4) is similar to that in the present text:
Mark 6:10: ὅπου ἐὰν εἰσέλθητε εἰς οἰκίαν
Luke 9:4: καὶ εἰς ἣν ἂν οἰκίαν εἰσέλθητε.
Luke offers no parallel for Mark 6:56 and 14:9—two other Markan
texts in which this combination appears, and in 9:39 Luke completely removes the nuance of repetition in the past time read in the
Markan parallel (9:18). On πορεύομαι as a substitute for ἔρχομαι,
see above on 22:8.

---

[34] Turner, *Style*, 59; Cadbury, *Style*, 133-134; Fitzmyer, *Luke*, 1:108.
[35] But, cf. Rehkopf, *Sonderquelle*, 10-11.
[36] E.g., Taylor, *Passion*, 45.

Luke's redactional activity in 22:10, then, is minimal, and may be explained in stylistic terms alone.

Luke 22:11: καὶ ἐρεῖτε τῷ οἰκοδεσπότῃ τῆς οἰκίας· λέγει σοι ὁ διδάσκαλος· ποῦ ἐστιν τὸ κατάλυμα ὅπου τὸ πάσχα μετὰ τῶν μαθητῶν μου φάγω;

Mark 14:14b: εἴπατε τῷ οἰκοδεσπότῃ ὅτι ὁ διδάσκαλος λέγει· ποῦ ἐστιν τὸ κατάλυμά μου ὅπου τὸ πάσχα μετὰ τῶν μαθητῶν μου φάγω;

Here, too, Luke follows the Markan text closely. Καί, from Mark 14:14a (unnecessary in Luke's earlier phrase), is now brought in. Luke is not fond of the aorist imperative of εἶπον (used only in 10:10; 13:32; Acts 24:20), and he uses the future instead. This change corresponds to Luke's treatment of Mark's text in the parallel story in Mark 11:3/Luke 19:31. This use of the future with imperatival force is reminiscent of OT legal language,[37] and it may be that Luke, who often follows the style of Septuagint Greek, has intended this implicit connection. That is, by his linguistic choice Luke has perhaps underscored the authoritative character of Jesus' instructions. This, taken together with Luke's amendment of the Markan word order, deletion of ὅτι, and addition of the unnecessary σοί (see above on 22:8), should be understood as another means of stressing Jesus' initiative and authority.

Plummer and Marshall suggest that οἰκοδεσπότης had lost its original force, and that this accounts for Luke's addition of the pleonastic phrase τῆς οἰκίας.[38] This may be, but it should not be overlooked that not even Luke is immune from what might be regarded as looseness in style (e.g. Acts 10:15; 14:10[D]; 18:21).[39]

Luke 22:12: κἀκεῖνος ὑμῖν δείξει ἀνάγαιον μέγα ἐστρωμένον· ἐκεῖ ἑτοιμάσατε.

Mark 14:15: καὶ αὐτὸς ὑμῖν δείξει ἀνάγαιον μέγα ἐστρωμένον ἕτοιμον· καὶ ἐκεῖ ἑτοιμάσατε ἡμῖν.

Luke's version is very close to the Markan, Luke having made only stylistic amendments. Κἀκεῖνος appears in the NT 23 times, 7 of which are read in Luke-Acts. Luke borrows the term from Mark 12:4 (Luke 20:11), though not from Mark 12:5. Mark's ἕτοιμον is unnecessarry and, in fact, stands in tension with the subsequent

---

[37] See BDF § 362.
[38] Plummer, *Luke*, 493; Marshall, *Luke*, 792.
[39] Cf. BDF § 484; Turner, *Style*, 19.

imperative, ἑτοιμάσατε. It is therefore ommitted. The καί and ἡμῖν of the Markan text are also unnecessary (on the pronoun as indirect object, see above on 22:8) and are deleted.

Luke 22:13: ἀπελθόντες δὲ εὗρον καθὼς εἰρήκει αὐτοῖς καὶ ἡτοίμασαν τὸ πάσχα.

Mark 14:16: καὶ ἐξῆλθον οἱ μαθηταὶ καὶ ἦλθον εἰς τὴν πόλιν καὶ εὗρον καθὼς εἶπεν αὐτοῖς καὶ ἡτοίμασαν τὸ πάσχα.

In this final verse of the pericope[40] Luke's use of Mark is again influenced by his stylistic preferences. Mark's καί parataxis has been dropped in favor of a participial phrase—a characteristic Lukan editorial move, with the result that the Lukan rendition is greatly abbreviated. Contributing further to the relative brevity of the Lukan text is Luke's omission of the redundant οἱ μαθηταί and εἰς τὴν πόλιν. Following his frequent practice Luke has used δέ in place of Mark's initial καί (see above on 22:7a). For Mark's εἶπεν Luke has substituted the pluperfect εἰρήκει. The pluperfect, while not popular among NT writers, is employed by the Third Evangelist in 4:29; 8:2, 29, 38; 11:22; 16:20; 19:15; 23:35, 49; Acts 8:24; 13:34; 17:28; 20:38.[41] Of course, Luke has inherited from Mark the motif of Jesus' prophetic foreknowledge which is underscored in this verse, but we may note that it dovetails nicely with the aforementioned Lukan interest in Jesus' initiative and control vis-a-vis his own passion.

3. Summary and Conclusion

We began our discussion of the Lukan narrative of the preparation of the Passover meal by noting the near-consensus among NT scholars that Luke has made use of the Markan narrative and no other written source material. Our analysis of the Lukan redaction has borne out this consensus while at the same time pointing out what Taylor called Luke's "considerable fidelity" to his Markan

---

[40] We take 22:14 to be the introduction to the meal-episode itself (i.e. associated most clearly with 22:15-18)—so also, e.g., Kurt Aland, et al., eds., *The Greek New Testament*, 2d ed. (London: United Bible Societies, 1966); Eberhard Nestle, et al., eds., *Novum Testamentum Graece*, 26th ed. (Stuttgart: Deutsche Bibelstiftung, 1979); Albert Huck, *Synopsis of the First Three Gospels with the Addition of the Johannine Parallels*, 13th ed., revised by Heinrich Greeven (Tübingen: J. C. B. Mohr [Paul Siebeck], 1981).

[41] BDF §347; Schürmann, *Paschamahlbericht*, 103-104.

source.[42] The vast majority of instances in which the Lukan rendition departs from the Markan are motivated by stylistic and not theological interests. (We include here the observation that Luke has "historicized" the event, bringing it into much closer relation to the chronology of the opening of the passion story.) Nevertheless, as we have observed, even in this pericope Luke is theologically motivated.

Above all, Luke has emphasized the role of Jesus in the passion account as an active agent—taking initiative, in control, exercising authority. However, we must not let the Lukan redaction blind us to the fact that this motif was present already in the Markan text, specifically in the detail about Jesus' foreknowledge. (If one denies that either evangelist is interested in Jesus' prophetic foreknowledge but, instead, presumes that Jesus has made prior arrangements with the "master of the house," our point still stands: Jesus has taken the initiative.) That is, Luke has emphasized this theme, but in doing so has only built on or enhanced an idea already present in his source.

At this juncture we should note that a parallel motif can be read in both the Lukan and Markan versions of the story of the preparation for Jesus' entry into Jerusalem. We have observed two points at which Luke may have had that earlier story in mind—(1) Jesus' initiative and (2) his "authoritative directive" (ἐρεῖτε). On the whole, however, influence from his reporting of that episode is at best minimal, and in any case it would be difficult to prove that influence was from the first preparation to the second and not vice versa—or, indeed, whether either directly influenced the other theologically at all.

The δεῖ-motif we noted in 22:7 is not unique to Luke either, generally speaking. From a tradition-historical point-of-view it is clear that the early church was from the beginning well aware of the scandal of the cross and was therefore motivated to come to terms with the cross-event in the context of the will of God. As Jürgen Roloff has suggested, this treatment of the problem likely took several forms before the writing of Luke-Acts.[43] Indeed, Luke's Markan source communicates this point clearly, albeit not in this

---

[42] Taylor, *Passion*, 46.

[43] Jürgen Roloff, "Anfänge der soteriologischen Deutung des Todes Jesu," *NTS* 19 (1972-73) 38-64.

pericope (cf., e.g., 8:31; et al.). In this case, then, Luke has only communicated this motif more pointedly, more pervasively, making it even more central to his understanding of the gospel than was the case with Mark.

The introduction of the names of Peter and John is a more substantive departure from the Markan narrative. Apparently this innovation should be credited to the fact that Luke wrote a Gospel in two volumes, and was therefore interested in showing the relation of the disciples' mission (in this case, the import of Peter and John as leaders) to the work and words of Jesus (in this case, Jesus' farewell instructions on servant leadership). Incidentally, this underscores the potential value of keeping the Acts of the Apostles in view when studying the theology of the Third Gospel.

Our investigation has thus suggested the fidelity with which Luke has followed his sources in this one pericope of the passion story. His redaction is largely stylistically motivated; when theological interests are in view Luke has for the most part only enhanced motifs already present in his sources. This raises important, programmatic questions about how the source-critical issue in the whole Lukan passion narrative, where Luke is obviously not so closely bound to his Markan source, might best be explained. Source- and redaction-critical work on the Lukan passion account should proceed with this illustrative model of Luke's fidelity to Mark in view.

THE GROWTH OF THE KINGDOM IN LIGHT OF ISRAEL'S REJECTION OF JESUS: STRUCTURE AND THEOLOGY IN LUKE 13:1-35

by

ROBERT J. SHIROCK

Aberdeen

Of the many puzzles surrounding the study of Luke's central section (Lk. 9:51-19:28), one of the most perplexing is the enigmatic character of the structure of the narrative.[1] Commentators agree that the framework of a journey toward Jerusalem forms the basis of the narrative. It is further agreed that on this scaffolding Luke has placed a large amount of varied material, much of which is unique to his gospel, in an arrangement which at many places appears to be somewhat haphazard.[2] It is common to read of modern commentators opting for *convenience* in the development of working outlines by which they may proceed with the analysis of the central section of the gospel.[3]

The problem of discovering Luke's organizing principles becomes acute when particular portions within the travel narrative are analyzed for structure and theology. At points he appears to have been more adept at collecting tradition than redistributing it in a unified whole. The feeling shared by many students of Luke

---

[1] For literature on the study of the travel narrative see the bibliographies in I.H. Marshall, *Commentary on Luke* (Grand Rapids: Eerdmans, 1978), p. 402: J.A. Fitzmyer, *The Gospel According to Luke I-IX* (New York: Doubleday & Co., 1981), pp. 830-32.

[2] C.F. Evans (*Saint Luke* [London: SCM, 1990], p. 433) notes that the section "has the appearance of a largely amorphous aggregate of material".

[3] After proposing an outline, E.E. Ellis (*The Gospel of Luke* [London: Marshall, Morgan & Scott, 1974]) remarks: "In any case it offers a convenient structure that probably is not far from the evangelist's intention" (p. 150). Fitzmyer offers a three part division but beyond this abandons the attempt to subdivide and gives a running account in fifty-eight parts. In the commentary proper he denies the reliability of even the three part division labelling it "a mere convenience" (p. 825). L. Morris (*Luke, Tyndale NTC* [London: IV Press, 1974]) provides a handy a-z outline of 9:51-19:44 which coincides happily with his a-z outline for 4:14-9:50.

is that from 9:51-19:28 we are dealing with a collection of
miscellanea. Luke had materials which he was reluctant to eject yet
he had no discernible method by which to shape these *miscellanea*
into a symphony. Luke 13:1-35 would on the surface appear to be
a portion at which the evangelist had reached the low-point in his
constructive creativity and had more or less dumped materials into
the story.[4]

Corollary to the structural problem is the theological one. When
structural discord is evident it becomes well-nigh useless to search
for themes and theological ideas which span a sequence of
pericopae. Enigmatic structural work leads to uncertainty and
disagreement among commentators who are seeking to understand
the narrative theology of the gospel writers. Thus, Marshall, aware
of the structural difficulties, urges caution with regard to the
theological analysis of material in Luke 13 and 14: "we should not
look for too connected a theme running throughout the section".[5]

The thesis of this paper is that Lk. 13:1-35 is to be understood
as a unit. It is tied together structurally and develops one major
theological theme. With Jerusalem and the consummation of Jesus'
earthly ministry looming in the near future of the narrative, Lk.
13:1-35 stands with purpose in the midst of the "toward
Jerusalem" section as an explication of the deteriorating relationship between Jesus and the Jews. Lk. 13:1-35 explains the progress
of the kingdom-of-God program in light of the Jewish rejection of
Jesus.

Our analysis will proceed in three stages. First, a proposal will
be made regarding the structure of Lk. 13:1-35. Second, a
theological analysis will be made based upon the proposed structure. Finally, the literary implications of this analysis will be

---

[4] At 13:10 Marshall remarks, "The connection of thought at this point in the
gospel is far from clear" (p. 556). On the broader relationships governing chapters
13 and 14: "Any division of the gospel into sections must show some arbitrariness,
and this is especially evident at this part of the narrative." And again, "... it is
debatable whether we should regard all of what is to be found here as being linked
in any kind of way ... It would appear that Luke has had to do his best with a
variety of material from more than one source ..." (p. 562). Evans (p. 544) cites
W.L. Knox (*The Sources of the Synoptic Gospels*, 2 vols. [Cambridge and New York,
1953, 1957], II, pp. 74-83) to the effect that 13:10-35 is "a collection of fragments
which Luke has inserted here for no particular reason; they were in his tradition,
and had to be put in somewhere."

[5] *Luke*, p. 562 (with reference to 13:22-14:35).

explored as far as they touch upon our broader understanding of
the material around Luke 13:1-35.

The Structure of Luke 13:1-35

Preliminary Observations

It has long been recognized that Luke has a tendency to present
things in pairs.[6] The pair of kingdom parables (Lk. 13:18-21) provides a classic example of this. The presence of these two *growth-of-
the-kingdom* parables causes us to ask a question about the surrounding materials: Are there any hints of parallelism or pairing between
the materials preceding and following the twin kingdom parables?
Or, to put it another way, Do these twin parables form the *center*
of a larger balanced block?

A brief glance at the opening (13:1-9) and closing (13:31-35)
pericopes reveals some interesting parallels. Both contain a report
made to Jesus concerning the murderous action or intentions of a
civil ruler. Both continue with a response from Jesus which comes
in the form of a double-pronouncement. Both are rounded off with
a metaphor/lament in which the sad condition of the nation Israel
becomes the object of her master's sorrow. Both contain a hint
about the future of Israel in the closing line.

The parallels noted so far are enough to urge us to look for
parallels between the remaining two pericopes of the chapter
(13:10-17 and 22-30). While exhibiting striking *formal* differences,
it will be observed that they do contain interesting pictorial or
thematic parallels. Both feature an authority figure who is seeking
to exclude certain people from something they want. In both scenes
the authority figure expresses, by means of direct speech, his intention to shut people out from that which they are seeking. Both
scenes show the reactions of the participants (shame, joy) and the
idea of reversal (humiliation, exaltation) is a strong element in
each. The patriarch Abraham is mentioned in both scenes and the
problem of hypocrisy or false profession on the part of some is twice
present.

---

[6] The classic work on duality in Luke is that of R. Morgenthaler, *Die lukanische
Geschichtsschreibung als Zeugnis: Gestalt und Gehalt der Kunst des Lukas* (Zürich: Zwingli,
1948).

Our preliminary observations reveal that Lk. 13:1-35 exhibits numerous indications of pairing, balance, contrast and symmetry. We may be dealing with a unit of material which, while consisting of diverse material, has been organized along the lines of a chiasm.[7] The material has been arranged in the following manner:

A   13:1-9
  B   13:10-17
    C   13:18,19
    C1 13:20,21
  B1   13:22-30
A1   13:31-35

We turn now to a closer examination of the parallels in the various members of Luke 13:1-35.

Parallels between 13:1-9/31-35

The opening and closing pericopae invite comparison under three headings: 1. The reports 2. The replies 3. The metaphors and laments.[8]

---

[7] M.D. Hamm ("The Freeing of the Bent Woman and the Restoration of Israel: Luke 13:10-17 as Narrative Theology", JSNT 31 [1987], 23-44)) has suggested that Luke 12:49-13:35 is arranged in chiasm (12:49-53/13:31-35; 12:54-13:5/13:22-30; 13:6-9/13:18-21; center 13:10-17). He devotes only two pages to the suggested structure and provides minimal support. A careful analysis of the parallels suggested by this scheme reveal that it is unworkable. What do sayings about household division (12:51-53) have in common with sayings about the destruction of Jerusalem (13:34-35)? Can 13:6-9 rightly be separated from 13:1-5, labeled a "growth parable" and then compared with the growth of the kingdom parables (13:18-21)? Are common words such as "west" and "south" (12:54,55/13:29 [12:55 has "south wind"]), "three" (years, 13:7) and "three" (pecks of meal, 13:21) significant enough to suggest intended parallelism? These are the sort of questions which any proposed chiastic scheme, including our own, should have to answer and Hamm's article simply does not address them. His attendant theological proposal—that since 13:10-17 is the centerpiece, the freeing of the bent woman is emblematic of the Christian community, the fulfillment of the expected end-time restoration of Israel (p. 39)—is to be rejected. Structure and theology stand or fall together.

[8] W. Grundmann (*Das Evangelium nach Lukas* [Berlin: Evangelische Verlags-anstalt, 1966]) thinks that 13:1-9 is parallel in form with 12:13-21 and 12:54-59: "Worte Jesu, in 12:13 wie hier durch eine an ihn herangetragene Mitteilung verursacht, und anschliessende Parabel" (p. 274). While there is vague formal similarity between 13:1-9/12:13-21, there is almost no observable structural parallel between 13:1-9/12:54-59. As we will show there is much greater similarity both in form and content between 13:1-9/31-35.

1. The reports 13:1/31

Both reports are introduced with similar time indicators (ἐν αὐτῷ τῷ καιρῷ/ἐν αὐτῇ τῇ ὥρᾳ) and indefinite references to the reporters (τινες/τινες Φαρισαῖοι). Both reports focus on the hostility of a civil ruler. Pilate has killed Galilean worshipers. Herod wishes to kill Jesus. Reports of this nature are rare in the gospels.[9] These two particular reports are unique to Luke. They are both used as a springboard for warnings from the lips of Jesus.

2. The replies 13:2-5/32-33

The introductory formulae are similar (καὶ ἀποκριθεὶς εἶπεν αὐτοῖς/καὶ εἶπεν αὐτοῖς). Most importantly, both replies contain double-pronouncements which focus attention sharply on the danger of imminent death.

In the opening scene Jesus' reply emphasizes the urgency of repentance for all the inhabitants of Galilee and Jerusalem (13:2-5). The double ἐὰν μὴ μετανοῆτε πάντες ... ἀπολεῖσθε heightens the warning concerning the urgent need for repentance.

In the closing scene Jesus uses a double-pronouncement reply (σήμερον καὶ αὔριον καὶ τῇ τρίτῃ ... σήμερον καὶ αὔριον καὶ τῇ ἐχομένῃ) to emphasize his resolve to finish the course of his ministry and to arrive in Jerusalem, the city of destiny for rejected prophets (13:32,33). When Jesus arrives in Jerusalem, he will perish (ἀπολέσθαι).

We note that both replies are composed of words of Jesus which are unique to Luke. The double-pronouncements lend a tone of urgency or certainty to the warnings. There is a marked contrast in the content of each reply. In the first it is Israel who is in danger of perishing, while in the last it is Jesus himself. The theme of imminent death is common to both.

3. The metaphors and laments 13:6-9/34-35

Both units conclude with a metaphor/lament combination with very similar foci. God is a troubled vineyard owner/Jesus is a frustrated mother hen. Israel is a fruitless tree/an unwilling brood. A future day of reckoning is coming between God and Israel: tree cut down/house left desolate.

---

[9] The report concerning the fate of the Baptist (Mt. 14:12) is comparable.

In the opening scene the parable of the barren fig tree[10] highlights God's disappointment with the fruitless nation. The owner verbally laments the tree but is persuaded by the keeper to leave it (ἄφες) for one more season. The parable concludes on a note of uncertainty. Perhaps the tree will bear fruit (= the nation will repent) and will not have to be cut down.

In the closing scene the metaphor of the bird wishing to gather her unwilling brood under her wing pictures Jesus' desire to draw Israel to himself.[11] Jesus verbally laments Jerusalem's unwillingness to accept the offer of salvation. The lament concludes on a prophetic note of certainty. Jerusalem will be left (ἀφίεται), abandoned by God as a judgment for her lack of responsiveness.

Other Miscellaneous Parallels between 13:1-9 and 13:31-35

Both units refer to "Jerusalem" with a representative nuance.[12] In 13:4 it is all those who live in Jerusalem who are sinners in need of repentance. In 13:33,34 Jerusalem (3 ×) is the representative entity for Christ-rejecting Israel. Thus, Jerusalem is depicted in these two scenes as the place where sinful men die by accident (13:4) and, ironically, where men sent from God (prophets) die by commen consent (13:33,34).

Both units show Jesus speaking with prophetic authority. In the opening pericope he warns the people of impending judgment (Do you suppose ...? No I tell you ... [2 ×].[13] In the final scene he ranks himself among the prophets who die in Jerusalem and he utters a prophetic oracle concerning the future of Israel.

A final point of comparison is both very interesting and problematic. The opening and closing scenes contain enigmatic time

---

[10] A majority of commentators recognize the connection between this parable and the preceding pronouncements so that 13:1-9 is rightly regarded as a unit.

[11] The structures of 13:6-9/34-35 are not identical. In the former the parable stands in the foreground with the lament (complaint?) taking up a subordinate position. In the latter (13:34-35) the lament occupies the prominent position and the metaphor is subordinate. Thus, the two pieces give slightly different impressions.

[12] The simple geographical sense is clear enough at 13:22 as well as most other places in Luke-Acts.

[13] Josef Ernst (*Das Evangelium nach Lukas* [Regensburg: Pustet, 1977], p. 420) speaks of Jesus' prophetic consciousness at 13:3,5.

references involving the number three.[14] The time indicators point to a day of reckoning. At 13:7 we learn that the owner of the vineyard had been coming for "three years" seeking fruit on the tree. The decisive year will be the fourth ("next year") at which time the tree's fate will be decided. Judgment will be passed on the fourth year. At 13:32,33 we have a time reference in the double-pronouncement reply of Jesus to Herod. There is reference to three days of ministry culminating in Jesus' arrival at Jerusalem, where his fate will be accomplished (i.e. on the fourth day).[15]

Parallels between 13:10-17/22-30

The parallels between 13:1-9/31-35 were both structural and pictorial. Now, however, we are confronted with two units which have very little in common by way of form. The first (13:10-17) is a controversy dialogue growing out of a miracle story.[16] The second

---

[14] It is difficult to know when a numerical parallel is intended or merely coincidental. For instance, the number eighteen occurs three times in Lk. 13:1-35 (vv.4,11,16) and the number twelve occurs twice in Lk. 8:42,43. Plummer warns that to suggest that these are intended parallels "is hardly sober criticism" (*Gospel According to S. Luke* [Edinburgh: T. & T. Clark, 1896], p. 342). Is it not possible, however, that these were actual historical details in the stories which were highlighted by the conveyors of the tradition for mnemonic purposes? Thus Fitzmyer, commenting on 13:11, equivocates saying "it is probably sheer chance that the number eighteen appears in this and the foregoing episode, though one cannot deny that it may have served as a catchword-bond for the episodes" (p. 1010). While the numbers may have been coincidental at the point of occurrence they have become, in the process of transmission, significant details which help to tie various units together.

[15] Our view is that the three days are to be viewed as days of *finishing the ministry* with the decisive events beginning to take place on the fourth day. This understanding seems probable if it be allowed that the second time-reference (v.33) was intended as a clarification of the first (v.32). R. Tannehill (*The Narrative Unity of Luke-Acts* [Philadelphia: Fortress Press, 1986]) notes: "Verse 32 is often understood as a reference to Jesus' death. However, in v.33 the sequence of three days refers to the time of travel to Jerusalem. It would be remarkably awkward and confusing for the narrator to refer to three day periods twice in adjacent verses, using largely the same wording, and yet intend to refer to different periods ... Verse 33 makes clear that Jesus' required goal is Jerusalem, and v.32 should be interpreted in light of this verse" (p. 154). Along different, but supporting lines, Marshall notes that Hebrew parallels to v.33 refer to a "decisive fourth day" (p. 572).

[16] Fitzmyer notes the difficulties which form critics have had in classifying this scene (p. 1010). The basic problem is that the narrative element has become dominant while the miracle has faded somewhat into the background. As we will argue, the narrative elements in the controversy provide the rich and careful pictorial parallels with the companion scene (13:22-30).

(13:22-30) is a brief discourse of Jesus which develops out of a question-answer sequence. If there are significant parallels here, they must be located in the imagery created by the pericopes.

Two Authority Figures and Their Words

In the synagogue scene the ruler of the synagogue (ὁ ἀρχισυνάγωγος) stands at the center of the controversy. There are other hostile people present (πάντες οἱ ἀντικείμενοι αὐτῷ [v. 17]) but it is this one key authority figure whose words and actions are highlighted for the reader. In the corresponding closed door scene, the head of the house (ὁ οἰκοδεσπότης) stands at the center.

The ruler of the synagogue is trying to restrict access to Jesus. Angered by Jesus' Sabbath-healing, he says, in effect, "Do not come in here on Sabbath days to get healed" (v.14). It is noteworthy that the ruler of the synagogue does not attack Jesus himself as in normally the case in Sabbath controversies.[17] Instead, he directly addresses those who are coming for healing. In the parallel closed door pericope, the head of the house is seeking to shut people off from entrance to the house. Again, the dialogue takes place between the head of the house and those seeking access.

Enter Through the Narrow Door

We note that Luke records narrow door/closed door imagery (vv.24,25) as opposed to Matthew's small gate/narrow way language (Mt. 7:13,14).[18] The narrow door imagery may allude to the synagogue scene with which it is matched. Although no door is mentioned in the synagogue pericope, it is known that there were small (narrow) and large doors in many ancient synagogues.[19] Different people, based upon their status in the community, entered the synagogue through various doors and were seated accordingly. The bent woman, being low in communal honor, may have entered the synagogue via a small, side entrance. This forms a picture of what Jesus says later: "Enter through the narrow door" (v.24).

---

[17] Compare Lk. 5:17-26; 6:6-11.

[18] Evans' remarks with regard to Luke's door imagery are typical: Luke's version "is plainly secondary, and is barely intelligible. For it is not the width or narrowness of a door which makes it a symbol of entry or not in salvation, but whether the door is closed or not (as in v.25)" (p. 556).

[19] W. Schrage, συναγωγή κτλ. TDNT VII, 798ff (esp. 816-818).

Reversal of Fortunes

Reversal of fortunes in light of the advent of the kingdom of God is a major idea in Luke-Acts.[20] Both the synagogue scene and the closed door scene picture the reversal in terms of the exaltation of the lowly and the humiliation of the proud. The sick woman in the synagogue represents the lower class of Jewish society. This lowly woman is lifted up by the Lord and given a share in the messianic blessings. In contrast, the ruler of the synagogue, who would have been high on the social ladder, is humiliated by Jesus' stern rebuke and the unveiling of his hypocrisy.

Similarly, in the closed door scene we also find the exaltation/humiliation motifs. Those who proudly assumed they would have access to the kingdom will be humiliated when they realize that they have been shut out. Those who are least expected to enter (from east, west, north, south) will be welcomed in. The statement at the close of the pericope sharpens the effect: "And behold, some are last who will be first, and some are first who will be last" (13:30).

Abraham's True Children

The name of Abraham is mentioned in both scenes.[21] The woman who was healed is called "daughter of Abraham". Near the end of the closed door scene Abraham is pictured in connection with the kingdom banquet (v.28). The patriarch and all of his true descendants (like the woman) will be gathered for the feast. The evildoers and hypocritical pretenders (like the synagogue ruler) will be shut out.

Rejoicing and Bitterness

Both units describe the emotional reaction of the crowd in response to what is happening in the respective scenes. There is a contrast here. At the end of the synagogue scene Luke notes that the multitude was rejoicing over all the glorious things being done

---

[20] Most recently, see John O. York, *The Last Shall be First: The Rhetoric of Reversal in Luke*, JSNTSS 46 (Sheffield: JSOT Press, 1991).

[21] Elsewhere in Luke: infancy narrative (1:55,73); John's preaching (3:8); genealogy (3:34); rich man and Lazarus (16:22,23,24,25,29,30); Zaccheus' salvation (19:9); dispute with Sadducees (20:37).

by Jesus (13:17). In the parallel scene, there is "weeping and gnashing of teeth" when many realize that they are not insiders after all (13:28).

Summary of Pictorial Parallels between 13:10-17/22-30

The fundamental issue in both scenes has to do with gaining access or entry into the sphere of messianic blessing. People are seeking to enter, but an authority figure stands in the way determining who will be allowed to enter. A great reversal is pictured as a result of which those who were outsiders will be let in, and those who thought they were in will be left out.

Parallels between 13:18,19/20,21

If Luke 13:1-35 is chiastic, it is not lacking for a strong center-piece with a forceful message. The structural parallels between these two parables are obvious. It is worth noting, however, that the pair is tied especially tightly together by Luke. This is evident first by their placement in the gospel. Only here do we find these two parables standing together in a unique place of their own.[22]

Luke's tight weaving of the parables is further evidenced by the simple form in which he has maintained them. Both develop in precisely the same sequence: introduction> object> actor> action> place> result.[23]

Summary of the Structure of Luke 13:1-35

Luke 13:1-35 has been arranged along chiastic lines with the two kingdom parables standing at the center. The other units of material have been placed in pairs, 13:1-9 going with 13:31-35 and 13:10-17 going with 13:22-30. The parallels are of different kinds. Highly formal points of contact are found at 13:18,19/20,21 and at

---

[22] In Mark the parable of the mustard seed is independent (4:31,32). In Matthew, they stand together in the midst of the large parable block (ch.13). In G. Thomas 96 the parable of the leaven is found with two others (woman with broken meal jar [97]; man wishing to kill powerful opponent [98]).

[23] Matthew also develops the two parables in the same sequence with the exception that between place> result he has inserted a description of the exceptional differential in size between the mustard seed and its full grown tree.

13:1-9/31-35. Pictorial parallels are found in all pairings. The units 13:10-17/22-30 depend upon pictorial features to establish their parallelism.

The Theology of Luke 13:1-35

Structure serves the pragmatic interest of rendering material more memorable for readers, hearers, or conveyers of the tradition. It is also widely recognized, however, that structure was a tool in the hands of the evangelists by which they communicated significant theological ideas.

Following our proposed structure, here are the basic ideas we see being developed in Luke 13:1-35:

13:1-9 Question: Will Israel repent and retain her place?
  13:10-17 Problem: The hypocrisy of Israel's leaders.
    13:18,19 Key idea: The certain growth of the kingdom.
    13:20,21 Key idea: The influence of the kingdom.
  13:22-30 Solution: Hypocrites shut out, others let in.
13:31-35 Answer: Israel will be judged by God.

The Future of Israel 13:1-9/31-35

The opening pericope (13:1-9) focuses on the urgency of repentance for the nation Israel. Unless swift repentance occurs, disaster will overtake the nation. She will be judged by God, cut down from her privileged position within His developing kingdom program. But the question lingers in the opening scene: Will Israel repent? She is in grave danger. Sufficient time has elapsed for her to begin to produce fruit (i.e. to respond positively to the message of the kingdom). Nevertheless, her fate is not yet sealed.

The closing pericope (13:31-35) focuses on the sad fate of the unrepentant nation. Historically, Israel has failed to repent in accord with the voice of God's prophets. She has consistently murdered the prophets and will do the same with the prophet Jesus. Thus, the question of Israel's repentance (13:1-9) is given a sad and decisive answer. Unrepentant Israel will continue in her hardness of heart, will murder the prophet Jesus and will, as a result, be given over to divine judgment. The intercessor, at the close of the scene, no longer pleads for time. He can only weep in sorrow at what is to come.

The Grand Reversal 13:10-17/22-30

The major theme communicated by the second set of pericopae is one of reversal of positions.[24] The kingdom of God will bring, and in fact has already begun to bring, a reversal of unprecedented proportions. Those who assume that they are "in" (i.e. religious leaders such as the synagogue official) will find that they are on the outside looking in. On the other hand, those who have long been considered outcasts (i.e. the bent woman) will joyfully find that they are insiders in God's kingdom. They who have entered through the small door will find, once inside, that they are to enjoy wonderful table fellowship with the true children of Abraham.

If a cause is to be sought for the exclusion of some, it is found in their hypocrisy[25] (13:15) and their false sense of security stemming from mere association rather than intimate acquaintance (13:26,27). It is not enough to be involved in religious things. To be an insider in the kingdom of God one must take delight in the fact that in the person and work of Jesus the kingdom of God is present. Kingdom inclusion comes when one enters by the narrow door which, in these two pericopae, is Jesus himself.

The Progress of the Kingdom 13:18,19/20,21

Israel is rejecting her God-sent deliverer and King. What are the implications of this for the development of the kingdom-of-God program? Is the program thrown off track by Israel's unbelief?[26]

The message of Luke 13:1-35, and especially of the two kingdom parables at the center (13:18-21), is that the kingdom will grow and advance with or without Israel at the center. God's plan will not be thwarted by Israel's hardness of heart. The idea of certainty or inevitability is prominent in the twin kingdom parables.[27] In other

---

[24] Ellis remarks that, beginning with 13:22 there is a major emphasis on the "principle of reversal" which will come to work in the establishment of God's kingdom. The churchmen of Israel "become 'the rejected-seekers' (13:22-30), 'the excluded guests' (14:1-24). And theirs is 'the Godforsaken city' (13:31-35)" (*Gospel of Luke*, p. 187).

[25] Preceding and succeeding units of the gospel deal with the issue of hypocrisy on the part of Israel's spiritual leaders (11:37-54; 14:1-24).

[26] Precisely the same issue is addressed in Romans 9-11. Interestingly, the same answer is given: Israel's unbelief does not nullify God's program. In fact, in the sovereign purposes of God, it advances it.

[27] "The stress is not so much on the idea of growth in itself as on the certainty that what appears tiny and insignificant will prove to have been the beginning of a mighty kingdom" (Marshall, p. 561).

words, the kingdom parables form the central message, the *assurance* as it were, that God's program will advance even though Israel will soon culminate the process of its rejection of God's chosen one. Although Luke 13 does not make this clear, it is difficult, given the broader message of Luke-Acts, not to see some allusion to the incorporation of vast numbers of Gentiles into God's kingdom program as a means by which the grand reversal will take place and the kingdom program will move forward.[28]

Literary Reflections

A number of literary implications grow out of the foregoing analysis which have a bearing on our understanding of the background of this material as well as the study of surrounding material in the central section of Luke.

First, concerning Luke's use of material common with Matthew: There is scattered material from Lk. 13:18-35 which Luke has in common with Matthew. We have commented above on the significance of Luke's placement of the twin kingdom parables. Our proposed structure makes good sense of his use of this material.[29] Further, we noted the appropriateness of the narrow door imagery over against Matthew's gate/way sayings. There is also the issue of Luke's placement of Jesus' lament over Jerusalem. Matthew places the lament at the end of Jesus' discourse in which he attacks the religious leaders of Israel (Mt. 23) and just prior to the Olivet discourse (Mt. 24). Matthew's setting for the lament seems very natural and, not surprisingly, most commentators feel that it is more likely to be the original setting. There is, therefore, a special task for students of Luke to explain the placement of the lament at this particular point in the central section.[30]

---

[28] The contrast in Lk. 13 is between lowly Israelites and hypocritical ones. One could argue, however, that 13:29 broadens the reference to Gentiles who will be incorporated into the kingdom program.

[29] Grundmann, while preferring that the twin parables be regarded as the final word of Jesus in a section running from 11:1-13:21 comments: "Dieses abschliessende Doppelgleichniss schlägt zugleich das Thema des Folgenden an" (p. 281).

[30] We would not wish to rule out the possibility that Jesus uttered this lament more than once. Israel's prophets often used stereotyped phrases on repeated occasions. The historical question aside, however, one still needs to account for Luke's decision to record it in the present literary context.

On our reading of this section, the lament accomplishes two things. First, it balances or answers the opening pericope in which the question still lingered concerning Israel's repentance. The lament is the perfect conclusion to the questions and issues raised by the chapter as a whole. Second, in the larger framework of Luke's "toward Jerusalem" narrative, the lament points the reader forward to the city of destiny and the fateful events to occur there. Thus, the lament sounds the final note in one section while turning the reader's attention forward to the subsequent material.

Second, concerning the broader structure of the travel narrative: As noted at the outset, the central section of Luke is notoriously difficult to outline. If the foregoing analysis is correct, we can mark off certain divisions running from 12:1-14:24. Chapter 12 is a self-contained sermon addressed primarily to the disciples, but concluding with a general call to the multitudes to take decisive action in light of Jesus' words. A new section begins at 13:1. While the initial theme of repentance (13:1-9) serves as a bridge from the previous sermon, the material in 13:1-35 has a structure and message of its own. Finally, at 14:1 a new section begins with the focus on meal-time interaction between Jesus and the Pharisees (14:1-24). Here, the issue of Israel's flawed leadership (13:15,26,27) is taken up more fully as Jesus dines with them and unmasks their hypocrisy.

Third, concerning the origin/tradition history of Luke 13:1-35: As indicated above, the entire passage is pervaded by a prophetic tone. In particular, the opening and closing scenes present an interesting mix of prophetic themes. Warnings of impending disaster are mingled with expressions of hope over the possibility of repentance. The closing scene sees the prophet himself being murdered and all hope being displaced by a prediction of calamity. The closing lament is much like an Old Testament prophetic dirge.

While a Hellenistic audience might find this material somewhat perplexing, a Jewish reader/listener would be quite at home here. Those familiar with the Old Testament prophets would not be surprised by the mixing of guarded hope with prophecies of doom. Such a mixing of themes was characteristic of the Hebrew prophets. A call to repentance would, in fact, often be immediately juxtaposed with a lament over the nation's failure to repent.[31] In short,

---

[31] The pattern is everywhere in the prophets, but see for example Isa. 1:16-20 followed by vv.21-26. Or Jer. 7:1-7 followed by vv.8-20.

Luke 13:1-35 has a very Jewish/prophetic character about it which may indicate that it either originally took shape under the supervision of Jews or that it was intended by the final editor to speak to Jews in particular about their need for repentance.[32]

Finally, if the chiasm is present, as we suggest, then Luke was not the haphazard editor, at least in this particular section, that many modern commentators make him out to be. Far from simply dumping *miscellanea* onto a journey scaffolding, he was utilizing and distributing unique material with great caution and skill. Here in the travel narrative, where presumably his editorial freedom was at its height, we meet a literary craftsman, not a careless compiler of random traditions.

Conclusion

As Jesus moves toward Jerusalem, the city of destiny, Luke 13:1-35 stands as a miniature narrative excursus on the deteriorating relationship between Jesus and the Jewish nation. It anticipates what will happen in Jerusalem—the murder of Jesus—and clearly sets forth God's judgment on this act of rebellion. It shows, however, that God's kingdom program will move forward with a grand reversal taking place. Outcasts will be placed in the center of God's dealings and the rebellious hypocrites will be cast out.

Paul expressed "sorrow and unceasing grief" over Israel's plight (Rom. 9:2). He was echoing what Jesus expressed before him (Lk. 13:34,35). And, as Paul could confidently declare, "But it is not as though the word of God has failed" (Rom. 9:6), Luke has told his readers, through the voice of Jesus the prophet, "The kingdom of God is like ... a mustard seed, which a man took and threw into his own garden; and it grew and became a tree; and the birds of the air nested in its branches." The program of Jesus, according to Luke 13:1-35, is much bigger than Israel's reaction to it.

---

[32] J. Duncan M. Derrettt (*New Resolutions of Old Conundrums: A Fresh Insight Into Luke's Gospel* [Warwickshire: P. Drinkwater, 1986], p. 102) comments: "The fact that Luke's gospel presents itself as an Hellenistic production has never lessened the intensive Jewishness with which the whole is penetrated."

THE "BOOK OF ACTS" THE CONFIRMATION OF THE GOSPEL

BY

W. C. VAN UNNIK

INTRODUCTION

The following contribution contains the text of two lectures which I was privileged to deliver in Cambridge University, january 1955, at the kind invitation of its Faculty of Theology, and afterwards in Durham and Manchester. They were not published at that time, because I hoped to expand them into a book. Lack of time has prevented the execution of this plan. Meanwhile various fresh studies about Acts have appeared, the most notable of which is Professor HAENCHENS great commentary. In connection with the "Lacan theology" in general more attention is paid to the theme of these lectures than before. But since the conclusion to which I was led, and the way in which it was arrived at, have not been proposed by other scholars, the publication of my solution seemed to be justified. For these reasons it will be understood that the original form of the lextures was kept.

I

THE PROBLEM OF THE PURPOSE OF ACTS

It was a most remarkable day in the history of Christianity when a certain man, called Luke, made and began to execute his plan to write a second[1]) book as a sequel to his gospel. In it he gave to the church a picture of the very beginnings of its existence, scenes from its first expansion into the world; he showed, how the message of salvation spread and was received in a great part of the Roman empire. This was remarkable, because no other religion of his time has done the same to the great regret of the students of the history of religions. Not even one of his fellow-christians, as far as we know, had tried it before. In writing his gospel Luke had his predecessors, because, as he himself confesses, "many had undertaken to compile a narrative of the things which had been accomplished among us" (Ev. i 1). Here he found a certain set form and kept himself within its limits, but nothing has survived of any attempt to write about the apostolic age, to the great regret of all

---

[1]) There are no valid reasons to doubt the correctness of Acts i 1.

New Testament scholars who miss the chance of a new "Synoptic Problem". And although a flourishing branch of litterature sprung up in the "Acta Apostolorum Apocrypha" of the 2nd century, these acts of Peter, Thomas, Paul etc. are so different in character and contents that they cannot be compared with Luke's second volume. Even if it could be maintained that the name πράξεις ἀποστόλων is authentic [1]), the fact that there apparently existed a kind of πάρξεις-litterature among the Greeks and Romans [2]) does not allow us to say that Luke imitated that *genre*. Luke's Acts is a unique achievement within and outside the borders of Christianity.

In continuing his story of Jesus by that of the first stages of the church he made it clear once for all that Christianity was a missionary religion, an apostolic message to the world with a task extended "to the end of the earth" (i 8) under the inspiring Spirit of the risen Lord. The legacy of this book remained a "pattern which was shown on the mountain" though it has not always been so understood. The present situation of the Christian church has opened our eyes— it may be better than before—to see the task, to feel the inspiration and to experience the comfort flowing forth from these pages. It was a remarkable day when the plan of this book was conceived, but like so many other important days in the history of our faith and of our world it remained unnoticed though its effect made itself felt afterwards right up to the present time.

In the preceding introductory paragraphs I have spoken about this book and its plan in a very general way as it is done so often. But it does not seem out-of-place or far-fetched to ask somewhat more precisely: what was in the author's mind when he started this new venture? He has brought together in his book much material of highly varying character, but what was his scheme and *purpose*? Or was he just compiling stories and speeches at haphazard?

This question of the purpose is always important because it brings to light the perspective in which the writer wants us to see his information. But in the case of Acts it is the more significant, since he wrote this book as a companion-volume to his gospel. Now it is generally agreed that the gospels do not contain a biography of Jesus, but proclaim the good news about Jesus, the *kerygma*.

---

[1]) Cf. P. Feine-J. Behm, *Einleitung in das Neue Testament*[9], Heidelberg 1950, S. 77.

[2]) A. Wikenhauser, *Die Apostelgeschichte und ihr Geschichtswert*, Münster i.W. 1921, S. 94 ff.

John's explicit declaration: "these are written that you may believe
that Jesus is the Christ, the Son of God, and that believing you may
have life in his name" (xx 31), can be applied to the synoptics as
well. What Luke offered his readers in his gospel was *kerygma*,
but what was he doing in giving them this continuation? Was this
just a piece of pious church-history, some stories and sayings of
highly respected founders of the church—in other words: was this
really a "metabasis eis allo genos"—or had it something to do with
the *kerygma* of the gospel? The answer to this question is, I think,
of great value for the exact interpretation of Acts and may bring
to light an essential feature of this interesting and puzzling book.

In these lectures I propose to discuss with you this question
of the purpose of Acts, its character and its connection with the message of the Gospel.

This theme in itself is not a new one. In the last century it was
hotly debated, largely because of the so called "Tübingen"-position.
But since that position ceased to be defended any longer, the interest flagged. It is a matter of course that whereas Luke himself
did not give a definite declaration, many scholars have tried to
find an answer. In every commentary and every textbook of
"Introduction" one will find some lines or pages about this question.
But it is a curious fact that, apart from these books which are bound
to pay some attention to it under penalty of incompleteness, so
little has been published about it in recent years. When MAC
GIFFERT gave his sketch of "Historical Criticism of Acts in Germany" [1]), he remarked at the end of his abstract from JOHANNES
WEISS' *Über die Absicht und den literarischen Charakter der Apostelgeschichte* that this book of 1897 was "the last elaborate discussion
of the purpose of Acts". These words were written more than
30 years ago, but in the meantime the situation has not considerably
changed. Many of you will have read HUNTER's instructive book
Interpreting the New Testament 1900/1950 [2]) and have noticed that
in the section on Acts this problem of the purpose is dealt with
in a very few lines,—while all attention is given to criticism of text
and sources, authorship and historical trustworthiness.

---

[1]) In: F. J. FOAKES JACKSON-K. LAKE, *The Beginnings of Christianity*,
Part I, *The Acts of the Apostles*, vol. ii, London 1922, p. 389.
[2]) A. M. HUNTER, *Interpreting the New Testament* 1900-1950, London
1951, p. 105 ff.

This sketch of the present situation is fully confirmed by the Belgian scholar Jac. Dupont in his indispensable book *Les problèmes du livre des Actes d'après les travaux récents* [1]). In this survey of more than a hundred pages only somewhat more than one page is allotted to our problem! A monograph *The Purpose of Acts* by B. S. Easton [2]) stands there "auf einsamer Höhe". So it cannot be called superfluous, if we submit the question to a fresh investigation at this moment, when, as was said by Paul Schubert recently, "new life has come to the study of Luke-Acts" [3]). In handling this subject the great respect due to previous generations of scholars and contemporary fellow-students bids us first see in what ways solutions have been sought for. This former lecture will be devoted to a survey of the keys put into our hands and to testing them. This will help us to discover more precisely the kind of lock by which the door is closed. For I must confess that in spite of much labour bestowed upon this question the problem has not yet been solved in a satisfactory way. Having thus cleared the point at issue I shall humbly submit to your judgement a suggestion for a new solution in my second lecture. In the present one we shall discuss: *the problem of the purpose of Acts*.

In reading the first sentence of Acts it seems as though these well-known words will give us the clue: "In the first book, o Theophilus, I have dealt with all that Jesus began to do and teach" (Τὸν μὲν πρῶτον λόγον ἐποιησάμην περὶ πάντων, ὦ Θεόφιλε, ὦν ἤρξατο ὁ Ἰησοῦς ποιεῖν τε καὶ διδάσκειν) i 1. The author addresses himself and therewith dedicates his book to the same person as his Gospel (Ev. i 1). In a few words he summarizes the contents of his former volume. It is clear that this phrase forms a very strong link between the two books: they are parts of one work. Luke does not say: once upon a time I wrote something about Jesus Christ, but he continues his story in one way or another. The whole passage is encumbered with all sorts of difficulties, set out quite recently by

---

[1]) J. Dupont, *Les problèmes du Livre des Actes d'après les travaux récents*, Louvain 1950, p. 19-21.

[2]) B. S. Easton, *The purpose of Acts*, 1936, now reprinted in his :*Early Christianity*, ed. F. C. Grant, London 1955, p. 33 ff.

[3]) P. Schubert, *The structure and Significance of Luke* 24, in *Neutestamentliche Studien für Rudolf Bultmann*, Berlin 1954, p. 165.—(This has also effected the present subject in the course of the last years; but see Introduction).

MÉNOUD in the *Bultmann-festschrift* [1]). But though, they may be admitted, the solution which MÉNOUD following Lake and Sahlin, proposes, viz. that this introduction was a later intrusion when Acts was admitted into the canon, and that Luke-Acts once formed one work without a break, not in two volumes, but in one I cannot accept. The Gospel as a special form was too well-fixed and it is impossible to see the contents of Acts brought into it. That．the end of the former and the beginning of the latter book are related is not startling and I doubt whether the so-called conflicting statements are really so. This manner of connecting separate parts of the same work is in accordance with the literary habits of ancient authors. A new book opens with a short survey of the preceding part (the so-called ἀνακεφαλαίωσις) and announces what may be expected in the following pages (the προέκθεσις). Besides the examples adduced by NORDEN [2]) we may compare the beginning of the second book of Josephus *contra Apionem* II 1, 1-2 which is very appropriate because Josephus is a younger contemporary of Luke: διὰ μὲν οὖν τοῦ προτέρου βιβλίου, τιμιώτατέ μοι ᾿Επαφρόδιτε, περί τε τῆς ἀρχαιότητος ἡμῶν ἐπέδειξα τοῖς Φοινίκων καὶ Χαλδαίων καὶ Αἰγυπτίων γράμμασι πιστωσάμενος τὴν ἀλήθειαν καὶ πολλοὺς τῶν ῾Ελλήνων συγγραφεῖς παρασχόμενος μάρτυρας, τὴν τ᾿ ἀντίρρησιν ἐποιησάμην πρὸς Μανέθων καὶ Χαιρήμονα καί τινας ἑτέρους. ῎Αρξομαι δὲ νῦν τοὺς ὑπολειπομένους τῶν γεγραφότων τι καθ᾿ ἡμῶν ἐλέγχειν κτλ. The first paragraph is a clear analogy to Luke's first sentence and the second shows what we might have expected from Luke. Had he given this προέκθεσις in a sentence with δέ which had been prepared by the hope-giving μέν, all would have been in order. But the trouble is, as many commentators have acutely remarked that this second clause with δέ is missing! In contrast with the beautiful preface of the gospel with its classical structure, and in contrast with the good start, the sequence is in absolute disorder [3]). *Hinc lacrimae!* It does not matter much whether some unknown Redactor spoilt the original writing, as NORDEN thought, or Luke himself went astray and has not properly finished the sentence (so most commentators), the opening paragraph does *not* reveal the object Luke had in view.

---

[1]) Ph. MÉNOUD, *Remarques sur les textes de l'ascension dans Luc-Actes*, in: *Bultmann-Festschrift*, p. 148 ff.

[2]) E. NORDEN, *Agnostos Theos*, Leipzig 1913, S. 312.

[3]) See K. LAKE, in: *Beginnings of Christianity*, vol. V, p. 1 ff.; FEINE-BEHM, *a.a.O.*, S. 77 speak of "der stylistisch verunglückte Anfang".

A clear objective statement is not given here nor anywhere else; henceforth the chase for the great Unknown is open.

Since it is an established fact that μέν and δέ introduce either half of a sentence containing a contrast, many commentators tried to reconstruct the "missing" words by an exegesis of the words in the first verse assuming that this contrast-working would yield good results. The word "began" in the clause "that Jesus began to do and teach" is underlined and it is then said that Luke wanted to explain in Acts what Jesus continued to do after His resurrection and ascension through His Holy Ghost by His disciples. This position is however open to criticism for the Book of Acts does not tell that Jesus *continued* to do and teach. In some places He acts directly as in the conversion of Paul and in some visions, but in many other places He is not mentioned at all. Missionary work, that is so prominent in Acts, is inspired by the Spirit, but if one would say that behind the Spirit Jesus stands, it must be observed that in many instances the progress of the Gospel comes about through persecution (ch. xiii-xvii). Sometimes the angel of the Lord takes action, giving his command to Philip or liberating Peter out of prison. The teaching of the apostles in their speeches is *concerning* Jesus, but that is not identical with His teaching. And it is rather mysterious, how the very long story of Paul's captivity in Jerusalem, Caesarea and his voyage to Rome which altogether occupies a quarter of the whole, can be explained in that way.

Before we now turn to other answers to our question it will be useful to put before us a table of contents. Since there is no clear and unambiguous statement of Luke, we shall have to look in the book itself and try to find out if its composition betrays its purpose and if the great Unknown has left some fingermarks. Unfortunately the way of comparing his account with that of others and thereby detecting his handling of the material, as can be done in long stretches of his gospel with their parallels in Mark and Matthew, is impracticable. At any rate it will be clear that the author's aim should be formulated in such a way that it explains how and why these stories and speeches suited his purpose and that a definition by which only part of the material is covered should be dismissed or at least be brought into a wider context. It is also clear that the goal is not reached by a rather vague and summarizing definition, such as: "the spread of the gospel from Jerusalem to Rome", for in that way we do not get an insight into the complicated and somewhat puzzling selection of the material. And that is exactly the interesting point! For our purpose it is better not to be content with a short formula, but to see the whole in its constitutive parts.

In following the description of Luke we see this series of pictures:

I. Introduction: Jesus' intercourse with His disciples after the resurrection, His last commandment and His ascension; the disciples remain in Jerusalem and choose a new apostle in Judas' stead.

II. Pentecost: the gift of the Spirit and Peter's speech showing the fulfilment of Joels prophecy; preaching Christ, rejected and raised; ending with a strong appeal of conversion; the effect of this sermon and the life of the new Christian community.

III. The healing of a lame man in the name of Jesus which is explained to the crowd; Peter and John therefore being arrested give their witness to the saving power of Christ and are released because the fact is undeniable, on condition of their silence; together with the other Christians they pray for boldness and their prayer is visibly answered. Then follows a short sketch of the "communism" of the community with the outstanding deed of Barnabas which introduces the story of Ananias and Sapphira. In a short passage the "signs" of healing by the apostles are mentioned, which leads to a new imprisonment of the Apostles, their liberation by an angel, their second examination before the Sanhedrin and their release through the advice of Gamaliel, closed with the information that they "did not cease teaching and preaching Jesus as the Christ".

IV. The choice of the 7 deacons from the Hellenistic part of the Church, among whom Stephen is the outstanding figure. These deacons are not concerned so much with the poor, but they are preachers—"evangelists" (xxi 7). Stephens' long discussions with the Jews whom he accuses of permanent rebellion against God from their own history; his martyrdom. Dispersion of the congregation leads to the spreading of the gospel; Philip comes to Samaria, controversy with the famous Simon Magus; the conversion of an Ethiopian eunuch.

V. Conversion of Paul on his way to Damascus as a persecutor of the Christians; his first work in Damascus and Jerusalem after some time of suspicion; his flight ultimately to Tarsus.

VI. Peter healing Aeneas and raising up of Tabitha in the coastal districts; his dealings with the "godfearer" Cornelius under divine guidance and his defence before the Jewish brethren.

VII. Spreading of the dispersed brethren to the North; the gospel reaches Antioch where Barnabas comes in company with his protégé Paul; their mission to Jerusalem in connection with a famine.

VIII. King Herod against the apostles; Peter escaped from prison by divine help—Herod is struck to death by an angel at the height of his glory.

IX. Under the guidance of the Spirit Paul and Barnabas are sent out to missionary work; they do it in Cyprus (conflict with Elymas at the court of the proconsul) and in the southern part of Asia Minor (preaching in the synagogue of Antioch of Pisidia— jealousy of the Jews; preaching to the gentiles; mistaken for pagan Gods because of a healing; way back to Antioch and institution of churches).

X. The conference in Jerusalem on the salvation of the Gentiles without circumcision; this is accepted by the Jerusalem circle which sends out a letter, the only condition being the upholding of some commandments for intercourse with Jewish christians.

XI. Judas and Silas are commissioned with this letter; quarrel between Paul and Barnabas, the latter going to Cyprus, the former to Asia Minor, visiting first the churches of the previous journey and continuing his way to the West coast; Pauls own plans cannot be carried out; a vision shows him the way to Europe—Work in Macedonia (Philippi: conversion of Lydia, healing of a slave girl and imprisonment where the fetters are broken through an earthquake; conversion of the jailor and release of the apostles with all sorts of excuses because they as Roman citizens have been maltreated); Thessalonica and Berea (driven from one place to the other by conflicts with the Jews)—Athens (conflict with contemporary philosophy); Corinth (activity of $1\frac{1}{2}$ years in and outside the synagogue after Paul's break with the Jews—he is comforted by a heavenly vision—attack of the Jews before the proconsul Gallio)—Paul leaves Corinth, passes through Ephesus and sails for Palestine—after a short visit to Jerusalem (which is not mentioned by name) he goes to his place of departure Antioch.

XII. A new journey through Asia Minor to Ephesus—This story is suddenly interrupted by some information about Apollos at Ephesus and his vovage to Corinth after being fully instructed—

Paul in Ephesus baptizes disciples of John the Baptist, preaches in the synagogue but withdraws from there and continues his preaching in the school of Tyrannus, more than two years. His healing-power brings a conflict with some Jewish Exorcists who are overcome by the name of Jesus—the magic power is broken, but Paul comes into conflict with the power of the state-cult in Ephesus. —After that he goes again to Macedonia and Greece to visit the churches—on his way back he spends a week in Troas and heals Eutychus on a Sunday during the service of "breaking of the bread". On his way to Palestine he bids farewell to the elders of Ephesus in a long speech: a defence of his behaviour as an apostle, a warning for coming dangers.

XIII. Paul goes to Jerusalem while "the Holy Spirit testifies in every city that inprisonment and afflictions await" him; some examples of it being given a.o. about Agabus. Paul is gladly received by the brethren in Jerusalem and asked to fulfil a requirement of the Jewish law to stop the slander of his adversaries. While in the temple he is the cause of an outburst of Jewish hatred, he is arrested and the rest of the book tells of his apologies before the Jewish people and leaders, before the highest Roman officers and king Agrippa; his Roman citizenship helps him because it entitles him to appeal to Caesar; in spite of the fact that his innocence is acknowledged he is sent to Rome; he reaches the capital of the empire after a long and dangerous journey which is told in great detail; in Rome he finds a Christian group—he has again discussions with the Jews; to them he applies the well-known words of Isaiah vi 9, 10 for they reject the salvation while the gentiles will hear. He lived in his own house during two years "preaching the kingdom of God and teaching about the Lord Jesus Christ quite openly and un-hindered". That is the somewhat unexpected end of the book.

In trying to understand the purpose of Luke we must read his book *as a whole*. I often have the feeling that this has not been done sufficiently, that commentators investigate it piece-meal looking for what is told about the church in Jerusalem, the controversy of Paul and the Judaizers etc. But then its unity is broken to pieces and we do, I think, a grave injustice to its author. For there are strong indications, as we shall see, that Luke wants us to see the book in its entirety. If we take it such as it is and read it from be-ginning to end, there are several facts which attract our attention:

1) there is, as HARNACK showed, a great unity in style and choice of words [1]). One has not the idea of reading a history covering a space of 30 years, but it is a more or less continuous story. Only in fixing the dates, so far as it goes, one discovers how long a period it describes; only by critical investigation it comes to light that the unity of the picture is not so strong as it appeared at first.

2) some parts of the story are told with great detail, while these drawings are connected with one another or are alternated by very general remarks such as: there they preached the gospel, or: they comforted the disciples etc. While the healing of the lame man in ch. iii is told in exact terms the description of the church in Jerusalem is given in very broad outlines which are of uncertain interpretation. Paul's stay at Ephesus lasted three years, but apart from two or three remarkable incidents in the apostle's conflict with paganism Luke is practically silent about the inner life and growth of the church there. This fact could be illustrated by scores of examples. If it is allowed to characterize his literary habit with an anachronistic comparison: Luke makes me think of a lecture with lantern-slides; the pictures are shown one after another illustrating the story the lecturer wants to tell while he makes the transition from one plate to another by some general remarks. It has struck me that in most commentaries these summaries and transitions are treated in a fairly perfunctory manner. Read e.g. the explanation offered at the passage where Luke describes the activity of the apostles (v 12-16); very little is said about it, but does that mean that it is something that can be neglected? Or take the verses about Paul's behaviour after his conversion (ix 23 ff.); there it is pointed out that this account largely differs from the information furnished by Paul himself (Gal. i, ii). But was that important for Luke? He says twice that Paul spoke with "boldness" (παρρησία) and introduces a key-word of the book. In my opinion these transitions are highly important to understand the train of thought in Acts and they deserve a special treatment.

3) in these last two examples Luke uses the words σημεῖα καὶ τέρατα and παρρησία respectively. This leads to another observation. In running through its passages we discover in Acts again and again the same words, motives and ideas. For the moment it will be

---

[1]) A. HARNACK, *Neue Untersuchungen zur Apostelgeschichte und zur Abfassungszeit der synoptischen Evangelien*, Leipzig 1911, S. 1 ff.

sufficient to mention some of them: μάρτυς-σωτηρία—"signs and wonders"—jealousy of the Jews, παρακαλέω, visions at decisive points, a sentence like this: "But the word of God grew and multiplied", which sounds like a chorus, etc. In the second lecture we will return to this point, because it is highly significant. Ancient books were written to be read aloud, for hearing, not for silent reading [1]). The audience was trained to take it up by the ear and not by the eye. It is like music, when one hears the themes returning in various passages and moments. If one begins with marking these "motives", it suddenly becomes clear what Luke wants us to hear.

4) we will try to understand the "mens auctoris", but then it is an urgent need to make a clear distinction. We have before us the story as told by Luke, but that is not the same thing as the factual event itself; it may be that even between the fact and Luke stands a long time of transmission. DIBELIUS applied his method of "Formgeschichte" also to this book [2]), but I wonder if this helps us to understand Luke's work, because this reconstruction is largely, if not wholly hypothetical and dissolves the unity of the literary structure. It is of course possible to deal with Acts as a historical account and then it turns out that there are many difficulties which are duly discussed by the commentators; then it may be that even the speeches which are largely Luke's own work do not fully serve the purpose of the moment as Dibelius pointed out [3]). It is however the question whether Luke wanted to be a historian in the first place; it may be that his story is composed to convey a message. Therefore it is not so important to see where he is contradicting Paul or even himself, if we only hear this message.

5) it is clear that this book shows many gaps from the point of view of history. If it were not for the detailed information of Paul we would not guess that between ix 30 and xi 24 more than 10 years have elapsed. What became of Simon Magus, the Ethiopian and Cornelius? How was Christianity brought to Rome, not to say a word on the absolute silence about Egypt; can we trust a doubtful reading of codex D in xviii 25, according to which Apollos learnt something of the Christian faith in Alexandria, but then who preached it there? Why does Peter so suddenly disappear?

---

[1]) Cf. M. HADAS, *Ancilla to classical reading*, New York 1954, p. 51.
[2]) M. DIBELIUS, *Aufsätze zur Apostelgeschichte*, Göttingen 1951, S. 9 ff.
[3]) M. DIBELIUS, *a.a.O.*, S. 141.

Why does Luke not tell anything about the adventures of Paul as related in 2 Cor. xi 23 ff.? Nothing is said about Paul's letters nor about the troubles in Corinth. And on the other hand: why is that story of Cornelius told twice over at great length, while so many other interesting items are passed by silently or in general terms? Why do we hear so much about the two deacons who do the work for which they are not elected, while the apostles like John, Thomas and others do not enter into the scene? Why that long story of the shipwreck, interesting though it be, while in other cases the journey is just indicated? This list can be made longer at liberty. There is no sign that Luke tried to cover these gaps. He just ends a certain story and passes over to a different subject. It cannot be maintained that these gaps are due to lack of sources, because we do not know anything about the sources of information Luke had at his disposal. The question whether Luke possessed no more or did not wish to tell more cannot be decided either way. The problem of the historical value of his material is different from that of the purpose with which we are concerned at present. He must have had his reasons for this, even if one takes into account that the arrangement of the material in many ancient writings is a weak spot.

6) we must further consider that Luke is often very short in his description leaving his readers to read between the lines. Let us take that scene in the house of Philip with the prophetic sign of Agabus and the brethren trying to restrain Paul from going to Jerusalem (xxi 10-14). The highly dramatic tension of that moment is not fully described, but just hinted at in the words of Paul: "What are you doing, weeping and breaking my heart?" It is sometimes said that Paul's interview with Felix and Drusilla (xxiv 24, 25) is not very pauline and is not an exposition of the Christian faith; words like δικαιοσύνη and ἐγκρατεια read as if a teacher of Hellenistic philosophy and ethics is speaking; but then the situation is misunderstood. In realizing what kind of fine company Paul was addressing, that low Felix and that noble Jewess Drusilla, one suddenly sees that Paul preaches here in a very concrete way *ad hominem*, and it is clear that Felix "was alarmed" hearing about the κρίμα τὸ μέλλον (not only future, but imminent). — The missionary activity of Paul at Thessalonica and Corinth is briefly told: "he argued with the Jews from the scriptures, explaining and proving that it was necessary for the Christ to suffer

and to rise from the dead, and saying: "This Jesus, whom I proclaim to you, is the Christ" (xvii 3, cf. xviii 4, 5). If we want to know how Paul argued, we have to turn to chapter xiii and even to the speeches of Peter in ch. ii, iii. Much knowledge is always presupposed; to many subjects only a passing reference is given; it is only mentioned so far as it suited the plan.

At this point something must be said about the closing chapter of the book, because it has sometimes been argued that it is defective. It is a wrong argument to say that neither the final judgement about Pauls trial nor his martyrdom is mentioned and that they alone could give a real conclusion. This is only true, if it was Luke's aim to give a biography of Paul in which the martyrdom was the goal or if his real interest was in the trial, but this supposition cannot be proved, is a fallacious hypothesis and a wrong standard of comparison, because it starts from false presumptions. On the other hand we find several important themes of the book here together (23 διαμαρτυρόμενος τὴν βασιλείαν τοῦ θεοῦ — πείθων τε αὐτοὺς περὶ τοῦ Ἰησοῦ out of the Scriptures; the dissension among the Jews, their judgment in the words which all the gospels use in the same way, and τὸ σωτήριον τοῦ θεοῦ to the gentiles; vs. 31). In a *grande finale* the book finds its end.

7) another characteristic fact we cannot pass by is this that Luke does not seem afraid of contradictions such as in the story of the "communism" in Jerusalem or—most remarkably—in the conversion-narratives of Paul (n.b. twice in speeches!) on the one hand, while on the other his "report" of the preaching of Peter and Paul shows a great conformity. These typical defects from the historical point of view once more signalize the fact that the message prevails over historical accuracy.

We have reviewed these aspects of the working-method of Luke, because they seem to me essential for an adequate understanding of his book. What was the thread by which this mixture of detailed information and summaries, of speeches, healing-stories, travels and conflicts are bound together? Or—in other words—what was the purpose of Acts?

This problem has been, says Dr. FOAKES JACKSON in his commentary[1] "the subject of much controversy". "Two views of

---

[1] F. J. FOAKES-JACKSON, *The Acts oft he Apostles*, London 1931, p. xvi f.

this", he continues, "may here be mentioned as characteristic of modern conjectures on the subject". As such he discusses the irenic and the apologetic motive which he both rejects. The former alternative maintains that Luke wrote to reconcile adherents of a Petrine-judaistic party and the followers of Paul's gospel free from the Law. Once the favoured solution of the so-called school of Tübingen, it does not find anymore supporters among modern scholarship. It may be convenient in this connection to quote Hunter again. Among the three conclusions on which in his opinion most scholars would agree the second one is: "Luke's primary purpose in writing Acts was not to produce some "Tübingenesque" *eirenikon*, but to record how Christianity spread from Jerusalem to Rome, under the power of the Spirit and the leadership of St. Paul. It is also widely held that Luke had in his writing a secondary apologetic purpose—to show that the new religion was not politically dangerous and to commend it to the Roman world" [1]). As far as my knowledge of modern litterature goes, this statement is a fair presentation of the situation, although it is not complete. But it may be asked, if these answers hold good. Therefore we shall subject them to a critical test.

I. *Description of the spread of Christianity from Jerusalem to Rome.*

This solution usually takes its starting-point in i 8 "and you shall be my witnesses in Jerusalem and in all Judea and Samaria and to the end of the earth", which at the same time reveals the plan of the book [2]). It is true that Jerusalem is the first centre in Acts and Rome is the final station, but if we look closer into the matter this answer is unsatisfactory. To begin with it is nowhere said in i 8 that Rome is the suitable end; in that way an eschatological term "to the end of the earth", derived from the prophets has lost its full force and is changed into a geographical term of doubtful interpretation because Rome was perhaps the centre of the world, but certainly not "the end of the earth" (ἕως ἐσχάτου τῆς γῆς) [3]). In the second place the book nowhere shows a special interest for the capital of the Imperium Romanum; if this book was to show

---

[1]) A. M. HUNTER, *l.c.*, p. III f.
[2]) So e.g. FEINE-BEHM, *a.a.O.*, S. 75, 80.
[3]) Cf. the quotation from Is. xlix 6 in Act. xiii 47, and Is. viii 8, lxii II; the parallel in Luc. xiv 47 f. has: εἰς π ά ν τ α   τ ὰ   ἔ θ ν η , ἀρξάμενοι ἀπό Ἰερουσαλήμ. ὑμεῖς μαρτύρες τούτων.

"der Siegeslauf des Evangelium" (WIKENHAUSER) [1]) to Rome, one would have expected that more about the effect of the preaching would have been recorded. In the third place if it was Paul who was to bring the gospel there, we must say that he "missed the bus", because there *was* a Christian *ekklesia* before his coming and Luke is fully aware of that (see xxviii 15). If Luke really wished to tell this story of the spreading of the Gospel, it is not clear why he did not tell something more about the missionaries of the dispersion (xi 19 ff.), about Egypt so important with its large Jewish colonies, why he did not tell more about the other apostles. Why that lengthly report of Pauls imprisonment, its discourses before Felix and Festus? Besides that it does not explain the selection of the material and the special features of the composition we sketched before.

2. *Missionary motive.*

Then i 8 is read as a command to go out into the world which is fulfilled by the disciples. It must, however, be noticed that the phrasing of this verse is quite different from that in Matth. xxviii 18. On this assumption it is interesting to see that the disciples are not obedient to their Lord, because they remain in Jerusalem, even after Pentecost, and that the persecution (viii 1 ff.) is necessary to remind them of their task. They are witnesses, but not immediately missionaries. Paul does not rush off to missionary work, but is specially called (xiii 1), in spite of the voice at his conversion. In this connection we may also dismiss the idea that Luke wanted to demonstrate the *transition from Judaism to Gentile Christianity*. It should be observed that although Paul officially separates himself three times from the Jews (xiii 46 ff.; xviii 6; xix 9), he is always going to the synagogue first in the next town. It is true that the salvation is also preached to the pagan population, but the gentiles are incorporated while the Jews become divided (Luke is here in the same line as Paul, Rom. ix-xi). Had he wished to show this, why did he not tell more about Philip and his companions?

3. *Apologetic motive.*

Under this heading one points to the favorable or neutral reactions of the many Roman officials which figure in these pages; their attitude is in flatt contrast with that of the Jewish authorities;

---

[1]) A. WIKENHAUSER, *Die Apostelgeschichte*[2], Regensburg 1951, S. 8.

in their eyes Paul is innocent and the author stresses his roman citizenship [1]). It is either an apology for Paul or for Christianity as a whole being presented as a *religio licita*. As we heard from HUNTER this is only a secondary motive. That is right, for it manifestly cannot explain such stories as that of Ananias and Sapphira. Would it be a recommendation of the Christianity for Roman officials if they read that one should be more obedient to God than to men? The picture of the Roman magistrates is at the highest neutral, but not extremely favourable.

4. *Anti-jewish motive.*

The only author who in recent years underlined this element was KLAUSNER in his interesting book *From Jesus to Paul*. According to him Luke wanted to recommend Christianity to the expense of Judaism after 70 A.D.: the Jews are always the black sheep. Against this opinion we may say that the links with the Jewish people are always upheld. They are called "brethren" who crucified Jesus in ignorance (iii 17); the apostles go out to win the Jews and Paul goes everywhere first to the synagogues, in spite of bad experiences at former occasions, see also xiii 26, xxii 1, xxiii 1, 5, even in the very last chapter there is an intimate contact xxviii 17 in Rome. Is it historically beside the mark that they opposed against Christianity, since it was in their circles that the new faith arose?

5. *Instruction and edification.*

Either of the individual Theophilus or of the church in general. This was the solution of FOAKES JACKSON and DUPONT who referring to KÜMMEL said: "il a écrit dans un but missionaire, les Actes sont destinées au communautés chrétiennes et à leur catéchumènes" [2]). This is quite simple, but in my opinion this is exactly the place where the unsolved problem itself begins: how did these materials serve the purpose? These words are open to so many interpretations that they hide the real question instead of answering. it.

6. *Preaching.*

This was specially brought to the fore by DIBELIUS in one of his *Studien zur Apostelgeschichte*. It is written in order to bring the

---

[1]) See xvi 35 ff., xxii 25 ff., xxiii 29, xxvi 31 f., xxviii 18, also the attitude of Gallio in xviii 14 ff.
[2]) DUPONT, *l.c.*, p. 20.

readers "to acknowledge in adoration what the gospel is and how it conquers men" [1]). It is interesting to notice that DIBELIUS ends by calling Luke a preacher in his article on "the first Christian historian".—Although I agree that this book has its aim in preaching and not in history for its own sake, and although the great learning of DIBELIUS has given us a wealth of many excellent observations, here arises the big question to which he gave us no answer: why was it necessary to write this book as a sequel to the gospel? was the gospel in itself not sufficient? for what reasons did Luke act as an historian of the early church? Or let me formulate it in another way: was it a mistake of the later generations that this "first christian historian" had to leave the name "Father of Church-history" to Eusebius while he had to share the name "evangelist" with three other men?

We have analysed these various solutions one by one, but it must be understood that most authors give a combination of them because of the complexity of the problem. But since they point in different directions and are not a sufficient explanation of the whole book or are based on incomplete exegesis, it will be not out of place if we try another track. It goes without saying that the motives we discussed did not grow out of nonsense; a certain amount of acute listening to the text is underlying them and we must take full account to that. At the same time we will pay due attention to the method applied by Luke, more than is generally done. It may be that we can raise our answer beyond the level of "conjectures", as FOAKES JACKSON called it [2]), because it offers a clue to the problem: why has Luke compiled this complex mass of material in this form to serve as a second part to his gospel?

II

THE SCOPE OF ACTS

The problem we shall try to solve is: what purpose was in Luke's mind, when he started to add this second volume to his Gospel; was it a book of a different character or not; how did the complex material he used serve his intentions?

It is not only for the sake of curiosity, neither for merely literary

---

[1]) M. DIBELIUS, a.a.O., S. 117.
[2]) F. J. FOAKES JACKSON, l.c., p. xvi.

reasons that we look out for an answer. The writings of early Christianity have their place in the life of the church, their "Sitz im Leben", to say it with an expression coined by DIBELIUS. They are not written for the joy of writing, but have a task in the edification of the church or in the propagation of the gospel. Their publication is an expression of the faith in order to build up that of other people.

That this general characteristic of early Christian literature can also be applied to our specific problem, is apparent from an article which the German scholar KÄSEMANN published under the title "Das Problem des historischen Jesus" [1]. According to KÄSEMANN the very fact that this continuation was written signalizes a complete change in the spiritual atmosphere of the early church, because this history of the apostles was possible only on condition that the eschatology out of which the first circle of Jesus' disciples lived had been replaced by quite another outlook. "Man schreibt nicht die Geschichte der Kirche, wenn man täglich das Weltende erwartet". Primitive eschatology was substituted by a history of salvation ("Heilsgeschichte"), because the expected parousia did not come and historical continuity was to be reckoned with. The work of Jesus becomes the "initium christianismi" and Acts shows the pictures of the sacred past [2]. In reading this one is reminded of the word of Loisy, that the Kingdom of God was announced in the Gospel, but that the church came into existance [3]. This view of KÄSEMANN is shared by various scholars in Germany. It is the idea developed by an influential author like BULTMANN in his *Theology of the N.T.* [4] and forms the basis of the research which CONZELMANN published in his *Die Mitte der Zeit, Studien zur Theologie des Lukas* [5]. The answer to our question has a bearing upon much wider issues, upon the whole course of theological thinking and Christian living in the N.T.

---

[1] E. KÄSEMANN, *Das Problem des historischen Jesus*, in: *Zeitschrift für Theologie und Kirche* LI (1954), S. 125 ff.

[2] E. KÄSEMANN, *a.a.O.*, S. 136 ff.

[3] A. LOISY, *Autour d'un petit livre*[2], Paris 1903, p. XXV: "l'Evangile, qui annonçait le prochain avènement du royaume de Dieu, a produit la religion chrétienne et l'Eglise catholique".

[4] R. BULTMANN, *Theologie des Neuen Testaments*, Tübingen 1953, S. 462 f. in a chapter on "die Wandlung des Selbstverständnisses der Kirche".

[5] H. CONZELMANN, *Die Mitte der Zeit, Studien zur Theologie des Lukas*, Tübingen 1954 (a 3rd revised edition appeared in 1960).

Although it can be appreciated that here Gospel and Acts are not separated, but taken in their unity, it must be said that I have several grave objections against this evaluation of Acts. The "via negativa" of their exposition will be a suitable path to our object.

1) KÄSEMANN defines Acts as a "pattern of what the Church should be and may be" [1]. This hardly covers the ground, where as a matter of fact so little is said about the church and so much about certain persons in the church. When does it appear that Luke contrasts the sacred past with this own times?

2) KÄSEMANN started with the preconceived idea that Luke wished to write a *history* of the apostolic age. Of course he uses historical material, but did it serve the aim of showing "wie es eigentlich gewesen ist" or is Luke a "laudator temporis acti"? If we think that Luke primarily was a historian, we must naturally give some explanation of this fact. But before this issue is settled as to what he wanted to do with his stories, we are wise to abstain from such far-reaching conclusions. Unfortunately the professor of Göttingen (now Tübingen) does not give us a clue. If it were true that this is church-history it may be said that it is bad church-history because there are too many gaps (see p. 36 f.).

3) The signal points of the "motives" are not taken into account Only two of them are hinted at. According to KÄSEMANN Luke looks back on the apostolic times as the "period of great miracles"[2], but why? The world of Luke within and outside the churches believed in and saw miracles everywhere; they in themselves were not so miraculous and distinctive of a special period. If Luke draws attention to the "signs and wonders", it has a particular reason to which we shall return later on. More important still is the other point: Luke puts the "history of salvation" in the place of the eschatology, so reads his main thesis. The use of words like σωτηρία, σώζω etc. is conspicuous in Acts, but is is there the same idea as is expressed by "salvation" (German: Heil, Seligkeit)? I must confess that I do not understand what KÄSEMANN exactly

---

[1] E. KÄSEMANN, *a.a.O.*, S. 137: "ein Modell dessen, was es um Kirche sein soll und sein darf".

[2] E. KÄSEMANN, *a,a.O.*, S. 137: the time of the apostles "tritt nun der eigenen Gegenwart des beginnenden Frühkatholizismus als heilige Vergangenheit, als die Epoche der grossen Wunder, des rechten Glaubens und der ersten Liebe entgegen".

means by "Heil", but from the antithesis we may deduce that is it not eschatological and therefore has that somewhat vague idea of happiness and blessedness which is so often found in Christianity. Neither he nor CONZELMANN gives an analysis of the word in Acts; had they done so, they would have discovered that σωτηρία is strongly bound up with eschatology and that therefore the whole antithesis falls to the ground.

4) This leads us to the point which is most important of all: the complete underestimation of eschatology. KÄSEMANN holds that Luke reduced this element to a somewhat general expectation of "the Last Day" at a rather uncertain date in future. But the eschatological element is far stronger, is decisive, as will be seen if one has got accustomed to Luke's manner of writing, in listening to his "undertones". He does not speak explicitly about the "Kingdom of God", but it is significant that it is mentioned in the first and the last chapter. It forms an essential part in the summary of Philip's message (viii 12) and of Paul's argument with the Jews (xix 8), the latter even addressing his audience as people "among whom I have gone about preaching the kingdom" (xx 25) [6]). How strong this idea was for Luke may be seen from xiv 22 with its remarkable first person plural: "through many tribulations we must enter the kingdom of God" (δεῖ ἡμᾶς εἰσελθεῖν εἰς τὴν βασιλείαν), strongly recalling sayings of Jesus. In the gospel much had been said about this kingdom that is here presupposed. What is rejected in ch. i 6 ff. is not the idea of the Kingdom, but the idea of Jewish nationalism and apocalyptic computation of the day. Gods kingdom is the βασιλεία over the whole world and His σωτήριον must extend to the end of the earth (xiii 47 cf. i 8). But the Kingdom is there as an eschatological factor. We may also point to other facts.—The outpouring of the Spirit in ch. ii is explained by the quotation of Joel which is the starting point for Peter's speech and fundamental for the whole book: "this is what was spoken by the prophet Joel: "And in the last days, it shall be" etc. (ἐν ἐσχάταις ἡμέραις). This is the perspective of Acts: they are living in the last days. The Holy Spirit is not a variation, a more divine edition of our human spirit, but it is the gift of the new age, the proleptic "atmosphere" so to say of the Kingdom, the signal of the new and eternal covenant. The fulfilment of the O.T. prophecy is seen in the healing of the lame man and the incorporation of an euneuch in the church. Of this eschatology the resurrection of the dead and future judgment

was part and parcel; this is the *real* point in the famous speech on the Areopagus (xvii 31). It was the stimulating power behind the call for repentance because it was imminent (xxiv 15-25 μέλλειν). In Acts as *a whole* the eschatological element is strong, but the early Christian church had a somewhat different idea of the "Naherwartung" than many N.T. scholars of the present time. The primitive church saw the daybreak of the New Age, but in stead of counting the hours they set out to proclaim the Gospel.

It may be true that one does not write history of the Church when one expects the final day every moment, but—was Luke really writing church-history? This again brings us to our problem.

Our first attempt to lift the veil from Luke's purpose was, as you will remember, a discussion of the opening verses. We saw that the beginning rouses our hope, but discovered that the outcome is disappointing, because the crucial phrase is missing. The usual completion by saying that "Jesus continued His work" in Acts does not stand the test of the facts as appearing in the book itself. Since this way leads to nothing, there are commentators who drop this explanation and hold that ἤρξατο here is pleonastic, for which they refer to the usage in later Hebrew and Aramaic; so *e.g.* WALTER BAUER [1]). Then this verse simply means: what Jesus did and taught. Though this pleonastic use of ἄρχομαι—שרי may be found in some places, this explanation cannot be accepted here, because this relative clause is too closely connected with the πρῶτος λόγος. It would only be acceptable, if there is no other way-out. Is there a third possibility which opens the road to an understanding of the following book while attaching the full force to the words? As fas as I am aware it has never been considered; yet it seems to me that *tertium datur*.

If Luke does not offer any help, it must be looked for elsewhere. If it is to answer the requirements, it ought to be a statement about something which was initiated by Jesus' activity (ὧν ἤρξατο ὁ Ἰησοῦς ποιεῖν τε καὶ διδάσκειν) and was carried on. That is found in the Epistle to the Hebrews [2]). Many difficult problems of this

---

[1]) W. BAUER, *Griechisch-deutsches Wörterbuch zu den Schriften des Neuen Testaments und der übrigen urchristlichen Literatur*[5], Berlin 1958, s.v. ἄρχω 2aβ.

[2]) It will be remembered that already Clement of Alexandria observed certain similarities between Acts and Hebrews; the words of Eusebius,

λόγος τῆς παρακλήσεως (xiii 22) can be left aside. For the present moment it is sufficient to recall that it is directed to people who are wavering in their faith and run the risk of loosing it (see especially x 26 ff.). According to the author the decisive phase of world-history has come since God ἐπ' ἐσχάτου τῶν ἡμερῶν τούτων spoke to us in the Son (i 1), who through His sacrifice "once for all at the end of the ages" (ix 26) brought the new and eternal covenant. Soon the judgment day will come and the readers are exhorted to be steadfast in the Christian faith, in order that they may enter the kingdom of God and not be doomed (x 19 ff.). In ch. ii he makes an urgent appeal on the conscience of his audience; with a "conclusio a minori ad maius", so typical a feature in this letter, he says referring to the O.T. law: "If the message declared by angels [1]) was valid (βέβαιος) and every transgression or disobedience received a just retribution, how shall we escape if we neglect such a great salvation" (ii 2-3), namely that decisive one brought by Christ (cf. vi 4-6). Of this salvation—σωτηρία—the following further explanation is given: ἥτις ἀρχὴν λαβοῦσα λαλεῖσθαι διὰ τοῦ κυρίου ὑπὸ τῶν ἀκουσάντων εἰς ἡμᾶς ἐβεβαιώθη, συνεπιμαρτυροῦντος τοῦ θεοῦ σημείοις τε καὶ τέρασιν καὶ ποικίλαις δυνάμεσιν καὶ πνεύματος ἁγίου μερισμοῖς [1]) (ii 4, 5).

The following facts make this text interesting for our problem:

a) ἥτις ἀρχην λαβοῦσα λαλεῖσθαι ὑπὸ τοῦ κυρίου is parallel to Acts i 1 περὶ πάντων ... ὧν ἤρξατο ὁ Ἰησοῦς ποιεῖν τε καὶ διδάσκειν. Here the work of Jesus is also the beginning of salvation.

b) This text combines a number of elements which are also "motifs" of Acts: σωτηρία - συνεπιμαρτυροῦντος - σημεῖα καὶ τέρατα - πνεύματος ἁγίου μερίσμοι. (cf. before p. 35 f.).

c) The activity of God as described here strongly recalls Act xiv 3 "speaking boldly for the Lord τῷ μαρτυροῦντι ἐπὶ τῷ λόγῳ τῆς

Hist. Eccl. VI 14, 2 are as follows: "And as for the Epistle to the Hebrews, he says indeed that it is Paul's, but that it was written for Hebrews in the Hebrew tongue, and that Luke, having carefully translated it, published it for the Greeks; hence, as a result of this translation, *the same complexion of style* is found in this Epistle and Acts" (tr. of H. J. LAWLOR-J. E. L. OULTON, London 1927, i, p. 188). As far as the historical circumstances are concerned, this was of course mere guesswork, but Clement saw certain parallels in style between the two books.

[1]) Cf. Acts vii 53; in ch. 1 the author has explained why the angels are inferior to the Son of God (vss. 4 ff.).

χάριτος αὐτοῦ, διδόντι σημεῖα καὶ τέρατα γίνεσθαι διὰ τῶν χειρῶν αὐτῶν.

d) The σύν—in the compound verb [1]) draws attention to the fact that there are other witnesses too; this must refer to the preceding verb ἐβεβαιώθη. Οἱ ἀκούσαντες—Jesus' disciples—are indicated as μάρτυρες which exactly corresponds to the task Jesus bequeathed to them Acts i 8 "and you shall be my witnesses" [2]).

e) This salvation which is expected (ix 28) took its beginning in the preaching of Jesus with which His suffering and ascension is closely connected (passim); therefore He is the ἀρχηγὸς τῆς σωτηρίας (ii 10, cf. Acts iii 15, v 31); it is made sure (ἐβεβαιώθη [3])) to these people who have not seen nor heard Him by those who heard Jesus, His disciples.

To sum up: our text says that *there is a solid bridge between the saving activity of Jesus and people living at a distance who have had no personal contact with the incarnate Lord.* The solidity of this bridge consists in the *confirmation* of the salvation by the apostles, sanctioned by God through miraculous gifts. But it is possible to reject this eternal salvation in Christ through unbelief, disobedience and sin (cf. ch. iii, iv). The exhortation of this letter is a call to firmness in the faith.

If we now return to Acts i 1 and the question of the link between the Gospel and Acts, it is obvious that the passage in Hebrews gives an excellent explanation. Not only the word ἤρξατο must be

---

[1]) It is a double compound, where both ἐπιμαρτυρέω and συμμαρτυρέω also exist (see BAUER, *a.a.O.*, Sp. 585 and 1541); with regard to the verb συμμαρτυρέω BAUER remarks: "Schon für Solon 24, 3 D² hat das συν- höchstens noch die Bedeutung der Verstärkung", but in such a double compound as we have here the συν- has its full force "together with . . .", as may be seen from 1 Clem. xxiii 5 and xliii 1 and other double compounds verbs as συμπαρακαλέω, συμπαραμένω, συναναπαύομα, συνεισέρχομαι, συνεπιτίθημι etc.

[2]) See p. 53 ff. about the prime importance of this idea of "witness".

[3]) See the comments of J. MOFFATT, *Epistle to the Hebrews*, Edinburgh 1924, p. 19: "If the Sinaitic Law ἐγένετο βέβαιος', the Christian revelation was also confirmed or guaranteed to us . . . ἐβεβαιώθη. It reached us, accurate and trustworthy. No wonder, when we realize the channel along which it flowed. It was authenticated by the double testimony of men who had actually heard Jesus, and of God who attested and inspired them in their mission".—The word βέβαιος is a favorite one in Hebrews iii 6, 14; vi 19; ix 17; the verb also xiii 9 and the substantive vi 16. H. SCHLIER, in his article on βέβαιος in: G. KITTEL, *Theologisches Wörterbuch zum Neuen Testament*, Bd. I, Stuttgart 1933, S. 600 ff., says: "Im ganzen tritt also bei dem Begriff βέβαιος im NT wieder der ursprüngliche Charakter, dass etwas *fest* ist *im Sinne eines festen Grundes*, hervor, bekommt aber in Verbindung mit bestimmten Substantiva den Ton von *gültig*" (S. 602).

emphasized, but the whole clause: "what Jesus began to do and to teach". These last words are a common Greek expression for all-round activity. Jesus' activity is saving, "for the Son of men came to seek and to save that which was lost" (Ev. xix 10). His coming to the world is announced by the message of the angel—familiar to us all—: "I bring you good news of a great joy which will come to all the people: for to you is born this day in the city of David a Savior, who is Christ the Lord". The aged Simeon said: "Mine eyes have seen thy salvation . . . a light for revelation to the gentiles and for the glory to thy people Israel" (ii 30-32). It is significant that the quotation from Isaiah xl 3 ff. in Luke's version is longer than in Mark-Matthew and ends with the words: καὶ ὄψεται πᾶσα σάρξ τὸ σωτήριον τοῦ θεοῦ (iii 6). In all the Gospels this tone of salvation is heard, but in Luke very markedly [1]). Here the great salvation Israel and the world had longed for took its beginning. "All things which Jesus began to do and teach", described in the first book were not just words and actions of a certain man Jesus, but a showing forth of His saving activity. This "Good News" was proclaimed by telling who Jesus was; not in the wearisome, boring way of some people who thrust their opinions upon you, who wish to be clear by repeating the same words but by simply telling what He did and said. This salvation is proclaimed in the world.

Dr. Dodd has so lucidly demonstrated that the *Kerygma* underlying the speeches of Acts is also the basis of the gospel [2]). The Gospel of salvation (in its eschatologycal sense) is the great gift to the world, made sure by His disciples, the "witnesses", and "the signs and wonders" of God, meeting on its way belief and un-belief, obedience of disobedience.

These words in the second half of this passage of the Epistle to the Hebrews may fittingly be used as a heading of Luke's second volume. I am firmly convinced that here we have found the scope of Acts, the angle under which we must see it to find the right perspective, or you may say: the hidden thread holding together the string of pearls.

It will be my present task to prove this thesis in confrontation with the contents of the book. These "motifs" will enable us to do

---

[1]) I may refer here to my article: *L'usage de ΣΩΖΕΙΝ "sauver" et ses dérivés dans les évangiles synoptiques*, in: *La Formation des Evangiles*, Bruges 1957, p. 178 ff.

[2]) C. H. Dodd, *The apostolic preaching and its developments*, London 1936.

so and will be discussed more in detail, but since such heavy words
as σωτηρία and μαρτύς are playing a part in it, these details will
more or less look like gentle hints, for otherwise I should have to
read out five or six monographs and Eutychus would have many
followers in this place.

1) The leading idea is σ ω τ η ρ ί α - σ ώ ζ ω. Peter's speech at
Pentecost opens with a quotation from Joel. The outpouring of the
Spirit is a sign that the last days "before the day of the Lord comes"
have dawned: the day of judgment and doom. "And it shall be
that whoever calls on the name of the Lord shall be saved" (ii 21).
This Lord, Peter continues, is Jesus who was rejected by the Jews,
but exalted by God. He can be appealed to as the Saviour (v 31),
for everyone who believes in him receives forgiveness of sins through
his name" (x 43). A summary of Peter's urgent appeal is: "Save
yourselves from this crooked generation" (ii 40) and the new community of the believers are called "those who are being saved".
The preaching of the Crucified and Risen Lord is always a call to
turn to Him the Saviour. The message Peter will bring to the house
of Cornelius will be one "by which you will be saved, you and your
household" (xi 14) and this message was exactly that *kerygma*
about Jesus. Paul in giving a sermon called a "word of exhortation"
(xiii 15), shows how the line of Israel's history leads up to the
Saviour; then after this historical introduction he directly addresses
his hearers: "Brethren, sons of the family of Abraham and those
among you that fear God, to us has been sent the message of this
salvation" (xiii 26) ὁ λόγος τῆς σωτηρίας ταύτης ἐξαπεστάλη (if
ὁ λόγος . . . ἐξαπεστάλη are really taken from Ps. cvii 20, as Nestle
indicates, it is remarkable that the words "of this salvation" are
inserted by Luke, see also p. 49 on Ev. iii 6) and gives the *kerygma*
about Jesus, ending with the words: "Let it be known to you therefore, brethren, that through this man forgiveness of sins is proclaimed to you".—This saving message is not confined to one people;
the words of the prophet Isaiah xlix 6 about the "light for the gentiles" receive a new meaning when the Jews reject it. It is significant
that this prophecy is quoted in the middle and at the end of the
book (xiii 47 and xvxiii 28), at a turning-point and the conclusion
of the work. Under this point of view Luke sees also the famous
discussion of the conference at Jerusalem. The issue is the question
whether the men from Judea with their teaching: "Unless you are
circumcised according to the custom of Moses you cannot be saved"

(xv 1) are right or not, and the answer of Peter is: "we believe that
we shall be saved through the grace of the Lord Jesus, just as they
will" (xv 11) and that is accepted under *proviso* of some regula-
tions for the intercourse with the jewish brethren. Paul is called
by the girl slave one who proclaims the ὁδὸς σωτηρίας (xvi 17) and
this way is shown to the jailer. He asking in a critical situation:
"what must I do (cf. ii 37 the question of the Jews!) to be saved",
receives the reply: "Believe in the Lord Jesus, and you will be
saved" (xvi 30-31). Here the salvation is always the core of the
message.

There are two interesting passages however where the word has
a somewhat different aspect. In ch. iv the disciples are examined
by the Sanhedrin for the healing of the lame man in the name of
the Lord. Peter asks with that bit of humour that is sometimes
found in Acts, if this good deed of healing is a reason for examination. He calls the man ὑγιής and then suddenly says: "there is
salvation in no one else (sc. than Jesus) for there is no other name
under heaven given by which we must be saved". This transition from
ὑγίεια to σωτηρία in itself is not strange [1]), because the latter word
can mean in Greek: bodily health [2]). But the remarkable thing is
that σωτηρία combines here the two meanings, which we usually
separate. This healing of the lame is a sign of the messianic era;
this healing of the body visualizes the totality of Christ's saving
power. The second passage is the famous story of the shipwreck
which has always puzzled the scholars. Why did Luke give this
story with such great detail? Presumably not to give students of
ancient history who are delighted by this information a chance
of reading the Scriptures. Did Luke use a piece of novel-writing [3])
to make his history more thrilling and did he intersperse it with
some Christian remarks? Even if this could be proved, the question
remains: why does it stand here in such an elaborate form? According to others [4]) its purpose was to show how many dangers Paul
had to pass before he reached his goal: preaching of the gospel in

---

[1]) In the Synoptic Gospels it is very frequently connected with healings,
see my article quoted in p. 49, n. 1.

[2]) Cf. H. G. LIDDELL-R. SCOTT, *A Greek-English Lexicon*[9], Oxford 1940,
II, p. 1751a.

[3]) E. NORDEN, *a.a.O.*, S. 313 f. gave a number of parallels; cf. also the
opinion of WELLHAUSEN, discussed by WIKENHAUSER, *Geschichtswert*, S. 413.

[4]) So e.g. F. W. GROSHEIDE, *De Handelingen der Apostelen* II, Amsterdam
1948, p. 415.

Rome. Harnack [1]) pointed to xxviii 14 "and so (οὕτως) we came to Rome", but according to Luke himself there was no hurry to reach Rome; they took things easily and in the meantime something had happened. οὕτως refers to the journey as a whole. If however the chapter is read with that double meaning of σῴζω in mind, it is striking that this stem is used seven times (xxvii 20, 31, 34, 43, 44, xxviii 1-4); this note of salvation, obscured by a translation like R.S.V. "escaped", is strong, as appears from the repetition in xxvii 44 and xxviii 1. It should be taken into consideration that the sea was an anti-divine power for the ancients; some demonic power in the service Δίκη, Justice (xxviii 4). The heart of the story however is the vision of the angel: "Do not be afraid, Paul, you must stand before Caesar, and so, God has granted you all those who sail with you. So take heart, men, for I have faith in God that it will be exactly as I have been told" (xxvii 24-25). About the purpose of Paul's journey we will speak presently, but here it must be noticed that God who also graciously spares Paul's companions, will let him reach the goal in spite of the anti-divine power and great danger, even the bite of a viper (with which compare the words to the disciples Luke x 19: "I have given you authority to tread upon serpents and scorpions and over all the power of the enemy, and nothing shall hurt you").

This salvation is the eschatological, ultimate activity of Jesus Christ; they alone who are believing in Him will escape the coming judgment of the "great and manifest day" of the Lord. The gentiles do not know God and walked "in their own ways" (xiv 16), in ἄγνοια serving idols (xvii 29 f.); the Jews transgressed because they rejected Him who was promised. Therefore they are called to "turn from these vain things to the living God" (xiv 15) and to repentance. That Jesus is the One appointed by God is manifest in His resurrection. "God, having raised up his servant, sent him to you first, to bless you in turning every one of you from your wickedness" (iii 26), is said to the Jews and for the philosophers in Athens the real message is: "The times of ignorance God overlooked, but now he commands all men everywhere to repent, because he has fixed a day on which he will judge the world in righteousness by a man whom he has appointed, and of this he has given assurance to all men by raising him from the dead" (xvii 30-31). The background

---

[1]) A HARNACK, *Die Apostelgeschichte*, Leipzig 1908, S. 7.

of all this is the O.T., the prophetic message and not a Hellenistic belief in saviour-Gods, the eschatological setting making all the difference. All the preaching in Acts serves this end, to make known what God has done in Christ Jesus and what will happen, since the "last days" are here. Luke uses a great many synonyms to describe this message (εὐαγγελίζομαι - λαλεῖν τόν λόγον - κηρύσσω - καταγγέλλω - διαμαρτύρομαι). It is the "word of life" etc. It has often been noticed that the speeches show a great similarity in train of thought; although there is some variation every time according to the audience. Ultimately all these sermons serve to insist upon the same fact: the need of salvation, the Man of Salvation, the way of salvation: rejection of God, the Saviour Christ, repentance and baptism. In this connection the observation of Dibelius [1]) is very much to the point, where he says that it is interesting to notice that the speeches in Acts are in the *oratio recta* and not *obliqua*, as often in pagan historiography; they are not a record of the message only, but a direct message itself.

If one reads Acts a great part of the material can immediately be subsumed under this heading: all *kerygmatic* passages are not Christological *in se*, but within this scheme: why He is the ultimate saviour; all conversion stories find here their place. This σωτηρία as an eschatological fact rests upon the resurrection of the rejected One and the gift of the Spirit. Step by step it becomes clear that "all flesh shall see the σωτήριον τοῦ θεοῦ": it comes to the Jews, but also to the Gentiles, the door of faith (xiv 27) is opened. The reality of this salvation becomes manifest in the healing of men, because it is the great restoration. Therefore the healing-stories can all be seen in this perspective: the saving name of Jesus. This σωτηρία is the determining and decisive factor of the book both in places when it is explicitly mentioned or indicated through the general pattern and parallelism of thought (e.g. the liberation of Peter (ch. xii).

But can men be sure about it? Is the enthusiasm of the Spirit no drunkeness (ii 13); was He who "hung upon the tree" not doomed (v 30); was the resurrection not a laughable story, rejected by leading Jews the Sadducees, the Greek philosophers (xvii 33) and Roman officials (xxvi 24)?

2) These questions are answered by a second fundamental con-

---

[1]) M DIBELIUS, *a a O*, S. 144.

ception: the *Witness* (μάρτυς). The following related words are
used: μαρτυρία - μαρτύριον - μαρτύρομαι - διαμαρτύρομαι - ἄμαρτυρος.

Many studies have been devoted to it, especially in connection
with the later development to "martyr" in its specific sence [1].
Except in these cases where it is used for somebody who is a man of
good repute (vi 3, x 22, xvi 2, xxii 12) it is always connected
with the revelation in Jesus the Christ. The word has its background
in the legal sphere, but is not confined to that. The best general definition of it is: to give an authentic statement concerning the truth, in
this case: concerning Gods salvation in Christ. Jesus had bequeathed
to his disciples the task of being His witnesses (Luke xxiv 47 -
Acts i 8) and this commandment of the Lord stands as a frontispiece
of the book. One passage of Peter's speech to Cornelius shows the
full force of its meaning: after having spoken about the man Jesus
Christ by whom the good news of peace is brought he continues:
"and we are witnesses to all that he did both in the country of the
Jews and in Jerusalem. They put him to death by hanging him on
a tree; but God raised him on the third day and made him manifest,
not to all the people but to us who are chosen by God as witnesses
... and he commanded us to preach to the people and to witness
most clearly that he is the one ordained by God to be judge of the
living and the dead. To him all the prophets bear witness, that
every one who believes in him receives forgiveness of sins through
his name" (x 39 ff.); 4 times in these 5 verses!

People who hear the message can be sure about it, because it
is guaranteed by the prophets as a promise of the coming salvation
and the actuality of the resurrection by those who saw it. In a
specific sense the apostles are the people who can bear witness
because they were eyewitnesses of the resurrection (i 22, iii 15,
v 32). Their work is διαμαρτύρεσθαι, that Jesus is the Christ, the
Anointed One (xviii 5) by the argument of the Scriptures and their
fulfilment. So Peter acts; in the same way Stephen is called "thy
witness" (xxii 20) because he has seen Jesus in glory (vii 56).
So the work of Paul is characterized. In his own words it is expressed: "to teach you in public and from house to house, διαμαρτυρό-

---

[1] R. SCHIPPERS, *Getuigen van Jesus Christus in het Nieuwe Testament*,
Franeker 1938 (thesis Free University, Amsterdam); H. STRATHMANN,
μάρτυς in: G. KITTEL, *Theol. Wörterbuch*, Bd. IV, Stuttgart 1942, S. 477 ff.,
who also mention other litterature. H. VON CAMPENHAUSEN, *Die Idee des
Martyriums in der alten Kirche*, Göttingen 1936, S. 30 ff.

μενος 'Ιουδαίοις τε καὶ 'Ελλήσιν τὴν εἰς θεὸν μετάνοιαν καὶ πίστιν εἰς τὸν κύριον ἡμῶν 'Ιησοῦν, it was the διακονία he had received from the Lord Jesus διαμαρτύρασθαι τὸ εὐαγγέλιον τῆς χάριτος τοῦ θεοῦ (xx 24) In accordance with his own statement (1 Cor. ix 5) Paul is regarded here as a witness, because he has seen the risen Lord. It is from this point of view that the long-winded story of Paul's trial in Jerusalem and Caesarea must be looked upon. Obviously these chapters xxi-xxviii the end of the book(!) do not contain much about the σωτηρία, but they are an assurance of Paul's activity. It is the typical discharge of his task which does not end with death in Jerusalem as he had expected (xx 22 ff.). In the first conversion-story his task is defined by the words: "a chosen instrument of mine to carry my name before the gentiles and kings and the sons of Israel" (ix 15); in the second account it reads: "you will be a witness for him to all men of what you have seen and heard"; in the third report he relates the words of Jesus: "for I have appeared to you for this purpose, to appoint you to serve and bear witness to the things in which you have seen me and to those in which I will appear to you" (xxvi 16). This is done before the Sanhedrin, the Roman governors and Agrippa. What he has done, was no evil, but the accomplishment of his task: "as I stand here testifying (διαμαρτυρόμενος) both to small and great, saying nothing but what the prophets and Moses said would come to pass: that the Christ must suffer and that, by being the first to rise from the dead, he would proclaim light both to the people and to the gentiles" (xxvi 22, 23). He brings this testimony even before the highest court in Rome. That happens most clearly as a work not of men, not even of Paul himself, but of God's will. In the beginning of his imprisonment at Jerusalem the Lord appeared to him in a vision; saying: θάρσει· ὡς γὰρ διεμαρτύρω τα περὶ ἐμοῦ εἰς 'Ιερουσαλήμ, οὕτω σε δεῖ καὶ εἰς 'Ρώμην μαρτυρῆσαι (xxiii 11). This is the deciding factor, the heading of the whole story.

What Jesus "had done and taught" (i 1) reflects itself in the witness of the apostles who are bound to speak "what they have heard and seen" (iv 20, xxii 15). Because it is the saving revelation of God They speak with παρρησία[1]), this frankness which is a standing

---

[1]) H. SCHLIER, παρρησία, in: G. KITTEL-G. FRIEDRICH, *Theol. Wörterbuch*, Bd. V, Stuttgart 1954, S. 869 ff.

characteristic of their preaching and a special gift of God (iv 29-31,
ix 27 f.) [1]). Quite plainly these uneducated men speak before the
Jewish leaders (iv 13), quite plainly they reveal the plan of God
(xiii 46-xiv 3). In the persons of these witnesses there is a remarkable
parallelism with the work of their Lord (healings - opposition),
most obviously in the death of Stephen, Mt. x 24, Joh. xiii 16,
xv 20, Luke vi 40 [1]).

This element of the "testimony" by the witnesses and its importance in the work of Luke comes to light in quite a different
manner namely in a formal characteristic of this book. The interesting parallelism between Peter and Paul has always attracted the
attention of scholars (the same preaching, even with the same
proof-texts; conflict with the magicians; healing of a lame man;
defence against the Jews). But this is not a special feature of these
two. There is much of this kind. From the 7 deacons two are
mentioned because of their preaching. Paul makes his first journey
with Barnabas, later he chooses Silas. The eye once being struck
by this fact discovers everywhere this repetition e.g. three times
Pauls conversion is told—twice the history of Cornelius; there are
scores of such double texts. Morgenthaler has made a careful
study of this phenomenon in his: "Die lukanische Geschichtsschreibung als Zeugnis" [2]) to which I may refer. He aptly sees behind
it the rule of the Torah, Deut. xix 15: "at the mouth of two witnesses, or at the mouth of three witnesses shall a matter be established", quoted elsewhere in the N.T. [3]). The whole book is meant
as a witness to the truth! And it will be remembered that Luke
himself declared it his aim ἵνα ἐπιγνῷς περὶ ὧν κατηχήθης λόγων
τὴν ἀσφάλειαν (R.V. the certainty). He used the historical
material for it according to the standards of his time, as they are
expressed by Josephus in his Contra Apionem [4]).

3) This witness is strong, because it is not only given by men, but

---

[1]) The parallelism between the death of Jesus and that of Stephen has
often been observed, see e.g. H. von CAMPENHAUSEN, a.a.O., S. 146 f.—
The theme "the apostle as imitator of his Lord" is a recurring one in Acts;
a treatment of it must, however, be postponed to a later occasion.

[2]) R. MORGENTHALER, Die lukanische Geschichtsschreibung als Zeugnis,
Zürich 1948, 2 volumes.

[3]) These texts have lately been discussed by H. VAN VLIET, No single
testimony, Utrecht 1958 (thesis Utrecht).

[4]) See my article: Opmerkingen over het doel van Lucas' geschiedwerk, in:
Nederlands Theologisch Tijdschrift IX (1955), blz. 323 ff.

it is *brought by God Himself*. This comes to light in several features
of Acts. In the light of Hebr. ii 4 the most important evidence of it
consists in the *"signs and wonders"*. They are announced in the
prophecy of Joel, wrought by Jesus as signs of the "last days"
(ii 22). Peter and his company did them (v 12) but they are not
done by the disciples themselves, their power and piety (iii 12);
they are a response to their prayer: "And now, Lord, look upon
their threats, and grant to thy servants to speak thy word with all
boldness, while thou stretchest out thy hand to heal, and signs and
wonders are performed through the name of thy holy servant
Jesus" (iv 29, 30). These signs are a confirmation of the word, as
appears also in xiv 3 "speaking boldly for the Lord, who bore witness
to the word of his grace, granting signs and wonders by their hands"
(cf. xv 12). This is the other side [1]) of the miracle-stories in Acts.

The gift of the Spirit is also a manifestation of Gods activity
(ch. ii, x). It is not man's design but God's that realizes itself
and men cannot stop it. The progress of the missionary work is not
planned by the disciples, but pushed along by God. The disciples
have to wait (i 8) before they can proclaim the mighty deeds of
God. They are not leaving Jerusalem to preach abroad, but a persecution is necessary (viii 1 ff.). Paul's great work does not take place
immediately after his conversion, but at least 10 years later and
a special and solemn instruction of the Spirit commands to send
him out and at the end "he declared all that God had done with
them" (xiv 27, xv 4) [2]). God was with them (cf. xi 26) as He was
with Christ (x 38) and Joseph (vii 9). The experience of Paul
(Rom. viii 28): "we know that in everything God works for good
with those who love him, who are called according to his purpose"
is confirmed here. Persecution, opposition and threats of the Jews
serve to the furtherance of the gospel (cf. ch. xiii-xiv, xvii-xviii).
It is God who adds to the church (ii 47 par.). Through heavenly
visions, also foretold as a sign of the "last days" the disciples are
encouraged (xviii 9, xxiii 11-27) and the way is shown to them
(ch. x very conspicuous - xvi). The plan of God is unfolded—again

---

[1]) They have of course also the character of demonstrating the saving
power of Jesus' work, see p. 51.
[2]) Since the delivery of these lectures I investigated this expression in:
Dominus Vobiscum, the background of a liturgical formula, in: *New Testament
Essays, studies in memory of T. W. Manson,* ed. A. J. B. Higgins, Manchester
1959, p. 270 ff.

and again δεῖ is used: in the life of Christ and in that of his disciples[1]).

4) The fourth point is the *reception of this message*. When it is proclaimed and manifests itself people are called to a decision; a division between men who reject and who accept it is to be seen (ii 12-13, xvii 4-5, 32, xiv 4, xxviii 25). On the one hand the admonition of Gamaliel not to fight against God does not do any good. The speech of Stephen is one continuous charge against the Jews because of their disobedience which showed itself in the types of Christ, Joseph and Moses: "You, stiffnecked people, uncircumcised in heart and ears, you always resist the Holy Spirit" (vii 51). The jealousy of the Jews against Paul, their plots against his life are prominent in the second part. In the sphere of paganism the opposition comes from the magicians, from the philosophers and the religion of the city-god, yea it comes from the church itself (xv 20). On the other hand there is a tone of gladness running through these pages: in Samaria when the word is preached there, and when they later on hear the reports of the growth of the gospel; when the gentiles receive the word (viii 14, xiv 27). The apostles are examples of obedience: Peter immediately after his liberation goes to the temple to preach—Philip follows up an in itself silly command to go to the deserted place where nobody could be expected (viii 26) and Paul declares: "I was not disobedient to the heavenly vision" (xxvi 19). It leads to growth in spite of the opposition, for mighty men like Herod are only straw in the hands of God; they die but the Word multiplies. This opposition is a strong temptation and therefore the churches are warned, admonished (παρα-καλέω) and strengthened by various visits.

The two volumes of Luke's work show: this is the way of the Word in this world, the Word of God, the Word of Salvation. These various motifs are not separate lines of thought, but various aspects of *one* great fact: God's plan of σωτηρία, how it came to the world in Jesus Christ and how it built the solid bridge across to them who did not see Jesus incarnate. Acts is the confirmation (βεβαίωσις) of what God did in Christ as told in the first book. The gospel is not the "initium christianismi", as Käsemann held [2]),

---

[1]) E. FASCHER, *Theologische Beobachtungen zu* δεῖ, in: *Bultmann-Festschrift*, p. 228 ff.

[2]) E. KÄSEMANN, *a.a.O.*, S. 137.

but the ἀρχὴ σωτηρίας and Acts confirms it as the word for the world.

Both Gospel and Acts are dedicated to a certain Theophilus who is an unknown figure, perhaps a Roman official (κράτιστος). Some years ago my compatriote Mulder tried to make it plausible from Acts that this Theophilus was a φοβούμενος τὸν θεόν [1]), a man who was on the brink of Christianity and wanted to have certainty. Our analysis of the book would excellently fit this theory, especially if we assume that this Theophilus lived in Rome, though we have no external evidence to make this certain. It may be that Luke compiled his book for people like those in Hebrews who were wavering in their faith. At any rate Luke calls on history as a sure foundation for the message: in these last days there is salvation for all who believe in Jesus Christ!

In these lectures I have strictly confined myself to the task of elucidating the purpose of Acts. We did not enter into the problems of historical criticism important though they are for a further study of the book. I hope that my conclusion: *this book is not a "metabasis eis allo genos", but a legitimate sequel and complement to Luke's gospel because it formed its confirmation,* may meet with your approval. For if it can be accepted it is not only a gain for N.T. theology, but also for the preaching of the gospel to-day.

---

[1]) H. MULDER, *Theophilus de "Godvrezende",* in: *Arcana Revelata, een bundel Nieuw-Testamentische studiën aangeboden aan Prof. Dr. F. W. Grosheide,* Kampen 1951, blz. 77 ff.

INDEX OF AUTHORS

Abel, F.M., 7n5, n6
Aberle, 90, 90n2
Aland, K., 166n40
Anderson, H., 23n1, 24, 24n3, 26, 26n2, n3, 27
Arndt, 47n1

Bailey, K., 69n1
Baird, J.A., 40
Baltensweiler, H., 40
Barrett, C.K., 91n6
Bauer, B., 117n1
Bauer, W., 204, 204n1, 206n5
Baur, F.C., 117n2, 118, 118n5
Beare, F.W., 26n2
Behm, J., 82n58, 185n1, 188n3, 197n2
Black, M., 36, 36n1
Blass, F., 7n5, n6, 90, 92n9
Bornhäuser, K., 6n3, 8n3
Boucher, M., 69n1
Bovon, F., 70n8
Brown, S., 71n9, 82n59, 88n72
Bruce, F.F., 93n15, 148n76
Büchele, A., 155, 155n5, 161n26
Büchler, A., 32, 32n1
Bultmann, R., 1, 4, 8, 9n1, 11n3, 12, 12n2, 21, 21n2, 26n2, 157n14, 201, 201n4
Burkitt, F.C., 158n18
Burrows, E., 3n2

Cadbury, H.J., 91, 91n4, n6, 93, 93n13, 158, 158n18, 160n21, 162n28, 164n34
Campenhausen, H. von, 212n1, 214n1
Catchpole, D., 155, 155n4
Conzelmann, H., 10n2, 25, 25n1, n2, 29, 29n2, n3, 30, 41, 48, 70n5, n8, 76n32, 81n55, 83n61, 91n8, 119, 156, 156n9, n10, 201, 201n5, 203
Corssen, P., 90, 90n1, 92
Creed, J.M., 70n6, 73n24
Crockett, L.C., 31n2, 32, 32n2, 34, 34n1, n2, n3
Cross, F.M., 129n38

Crossan, J.D., 69n1, n2, n5, 77n36
Crystal, D., 103n47, 106n58, 107n59, n60

Dahl, N.A., 85n67, 128n32
Davies, J.H., 133n46
Davies, W.D., 65
Davy, D., 103n47, 106n58, 107n60
Debrunner, A., 7n5, n7, 92
Deissmann, A., 105n54
Derrett, J.D.M., 183n32
Dibelius, M., 1, 2n5, 12, 12n2, 21, 21n2, 194, 194n2, n3, 199, 200, 200n1, 201, 211, 211n1
Dillon, R.J., 72n17, n18, n22
Dodd, C.H., 70n8, 76n32, 139n62, 207, 207n2
Dupont, J., 64, 69n4, 70n8, 73n24, 81n54, 82n59, 84n62, 187, 187n1, 199, 199n2
Düring, I., 110n65

Easton, B.S., 70n6, 187, 187n2
Edelstein, L., 110n66
Elliot, J.H., 122n23
Ellis, E.E., 70n6, 79n41, 169n3, 180n24
Ernst, J., 174n13
Eucken, C., 96n22
Evans, C.F., 169n2, 170n4, 176n18

Fascher, E., 146n72, 216n1
Feine, P., 185n1, 188n3, 197n2
Filson, F.V., 146n69
Finkel, A., 35, 35n2, n3, n4, 36, 36n2
Fitzmyer, J.A., 38n2, 91n8, 132n45, 133n48, 155, 155n5, 157n14, 160n20, n23, 162n27, n28, 163, 163n29, n32, 164n34, 169n1, n3, 175n14, n16
Flender, H., 25, 25n3, 26, 26n1, 27n2, 29, 30, 30n1, 70n6, 71n9, 91n7, 156n10
Foakes Jackson, F.J., 186n1, 196, 196n1, 199, 200, 200n2
Franklin, E., 70n7
Friedländer, P., 96n21, n22, 98n27

Fuhrmann, M., 105n55, 111n69, 113n77
Fuller, R.H., 157n13
Funk, R.W., 92n9
Furnish, V., 65

Gächter, P., 3n2
Gaston, L., 163, 163n30
Geyser, A.S., 1n1, 3n3
Gingrich, 28n1
Glockmann, G., 109n63
Godet, F., 159n19
Goulder, M.D., 70n6, n8, 146n70
Goulding, A., 31n1, 32, 33n1, 34n2
Grant, F.C., 103n44
Green, J.B., 158n17
Greven, H., 166n40
Grosheide, F.W., 209n4
Grundmann, W., 27n1, 70n6, 71n9, 119, 172n8, 181n29

Hadas, M., 194n1
Haenchen, E., 23n4, 91n6, 92n10
Hamm, D., 72n19, 172n7
Hamman, A.-G., 104n50
Harnack, A., 42, 193, 193n1, 210, 210n1
Hawkins, J.C., 155, 155n5
Hayes, W., 6n4
Heiberg, J.L., 100n37, n38, 101n40
Hennecke, E., 6n4
Herkommer, E., 97n24
Hiers, R., 70n8, 81n55
Higgins, A.J.B., 215n2
Hock, R., 112n73
Howland, R.L., 96n22
Huck, A., 166n40
Hunter, A.M., 186, 186n2, 197, 197n1, 199

Jaeger, W., 98, 98n29, 100n36, 114
Janson, T., 98n30
Jeremias, J., 22, 22n4, 23, 24, 26, 29, 65, 69n5, 70n5, n8, 76n32, 77n37, 134n49, 154, 155, 155n3, 157n14, 163, 153n33
Jervell, J., 74n26, 82n59, 85n67, 164
Johnson, L.T., 71n15, 72n19, n21, 73n23, 75n29, n31, 87n70, 122n22, 124n27, 125n29
Jonge, M. de, 38n2
Joüon, P., 69n3, 75n28
Judge, E.A., 93n15

Kaestli, J.D., 70n8, 73n24
Kamlah, E., 70n6, n8
Karris, R.J., 72n16
Käsemann, E., 201, 201n1, n2, 202, 202n1, n2, 203, 216, 216n2
Keck, L.E., 128n32
Kenyon, F.G., 96n19, n21
Klausner, 199
Klein, G., 91n7
Klostermann, E., 70n6, 73n24, 93n13
Knox, W.L., 26n2
Kodell, J., 87n70
Koester, H., 112n70
Kreissig, H., 104, 104n53
Kudlien, F., 100n36
Kühn, C.G., 101n41, 112n72, 116
Kümmel, W.G., 199

Lagarde, P. de, 106, 106n56
Lagrange, M.-J., 7n5, n7, 9n3, 22, 22n3, 65, 70n7
Lake, K., 186n1, 188, 188n3
Lampe, G.W.H., 42, 120n14
Laurentin, R., 1n1, 3, 3n2, n3, 4n1, n2, 13n2, 14n1
Lawror, H.J., 205n2
Leaney, A.R.C., 21n1, n4, 22, 22n1, 26n3, 33n1, 34, 35, 35n1, 42
Liddell, H.G., 80n51, n52
Lightfoot, R.H., 21n3, 22n2
Linnemann, E., 69n1
Lohse, E., 161n26
Loisy, A., 70n6, 201, 201n3
Lyonnet, S., 3n2

Mac Giffert, 186
Malherbe, A., 103, 103n45, n46, 104, 104n48, 109n63
Manitius, C., 101n39
Mann, J., 18n2, 18n3, 32, 32n3
Manson, T.W., 58
Marsden, E.W., 100n36
Marshall, I.H., 70n6, n7, n8, 71n9, 74n26, 81n57, 93n15, 133n48, 156, 156n10, n11, 157n12, n14, 158, 158n16, 160n20, 161n26, 163, 163n31, 165, 165n38, 169n1, 170, 170n4, 175n15, 180n27
Martyn, J.L., 128n32
Matera, F.J., 155, 155n6
Mattill, A.J. Jr., 118n9, 146n70
Meeks, W.A., 104, 104n49, n50, n52, n53, 105n54, 112, 112n71

Menoud, Ph., 188, 188n1
Milligan, G., 80n46
Minear, P., 72n20, 120, 125n29
Moessner, D.P., 130n39, 132n44, 134n51, 142n64, n66, 146n70
Moffatt, J., 206n3
Morgenthaler, R., 6, 7n1, 11n2, 171n6, 214, 214n2
Morris, L., 31n1
Mosely, A., 75n30, 77n37
Moulton, J.H., 80n46, 158n18
Muhlack, G., 119n12
Mulder, H., 217, 217n1

Nestle, E., 114, 166n40, 208
Neyrey, J., 155, 155n7, 156
Nicholson, E.W., 129n38
Norden, E., 92n9, 93, 93n12, 188, 188n2, 209n3

Ollivier, M.J., 69n3
Oulton, J.E.L., 205n2
Overbeck, F., 118n8

Palm, J., 93n14
Patte, D., 69n1
Plümacher, E., 9n6
Plummer, A., 7n2, 7n4, n7, n8, 9n3, 59, 70n5, 71n9, 74n26, 78n38, 159n19, 165, 165n38, 175n14
Prast, F., 72n19, 83n60, 87n71

Rackham, R.B., 118n9, 146n70
Radl, W., 117n1, 118n5, n8, 119, 119n12, n13, 120n14, 146n70
Rajak, T., 92n9
Reicke, B., 40, 139n62
Reiling, J., 67
Rehkopf, F., 163n31, 164n35
Richard, E., 124n27
Robbins, V., 91n8
Roberts, C.H., 104, 104n53
Roloff, J., 119n13, 167, 167n43
Ruch, M., 98n28
Rydbeck, L., 102, 103, 103n43

Sahlin, 188
Sandmel, S., 160n20
Schippers, K., 212n1
Schlatter, A., 138n60
Schlier, H., 206n3, 213n1
Schmidt, W., 101n41, 116

Schneckenburger, M., 118, 118n6
Schneemelcher, W., 6n4
Schneider, G., 69n4, 70n8, 72n16, 154, 154n1, 155, 157n14
Schneider, J., 162n27
Schrage, W., 176n19
Schramm, T., 160n24
Schubert, P., 72n20, 133n46, 187, 187n3
Schürmann, H., 160n21, n22, n24, 162n27, 163n30, 166n41
Schütz, J., 104n49, 105n54
Scott, R., 80n51, n52, 209n2
Scroggs, R., 104n49
Shuler, P.L., 90n3, 111n70
Smith, M., 106n57, 107n59
Smith, J.Z., 104n49
Sparks, H.F.D., 23, 23n2
Stählin, G., 119n12
Steck, O.H., 122, 122n23, n24, 127n31, 136n55
Steinmetz, P., 111n69
Strathmann, H., 23n5
Streeter, B.H., 42
Suggs, J., 64, 65
Swellingrebel, J.L., 67

Talbert, C.H., 110, 110n64
Tannehill, R., 175n15
Taylor, V., 154, 154n2, 155, 157n14, 164n36, 167n42
Temple, P., 13n1
Theissen, G., 104n49, 105n54
Thiessen, H., 69n3
Tiede, D.L., 71, 71n12, n13, n14, 72n20, 74n25, 120, 121, 121n20, 122n21, 161n26
Tolbert, M.A., 69n1
Toynbee, A.J., 91n6
Trocmé, E., 157n15
Tuckett, C.M., 158, 158n17
Turner, N., 158n18, 160n21, n23, 163n29, 164n34, 165n39

Unnik, W.C. van, 38n1, 91n8, 92n10

Via, O., 69n1
Violet, B., 22
Vliet, H. van, 214n3

Weichert, V., 115
Weinert, F.D., 69n4, 71, 71n10, n11, 74n27

Weiss, J., 186
Wellhausen, J., 209n3
Wiener, A., 133n47
Wifstrand, A., 92n9, 102
Wikenhauser, A., 185n2, 198, 198n1,
    209n3
Wilckens, U., 72n19
Wimmer, F., 99n32

Winter, P., 13n2
Woude, A.S. van der, 38n2, n3

York, J.O., 177n20

Zeegers-Vanderhorst, N., 109n63
Zeller, E., 118, 118n8
Zerwick, M., 69n4

INDEX OF BIBLICAL REFERENCES

Genesis

9.5	136n55
27-43 ch	14, 15, 18
27.1	18
27.28	18
28.10	18
28.12	15, 18
28.13	15
28.13-15	18
28.14	15
28.15	15
28.19	15, 18
28.21	15, 18
28.30	18
28.31	15
28.32	15
29.1	15
29.4ff	15
29.31	14, 19
29.32	16
30.2	15, 19
30.3	15
30.13	16, 19
30.22	14, 16, 19
30.23	16
30.25ff	16
30.33	17
30.35	15
31.3	19
31.17ff	14, 16
31.42	16, 19
32.3ff	14
32.4	19
32.11	16
32.12	19
32.17	17, 19
32.29	16
32.30	16
33.1ff	17
33.11	16
33.18	19
35.9	19, 32, 35
35.19	17
37.1	19, 32
37.2	17, 19
37.11	17, 19
38.1	19, 32
38.3	17, 19
39.1	17, 19
40.1	19
41.1	19
41.28	17
41.38	19
42.1ff	17
42.18	21
42.22	136n55
42.23	17, 19
42.28	17, 18, 19
42.38	18, 19
43.7	17, 19
50.24-25	138

Exodus

3.16	138
12.6	161n25
32.11-33	133n47

Leviticus

9:1	32
12.1	32
13.29	32
14.1	32
14.9	33
25 ch	38
25.10	27

Deuteronomy

1.12	134
4.6	142n64
4.25	142n64
5.23-31	142n43
5.24	132
6.5	5n1
7.12	32
9.1	32
9.4-5	142n64
9.18	142n64
9.27	142n64
10.1	32
11 ch	33, 33n1
11.2	142n64
11.10	32
11.17	33
13.5	142n64
13.11	142n64
15.9	142n64
16.9-12	150
18.15	126
18.15-18	120
18.15-20	132
18.15-22	132n43
18.16b-20	132
18.19	136n55
18.20	142n64
18.22	142n64
19.15	214
19.16	142n64
25.2	142n64
28.45a	127n31
28.45b	127n31
28.46	127n31
28.47	127n31
28.48-57	127n31
28.59-62a	127n31
28.62b	127n31
28.63b-68	127n31
32.5	142
32.28	142n64

Judges

11.1f	22

1 Samuel

2 ch	4n2

2 Samuel

4.11	136n55
11.2	32

1 Kings

8.35	33
8.56-58	32
17 ch	33
17.9	23
18.1-39	153

19.4-18	133n47	9.29-30	142n67	61.1f	37
19.19-21	135n52	9.29-30a	127n31	61.1ff	35
		9.30	128n35	61.1-2	24, 32,
2 Kings		9.30b	127n31		33
		9.32	127n31	61.1-5	38
1.2-16	135n52	9.33b-35	127n31	61.1-7	36, 38
5 ch	32, 33,	9.36-37	127n31	61.2	34, 33
	33n1			61.3	35n4
7 ch	32, 33n1	*Job*		61.5-6	35n4
7.9	33n1			66 ch	32
8.3	33	11.18	80n49		
9.7	136n55	13.18	80n49	*Jeremiah*	
13.23	32, 33				
17.7-17	127n31	*Psalms*		2 ch	32
17.18	127n31			6.6-21	138
17.19	127n31	9.12(13)	136n55	6.15	138
17.20	127n31	79.1-5	127n31	7.1-7	182n31
18.14	128n33	79.7	127n31	7.8-20	182n31
		79.8a	127n31	7.24	128n33
2 Chronicles		106.6-7	127n31	7.25-28	127n31
		106.13-14	127n31	7.26	127n31
5.26	33	106.16	127n31	7.32-34	127n31
7.13	33	106.19-21a	127n31	7.34b	127n31
24.18-22	127n31	106.24-25	127n31	12.7	136n56
24.20-22	136n55	106.28-29a	127n31	22.5	136n56
24.23-24	127n31	106.32-39	127n31	25.3-7	127n31
25.12	33	106.40-42	127n31	25.8-14	127n31
36.12-16a	127n31	107.20	208	25.11	127n31
36.16b-21	127n31	118.22	141	26.2-5	127n31
36.21b	127n31			26.6	127n31
		Isaiah		29.17-18	127n31
Ezra				29.19-20a	127n31
		1.16-20	182n31	29.30b	127n31
9.7a	127n31	1.21-26	182n31	35.13-15	127n31
9.7b	127n31	4.6	32	35.17	127n31
9.9a	127n31	6.9-10	151, 192	44.2	127n31
9.10b-11	127n31	8.8	197n3	44.3-5	127n31
9.13	127n31	29.1-4	138n59	44.6	127n31
9.14b	127n31	29.6	138	44.7-10	127n31
9.15b	127n31	32.18-33.15	32	44.11-15	127n31
		40.3ff	207	66.1	128
Nehemiah		42.1	133n48		
		42.11	197n3	*Ezekiel*	
1.7-8a	127n31	43.1-21	32		
1.8b	127n31	49.6	151,	29.2	127n31
9.13-14	127n31		197n3,	33.6	136n55
9.16-17a	127n31,		208	33.8	136n55
	128n33	49.8	27	38.2	127n31
9.18	127n31	52.7	38, 38n2		
9.20	128n35	54.2-55.6	32	*Daniel*	
9.26	127n31,	58.6	24, 27, 33		
	142n67	61 ch	38, 38n2,	9.5-6	127n31
9.26-30	129n36		39	9.7b	127n31
9.27a	127n31	61.1	24, 32,	9.8	127n31
9.28a	127n31		33, 33n1,	9.9b-11a	127n31
9.29	128n33		35n4, 36		

9.11b-14a	127n31
9.14b	127n31
9.15b	127n31
9.16	127n31
9.17b	136n56
9.17b-18a	127n31
9.25	38

Joel

3.4	79

Habbakuk

2.11	138

Zechariah

1.2	127n31
1.3-4	127n31
1.6	127n31
7.8-14	129n36
7.11-12b	127n31
7.12b	128n35
7.12c-14	127n31
7.14	127n31
7.14a	127n31

Malachi

3.1	4n2
4.5-6	133n47

Sirach

48.7-8	133

Baruch

1.19	128n34
1.20	127n31
2.1-5a	127n31
2.6-7	127n31
2.9	127n31
2.13-14	127n31
2.20-26	127n31
2.26	136n56
2.29-30	127n31
2.30	128n33
2.33	128n33
3.4b	127n31
3.7a	127n31
3.8	127n31

Tobit

3.4b	127n31

Psalms of Solomon

8.28	127n31
9.1a	127n31
9.1c	127n31
9.2a	127n31
17.20	127n31

Matthew

1 ch	4
4.25-5.1	63
5 ch	65
5.1	42
5.3-12	35
5.8	36
5.18	59
5.25f	55
5.32	59
6 ch	55
6.22-23	52
6.33	84n65
7.13-14	176
7.22f	56
7.28	42
8.19	164
9.15	159
9.33 par	5n3, 6n1
9.37-10.1	44
10 ch	55
10.24	214
10.26f	54
11.12f	59
11.25 par	2n4, 5n1
11.25-27	44
11.27	13
12.23	5n3, 6n1
12.24	52
12.31	54
12.32	54
12.33	5n3
12.38f	55
13.13 par	5n1
13.14-15	5n1
13.14f	50
13.19	5n1
13.23 par	5n1
13.31-33	84n66
13.50	74
13.53-58	20
13.54ff	31
13.55 par	13
13.54-56	13
14.12	173n9
14.33	5n5

15.10 par	5n1
15.31	5n4
16.1f	55
16.5f	54
16.12	5n1
19.1	45
19.28	73
21.18	56
21.19	56, 78
21.20	5n3, 6n1, 78
22.7	127n31
22.13	74
22.33	6n1
23 ch	181
23.1-36	53
23.29-31	127n31
24 ch	55, 181
24.1-51	73
24.51	74
25.1-30	73
25.14-30	69, 73
25.19	73
25.21	73
25.23	73
25.30	74
25.44	59
27.25	50
28.18	198

Mark

1.21	21n1
1.22 par	5n3, 6n2
1.27 par	5n3, 6n2
1.32	160
2.12 par	5n3
2.19	159
2.25	160
3.7-10	63
3.20-21	9n2
3.22	52
3.28-30	54
3.31-35 par	9n2
4.6	160
4.30-32	84n66
4.41 par	5n3, 6n1
5.15	5n3, 6n1
5.20	5n3, n6
5.42 par	5n3
6.1-6	20, 21, 26n2, 31
6.2 par	5n3, 6n2
6.2-4 par	9n2

6.4	11n2, 26n2	*Luke*		1.68	51
6.5	21	1 ch	4	1.68-79	14
6.5b	26n2	1-2 ch	3n5, 4,	1.69	78n40, 85
6.10	164		14, 15,	1.71	16, 19,
6.21	160		18, 47		78n40
6.34	59	1-3 ch	2	1.72	16
6.51 par	5n3, 6n1	1.1	184, 187	1.73	16, 177n21
6.56	164	1.1-3	18, 92,	1.75	17
7.6	50		98, 101,	1.76	17, 19
7.17	160		102, 106,	1.77	51
7.37 par	5n3, 6n1		114	1.79	17, 79
8.11f	55	1.3	72,	1.80	2, 12n1
8.14f	54		76n34	2.1-5	19
8.17	5n1	1.5	109	2.2	17
8.19	160	1.5-25	18	2.6-14	19
8.20	160	1.5-2.39	3, 4	2.9-12	4n3
8.21	5n1	1.9	7n4	2.11	85
8.31 par	10n2	1.10	51	2.13-14	4n3
9.1-23	53	1.11-20	4n3	2.14	82
9.11 par	10n2	1.17	51	2.15	17, 19
9.32	5n1	1.21	5n3	2.15-20	19
10.1	45	1.26	15, 18	2.18	5n3
10.24-32	5n3, 6n1	1.26-38	4n3, 18	2.19	12n1, 17, 19
10.30	159	1.28	15, 18	2.21	17, 19, 160
11.3	165	1.30	15, 18		
11.12-14	56	1.31	15, 18	2.22	17, 19, 160
11.18	5n3	1.32	84, 85, 87		
12.4	165			2.22-24	19
12.5	165	1.33	15, 18, 81, 84	2.22-28	146n21
12.9 par	127n31	1.36	15	2.25	4n4
12.17 par	5n3	1.38	15	2.25-35	19
12.32	43	1.39	15	2.26	4n4
12.33	5n1	1.39-45	19	2.27	4n4
12.34	43	1.41	4n4	2.29-32	14
13.7 par	10n2	1.42	15, 19	2.30	78n40
13.10	10n2	1.45	16, 19	2.30-32	207
14.9	164	1.45-46	19	2.31	50
14.12	158n15	1.46	16	2.31-32	152, 153
14.12a	159	1.46-55	14	2.32	14, 41, 51,
14.12b	160	1.48	16		142n65,
14.12c	163	1.54	14, 16		151
14.13b	164	1.55	16, 177n21	2.33	5n3
14.13c-14a	164			2.34	41, 86
14.14a	165	1.57-66	19	2.35	87
14.14b	165	1.58	11n2	2.36	4n4
14.15	165	1.61	11n2, 16	2.36-38	19
14.16	166	1.63	5n3, 16	2.39-41	19
14.17	161	1.64	16	2.40	2, 12,
14.41	159	1.65	16, 19		12n1,
15.5 par	5n3	1.66	16		17, 19,
15.20	160	1.67	4n4, 16		126n30
15.22	161	1.67-80	19		

2.41	3	3.8	48,	4.39	78n39		
2.41-42	12		177n21	4.40	160		
2.41-43	12	3.11	162	4.42	41, 48,		
2.41-45	3n1, 5	3.14	163		163		
2.41-51	146n71	3.15	51	4.43	83, 84		
2.41-51a	1, 3,	3.18	51	5.1	41, 48,		
	3n1, 4,	3.21	51		43, 63		
	6, 8, 10,	3.22	153n48	5.1f	48		
	12	3.22b	148n76	5.3	41, 48		
2.41-52	1	3.34	52,	5.8	5n5		
2.42	3, 7n4,		177n21	5.15	43, 48,		
	160	4 ch	38, 49		63		
2.42-43	3n4	4.3	163	5.17-26	117, 176		
2.42-52	19	4.9-12	146n71	5.17-6.6	141n63		
2.43	3n4, 9	4.10	160	5.18-19	11n3		
2.44	3n4, 4,	4.13	162	5.24	163		
	6, 7n3,	4.13-15	21n1	5.25	78n39		
	11, 12	4.14	21n1	5.27	163		
2.45	3n4, 11	4.14-15	21n1, 30	5.29	48		
2.45-46	12	4.14-9.50	169n3	5.29 par	47		
2.46	3n1, n4,	4.16	23, 35	5.35	159		
	17, 19	4.16-20	35	6 ch	63		
2.47	1, 2n4,	4.16-30	11n3, 20,	6.1	46		
	3n1, n4,		22, 23n1,	6.1f	67		
	5, 6, 8,		31, 32,	6.1-11	63		
	9, 10,		33, 33n1,	6.2	42		
	11, 11n1,		34, 36,	6.3	160		
	12, 17		37, 86	6.6-11	176		
2.47-48	19	4.17	11n3	6.7	141n63		
2.48	3n4, 4,	4.18-19	24, 33	6.10	164		
	8, 9, 11,	4.19	162	6.13	46, 63,		
	18	4.20	11n3, 24		160		
2.48-49	8, 13	4.21	35,	6.17	43, 46,		
2.48a	5		78n40		48, 50,		
2.48b	5	4.22	5n3, 6n1,		60, 63,		
2.49	8, 9, 10,		22, 23,		64, 65,		
	12, 13n2		24, 35,		67		
2.50	2n4, 4,		36	6.18	64		
	8, 12	4.22-24	21	6.19	48, 63		
2.51	3, 12,	4.23	21, 21n1,	6.19 par	47		
	18, 19		n2, 25,	6.20	84		
2.51b	2n6		25n1, 27,	6.20-23	35, 55,		
2.51b-52	12		30		63, 65		
2.51c	2, 12n1	4.24-28	35, 36, 37	6.20-26	67		
2.51c-52	2	4.25	33, 160	6.20a	66		
2.52	12n1,	4.25-27	22	6.22	66		
	126n30	4.25-28	36	6.23	65		
3.1	162	4.26	23n3	6.24	65		
3.3	162	4.27	33	6.24-49	65		
3.6	207, 208	4.28f	50	6.26	65, 66		
3.6-8	162n40	4.29	11n3, 33,	6.27	63, 65,		
3.7	47, 48		166		66		
3.7-21	47	4.31-32	178n22	6.27-38	57		
3.7	86n69	4.31ff	30	6.27-49	64		

Reference	Page	Reference	Page	Reference	Page
6.27f	65, 67	8.48	163	9.45	5n1, 134
6.27a	64, 65, 66	8.55	162n39	9.46-48	134, 140
6.28	65	9.1	84	9.48	134
6.32-34	64	9.1-17	59	9.49	134, 134n50
6.35-38	64	9.1ff	87		
6.39	163	9.2	83, 87	9.51	45, 132, 135, 139, 146
6.40	214	9.3f	60		
6.46-49	67	9.4	164		
7.1	50, 63, 64	9.8	79n42	9.51-62	45n4
7.1-10	11n3	9.10-17	48	9.51-18.30	45
7.1-23	64	9.10f	47	9.51-19.28	169, 170
7.6	163	9.11	87	9.51-19.44	135, 169n3
7.9	48	9.11f	48		
7.11	63	9.12	48, 163	9.51-19.46	152, 153
7.11-17	11n3, 117	9.12-17	87	9.51ff	71
7.13	163	9.13	50	9.52	44
7.18	46	9.18	41, 48, 164	9.52-56	146
7.22	163			9.52a	44
7.24	47, 48	9.18 par	47	9.53	135n53
7.28	67, 84	9.18f	47	9.54	135n52
7.29	47, 48, 63, 64, 65	9.20	141	9.57	44, 164
		9.20-22	143, 161	9.57-62	44
		9.20-27	141	9.57a	45
		9.22	132, 134, 161	9.59-62	135n54
7.29-30	86	9.23	135n54	9.60	44
7.30	43, 65, 86	9.23-25	139n49	9.61-62	135n52
		9.26	162n40	9.62	59
7.36-8.3	11n3	9.28	132, 162	10 ch	42
7.42	48	9.29-35	152	10.1	42
7.45	48	9.30-32	141	10.1-9	60
7.56	87	9.31	132, 143, 152	10.1-16	135n54
8.1	63, 84			10.1-24	44
8.1-3	86	9.31-50	152	10.2	42
8.4ff	64	9.32	133, 144, 152	10.5	42
8.6	160			10.5-7	43
8.8	43, 47, 66	9.32a	133	10.3	42
		9.33	48	10.4	42
8.9	160	9.33b	132, 133, 140, 148	10.7f	60
8.10	5n1, 84			10.9	42, 60, 83, 84n64
8.12	66	9.34b-35	133		
8.15	66	9.35	133n48, 152	10.9-13	42
8.18	76n33			10.10	165
8.19	48	9.35-36	145	10.11	84n64
8.19-21	47	9.35b	133	10.13	42
8.21	66	9.37f	47	10.17-23	42, 53
8.25	163	9.38	54	10.17-24	53
8.31	168	9.39	164	10.19	42
8.40-56	117	9.40b	134	10.21-24	44
8.42	41, 48	9.41	134, 142, 148	10.22	46
8.44	78n39			10.23	43, 44, 46, 61
8.45	48	9.43	5n3, 6n1	10.24	61
8.47	36, 48, 78n39	9.44	140, 141	10.25	43
		9.44b	134	10.25-37	43

10.28	77	11.46	53, 136,	12.54-59	172n8
10.29	43		141n63	12.54-13.5	172n7
10.30-35	77	11.46f	54	12.54-13.30	54, 55
10.36	76n34	11.47-48	117	12.55	172n7
10.36-37	77	11.47-51	136, 139	12.56	137
10.37	58	11.47-12.1	137	12.57	55
10.38	43, 58,	11.48f	53	12.57f	54
	135n53	11.49	136	12.58	55
10.38-11.13	43	11.50-51	136,	13 ch	178n22,
11.1	43, 46,		136n55,		181,
	160,		139		181n28
	181n29	11.52	53, 59,	13-14 ch	170,
11.2	84		136		170n4
11.7f	43	11.52-12.1	136	13.1	173, 182
11.11	42	12 ch	182	13.1-5	54, 56,
11.12	42	12.1	45, 52,		77,
11.13	42,		53, 135,		172n7
	181n29		141n63	13.1-9	171, 172,
11.14	41, 48,	12.1-12	53		172n8,
	52	12.1-13	53		174,
11.14-36	52, 136	12.1-13.9	136		174n10,
11.14b	136	12.1-14.24	182		175, 178,
11.15	52, 136	12.1b	136		179, 182
11.16	52, 136	12.2	53	13.1-35	169, 170,
11.20	52, 84	12.3	53		171, 172,
11.21	181n29	12.4f	53		175n14,
11.22	166	12.8-10	78n40		178, 179,
11.23	52,	12.10f	53		180, 182,
	135n54	12.13	54, 55,		183
11.26	163		77,	13.2	76n33
11.27	52, 54		172n8	13.2-5	173
11.27-28	9n2, 136	12.13-21	172n8	13.3	137,
11.28	52, 64,	12.15-21	59		174n13
	66	12.16	77	13.4	76n33,
11.29	52, 135,	12.20	84		174,
	136	12.22	55, 84		175n14
11.29-32	136	12.22-53	54	13.5	137,
11.30	138	12.28	54		174n13
11.30ff	52	12.32	59, 84	13.6-9	77,
11.32	138	12.32-34	135n54		172n7,
11.33-36	52	12.35-40	55		173,
11.37	136	12.40	76n33,		174n10
11.37-54	53,		78n40	13.7	172n7,
	141n63,	12.41	77, 87		175
	180n25	12.42	87	13.10	170n4
11.37-12.1	137	12.42-48	77	13.10-17	56, 171,
11.40f	53	12.46	54		172,
11.42	161n25	12.49-50	147		172n7,
11.43	140,	12.49-53	172n7		175, 178,
	141n63	12.49-13.35	172n7		179, 180
11.43-44	136	12.51-53	172n7	13.10-21	136
11.44	53	12.54	54, 55	13.10-35	170n4
11.45	53	12.54-55	172n7	13.11	175n14
11.45f	43	12.54-56	54	13.14	41, 48, 55,

	161n25, 176		179, 180n24	14.47f	197n3
13.15	180, 182	13.31-15.32	56	15 ch	59
13.15-16	86n69	13.32	165,	15.1	43, 58,
13.16	78n40,		175n15		64
	175n14	13.32-33	173, 175	15.1-2	137
13.17	41, 48,	13.32b	139	15.1-3	75, 77,
	55, 56,	13.33	135n53,		86
	176, 178		139, 161	15.1-32	57, 58,
13.18-19	172, 178,	13.33-35	136		141n63
	179, 180	13.33b	137, 149	15.4-7	77
13.18-21	84, 171,	13.34-35	136,	15.7	58
	172n7,		172n7,	15.8-10	77
	180		173,	15.10	58
13.18-35	181		174n10,	15.11-32	77
13.20-21	172, 178,		n11, 183	15.18f	58
	179, 180	13.34a	149	15.24	163
13.21	172n7	13.35a	139	15.30	160
13.22	135,	13.35b	138	15.42	160
	135n53,	14-15 ch	77	16.1-13	58, 59
	163,	14.1	182	16.14	59
	174n12,	14.1-6	57	16.14-15	76,
	180n24	14.1-24	141n63,		76n35
13.22-30	56, 136,		180n24,	16.14-18	137
	171, 172,		180n25,	16.14-31	59,
	172n7,		182		141n63
	175,	14.3	43	16.15	76
	175n16,	14.4	77	16.16	84n64,
	176, 178,	14.7	77		86n69
	179, 180,	14.7-11	57, 140,	16.19	59
	180n24		141n63	16.19-31	59, 76,
13.22-14.35	170n5	14.12	11n2		137
13.23	56, 85	14.12-14	57	16.20	166
13.24	176	14.12c	163	16.22	78n40,
13.25	176,	14.15	77		84,
	176n18	14.15-15.32	135n54		177n21
13.26	182	14.16-24	77	16.23	177n21
13.26-27	180	14.21	57	16.24	177n21
13.27	182	14.24	57, 58	16.25	177n21
13.28	74,	14.25	135,	16.29	177n21
	78n40,		135n53,	16.29-31	65
	177, 178		137	16.30	177n21
13.29	172n7,	14.25-27	141	16.31	56, 137
	181n28	14.25-33	77	17 ch	60
13.30	54, 177	14.25-34	64	17.1	59
13.31	137, 173	14.25-35	57	17.1-18.30	59
13.31-33	141n63	14.26	58	17.5	59
13.31-35	57,	14.26-33	46	17.6	60
	135n54,	14.27	57	17.8	43
	139, 147,	14.33	58	17.9	60
	171, 172,	14.34	57	17.11	60,
	172n7,	14.35	43, 57,		135n53,
	n8, 174,		66		136
	175, 178,	14.35b	58	17.11-19	60, 137
				17.14	60

Ref	Page	Ref	Page	Ref	Page
17.17	60	19.9-10	78n40, 86n69	20.45-47	141n63
17.18	60			20.47	141n63
17.19	60	19.10	78n40, 207	20.47b	141n63
17.20	60			21.6	140, 159
17.20-21	84n64, 85, 137	19.11	70, 74-84, 89, 135n53, 138	21.15	126n30
17.21	138			21.16	11n2
17.22	61, 78n40, 159, 160			21.22	51
17.23	138	19.11-27	69	21.31	83
17.24	78n40	19.14	74, 86	21.38	64
17.25	61, 134n49, 138, 147	19.15	74, 85, 166	22 ch	140
		19.17	74	22-23 ch	155, 159
17.25-30	137	19.18	48	22.1	159, 160n20
17.26	78n40	19.19	74	22.2	51
17.30	78n40	19.28	135n53, 160	22.3	140
18.1	61, 76			22.7	158n15, 160, 161, 167
18.2	166	19.29-40	162		
18.8	61, 78n40	19.31	75, 165	22.7-13	154, 157, 159, 166
		19.37	86, 138	22.7a	159, 166
18.9	61, 76, 76n35	19.37-39	46	22.7b	160
18.9-14	61, 141n63	19.38	80, 81, 82, 88, 138	22.8	161, 163-166
18.10-14	58	19.38b	138	22.8b	163
18.15	61	19.39	86, 140n63	22.9	163, 164
18.15ff	61			22.10	165
18.16-17	84n64	19.39-40	141n63	22.10a	164
18.18-30	62	19.40	138, 140	22.10b	164
18.24	83, 84n64	19.41	47, 135n53	22.11	46, 165
18.26	62	19.41-44	138, 139	22.12	165
18.27	62	19.42-44	71	22.13	166
18.28	62	19.42a	138	22.14	158n15, 161, 166n40
18.29	63, 84n64, 166	19.44	138, 140		
		19.44a	138		
18.30	159	19.45	139	22.14-38	140
18.31	62, 76, 135n53	19.47	51	22.14ff	60
		19.47-48	139	22.15	158n15
18.31-33	143	19.47-20.47	151	22.15-18	166n40
18.31-34	75, 138, 147	19.48	64	22.16	83
		20-24 ch	50	22.18	83
18.32	141, 149	20.1	51	22.22	161, 163
18.34	5n1	20.1-21.4	139	22.24	162
18.36	75	20.6	48	22.24-27	87, 140, 162
18.37-39	75, 85	20.9-18	87	22.25-27	163
18.38	166	20.11	165	22.25a	140
19-24 ch	47	20.19	48, 87	22.26	43, 59, 140
19.1-10	11n3, 75	20.20	141		
19.7	75, 85	20.26	10	22.28	88
19.9	79, 86, 177n21	20.37	177n21	22.29	82, 85, 88
		20.41-44	85	22.29-30	87
		20.45	48, 50, 64	22.31	140
				22.32	140, 149

22.33	163	24.25	5n1	1.25	59
22.35	160	24.26	143, 153, 161	2 ch	55, 203, 205
22.37	161			2-3 ch	196
22.39	7n4, 46	24.26-27	141	2.2-3	205
22.40-46	140	24.27	141	2.4-5	205
22.45	46	24.30	83	2.5-36	141
22.47	47	24.34	141, 143	2.10	206, 215
22.47-48	162	24.37	5n3, 6n1, 76n33	2.12-13	216
22.47-23.49	117			2.13	211
22.54-62	140	24.41	5n3, 6n1	2.20	79
22.56	24n1	24.43	83	2.21	208
22.66	60	24.43	161	2.22	215
22.66-23.25	150	24.44-48	117	2.23	122n21
23 ch	155	24.45-47	153	2.30	87
23.1-25	150	24.46-47	151	2.34	85
23.1	51, 82, 151	24.47	117n3, 212	2.37	209
23.2b-3	140	24.53	141	2.38	141
23.2ff	85			2.38a	143
23.4	47	*John*		2.39	141
23.5	51, 151	1.22	10	2.40	142, 208
23.6-12	11n3	2.4	9n2	2.40b	142
23.8	140	7.3-10	9n2	2.41	141
23.9	131, 140	12.26	59	2.46	51, 141
23.11	140	14.22	7n5	2.47 par	215
23.13	48, 51	18.15	7n3	3 ch	55
23.13-25	141	18.16	7n3	3-4 ch	206
23.14	48, 151	19.9	10	3.1	141
23.21-22	141	21.16	59	3.1-10	117
23.25	141			3.4	24n1
23.27	51	*Acts*		3.7	78n39
23.29	159			3.9	51
23.33	161	1.1	91n6, 101, 102, 117, 184n1, 187, 205, 206, 213	3.11	51, 141
23.34	131			3.12	41, 215
23.35	50, 166			3.12f	41
23.37	85			3.13	143
23.36	85			3.13-14	142
23.40	141			3.15	212
23.42	82, 85	1.4	83	3.17	199, 206
23.43	82	1.4ff	205	3.17-19	142
23.46	131	1.6	81	3.18	125, 143
23.49	7n3, 43, 160, 166	1.6-8	85	3.19	143, 159
		1.6ff	203	3.20	159
23.55	43	1.8	151, 184, 197, 198, 203, 206, 212, 215	3.21-25	125
23.56	43			3.22	142, 152
24.6	46			3.22-26	152
24.7	141, 161			3.22b	142
24.10	43	1.10	24n1	3.23	41, 51, 87
24.11	79n33	1.13	162		
24.13-35	11n3	1.15	50	3.24	143
24.19	50, 51, 141	1.15-26	141	3.26	143, 152, 210
		1.16	161		
24.19-21	141	1.17	59	3.26a	142
24.20	141	1.22	212	3.26b	142, 143

4.1-22	117	7.4	125	8.5	49
4.5-20	141	7.5	125	8.12	83, 85,
4.5-31	144, 153	7.7	128, 129,		203
4.7-10	117n3		130, 152	8.14	216
4.10	41, 51	7.7b	126	8.24	166
4.11	141	7.9	215	8.26	216
4.13	214	7.9-16	126	8.28	125
4.20	213	7.10	126n30	8.36	44
4.21	51	7.17	126, 128,	8.39	44
4.23-31	88		129, 152	9.1	46, 144,
4.27	51, 150	7.17-45	129		145
4.29-30	215	7.20	126	9.1-2	124, 145
4.29-30	214	7.21	126	9.1-19	144
4.32-37	88	7.23-43	153	9.2	44, 144
5.1-11	88	7.25	126	9.3-6	144
5.10	78n39	7.27	126	9.3-15	152
5.12	215	7.29-34	126	9.4-5	145
5.12-16	51, 193	7.30-32	152	9.7	144
5.12-42	88	7.34	41	9.13-14	145
5.17-41	149, 153	7.35-36	126	9.14	144
5.20	41, 141	7.35-45	126	9.15	152, 213
5.25	41	7.35-47	152	9.15-30	153
5.26	87	7.37	125, 126,	9.16	145, 147
5.28	117n3		143	9.17	46
5.30	211	7.38b	132	9.23-25	145
5.31	206, 208	7.39	127	9.23ff	193
5.32	212	7.39-43	130	9.25	46
5.34	51	7.41	127	9.26	46, 205
5.37	41	7.42-43	127	9.27	144, 145
5.41-42	87	7.44	127	9.27f	214
5.42	141	7.44-47	129	9.28	206
6 ch	124	7.45	85	9.29	145
6.1	46, 145	7.45-47	128	9.30	194
6.1-6	60	7.46	126n30	9.36	46
6.1ff	88	7.48-50	128	9.36-43	117
6.3	126n30,	7.51	128, 216	9.38	46
	212	7.52	125, 129,	10 ch	117, 215
6.4-6	205		143	10.15	165
6.7	46, 50,	7.52b	152	10.19ff	205
	124	7.51-53	153	10.22	212
6.8	51,	7.53	130, 205	10.26ff	205
	126n30	7.54-8.4	153	10.38	215
6.8-14	145	7.55	24n1	10.39ff	212
6.10	126n30	7.55-56	152	10.40	79n42
6.11	131	7.56	212	10.41	51
6.12f	51	7.58	144	10.43	125, 208
6.13-15	131	7.59	131	11.6	24n1
6.14	150, 151	7.60	131	11.14	208
6.15	24n1	8.1	144	11.18	56
7 ch	124	8.1-4	124, 152	11.19	124
7.2	125	8.1a	131	11.19-20	125, 152
7.2-50	129	8.1ff	198, 215	11.19-30	152
7.2-8.3	125	8.3	144	11.19ff	198
7.3	125	8.4-40	144	11.21	49

11.24	50, 194	14.20	46
11.25-26	146	14.21	147n74
11.26	46, 215	14.21-22	83
11.28	68	14.22	46, 83,
11.29	46		203
11.30	152	14.22b	147
12 ch	211	14.27	211, 215,
12.1-17	153		216
12.1-19	146	14.27-28	125
12.9	76n33	14.28	46
12.20-24	146	15.1	209
12.22	78n39	15.4	215
12.25-15.35	146	15.5	161n25
13 ch	196	15.10	46
13-14 ch	215	15.11	209
13-17 ch	189	15.12	215
13.1	125, 198	15.14	41
13.1-3	125	15.15-18	125
13.2-19.20	152	15.16	41, 85
13.7	5n1	15.20	216
13.9	24n1	15.22ff	76n34
13.13	147	15.36	147,
13.15	41, 208		147n74
13.17	41	15.36-19.20	146
13.22	205	15.38	147
13.24	41, 51	15.41	147n74
13.26	41, 199,	16 ch	215
	208	16.1	147n74
13.27	125	16.2	212
13.34	166	16.4	147n74
13.40-41	125, 152	16.4ff	104n51
13.42-45	49	16.6	147
13.44	159	16.17	209
13.45	147	16.22	49
13.46-47	152	16.30-31	209
13.46-14.3	214	16.35ff	199n1
13.46ff	198	17-18 ch	215
13.47	142,	17.2-3	147, 161
	197n3,	17.2-5	149
	203, 208	17.3	196
13.50-51	147	17.4	147n73
13.52	46	17.4-5	216
14.2	147	17.7	85
14.3	27, 215	17.8	49
14.4	216	17.10-12	147
14.5-6	147	17.10b-11	147
14.8-18	117	17.13	49
14.9	24n1	17.16-33	117
14.10	165	17.18	76n33
14.11-19	49	17.28	166
14.15	210	17.29f	210
14.16	210	17.30-31	210
14.18	49	17.31	204
14.19	49	17.33	211
14.19-20	147	18.3	104n51

18.4	147n73
18.4-5	147, 196
18.4-6	149
18.5	212
18.6	147, 152,
	196
18.9	215
18.9-10	147
18.10	41
18.12-17	147
18.14ff	199n1
18.21	147,
	147n74,
	161n25,
	165
18.23	147n74
18.25f	44
18.28	147
19.1	46
19.8	83, 203
19.9	44, 46,
	142, 198
19.13-17	147n75
19.21	146, 149
19.21-28.31	146, 152,
	153
19.21b	146
19.23	44
19.23-41	146, 148
19.23-20.1	125
19.30	46
19.33	49
19.35	49
20.3	148
20.6	160n20
20.7-12	117
20.16	125, 145,
	148, 150
20.17-38	148
20.17ff	141
20.18-20	148
20.19-20a	148n77
20.21b	148,
	148n77
20.22	149
20.22-25	147, 148
20.22ff	213
20.23	149
20.23-25	148n77
20.24	27, 213
20.25	83, 203
20.26	152
20.26-31	148,
	148n77
20.28	59

20.28b	148n76	22.21	145,	26.16-23	153
20.29-30	148		147	26.17	41, 147
20.30	148	22.25ff	199n1	26.17b-18	152
20.32	27	22.29	150	26.19	216
20.38	148, 149,	22.30	150	26.21	150
	166	22.30-25.5	147	26.22-23	125, 153,
21-28 ch	213	23.1	199		213
21.3	79	23.1-5	150	26.22b-23	150
21.4	147.149	23.5	199	26.23	41, 142
21.7	190	23.11	147,	26.24	211
21.8-14	149		150, 213	26.27	122
21.10-14	147, 195	23.11-27	215	26.31f	199n1
21.11	149	23.12-22	150	27.10	147
21.13	149	23.13	117n3	27.13	76n33
21.14b	149	23.15	79n42	27.20	79
21.15-36	149	23.22	79n42	27.24-25	210
21.21	149, 150	23.29	199n1	27.31	210
21.21-28.31	152	24.1	79n42	27.34	210
21.24	150	24.1-9	150	27.43-44	210
21.27	49	24.5	151	27.44	210
21.27-28	149	24.6	150, 151	28.1	210
21.27-31	150	24.11	145	28.1-4	210
21.27-22.29	117	24.12	49	28.4	210
21.28	151	24.14	44, 125	28.14	210
21.28b	149	24.15-25	204	28.15	198
21.30	41	24.17-18	145	28.17	150, 151,
21.30-32	150	24.18	49, 125		199
21.31a	149	24.19b-20	149	28.17-19	150
21.34-36	49, 150	24.20	165	28.18	199n1
21.36	41, 150	24.22	44	28.23	83, 85,
21.39-40	150	24.24-25	195		196
21.40-22.1	150	25.1-12	150	28.25	194, 216
22.1	199	25.2	79n42,	28.25b	151
22.4	44		150	28.26	5n1
22.4-5	145	25.3	44	28.26-27	151
22.5	144	25.8	151	28.28	208
22.6-15	152	25.15	79n42,	28.29b	151
22.6-21	144		150	28.31	83, 85,
22.7	144	25.18-20	150		196
22.7-8	145	25.24	149		
22.8	151	25.24-25	150	*Romans*	
22.11	145	25.27	76n34		
22.12	212	25.30-31	150	8.28	215
22.12-15	150	26.3	150	9.2	183
22.13-15	144	26.6-8	150	9.6	183
22.14	145n68	26.9	76n34,	9-11 ch	180n25,
22.14-15	144		151		198
22.14-21	153	26.9-11	145	11.13	59
22.15	213	26.12	144		
22.15-21	152	26.12-23	144	*1 Corinthians*	
22.17-21	145	26.13-14	144		
22.18	145,	26.13-18	152	1.19	2n4, 5n1
	145n68,	26.14-15	145	3.6-9	59
	147	26.16	144, 145,	9 ch	60
22.20	212		213	9.5	213

9.7	59	4.14	104n51,	*Titus*	
9.10	59		108	2.11	79
				2.13	79
2 Corinthians		*1 Thessalonians*		3.4	79
11.23ff	195	2.16	127n31	*Hebrews*	
Galatians		*2 Thessalonians*		2.4	215
				3.6	206n3
1-2 ch	193	2.8	79	3.14	206n3
				6.19	206n3
Ephesians		*1 Timothy*		9.17	206n3
3.4	5n1			13.9	206n3
4.2	59	6.14	79	*1 Peter*	
Colossians		*2 Timothy*		5.2	59
1.9	5n1	1.10	79	*Revelation*	
1.19	2n4	2.7	5n1		
2.2	5n1	4.1	79	10.11	68
2.2-3	2n4	4.14	104n51	11.6	33